Business Administration

Second Edition

ARLENE DOUGLAS

GILL & MACMILLAN

Gill & Macmillan Ltd
Hume Avenue
Park West
Dublin 12
with associated companies throughout the world
www.gillmacmillan.ie

0 7171 3500 4
Print origination in Ireland by
Paradigm DTP, Co. Cork

*The paper used in this book is made from the wood pulp of managed forests.
For every tree felled, at least one tree is planted, thereby
renewing natural resources.*

A catalogue record is available for this book
from the British Library

*This book is dedicated to my parents Shelia and Oliver, to my
husband Jim, to my sons Ciarán, Séamus and Colm and to
my twin girls Dearbhla and Róisín.*
*I wish to sincerely thank all the organisations and individuals
that contributed information to this book, in particular the
Independent Newspaper Group and the Sunday Tribune.*

Contents

Preface   vii

1. The Organisation   1
- Organisations in Ireland – Citizens Information   1
- What is an Organisation?   2
- Sole Trader   3
- Partnership   4
- Companies – State, Semi-State, Private and
  Public Company Information   6
- Friendly Societies   10
- Features of Different Types of Organisational Structures   14
- Environmental Features affecting an Organisation   20
- Importance of Effective Communication
  within an Organisation   22
- Knowledge Management   24
- The Need for Quality within an Organisation   26
- How Students Can Research Organisations   32
- S.W.O.T. and P.E.S.T. Analyses   35
- Sample Assignment Brief   37
- Sample Questions for Student Research
  on 'The Organisation'   37
- Student Analysis   39
- Simple Ways to Illustrate the Results of Research   40
- Sample Assignment Brief 'The Organisation'   42
- Sample Assignment – The Organisation   42

2. Finance, Business Controls and Ratios   51
- Why is Control So Important in Business?   51
- Ordering Stock – Re-order Levels and Quantities   55
- Breakeven Charts   61
- Sources of Finance for Business   65
- Commencement and Development Finance   69
- Matching the Sources of Finance with Particular Needs of
  the Organisation or the Individual   70

- Cash Flow Forecasts   70
- Impact of Credit Control Policy on the Liquidity
  and Profitability of a Business   75
- Unit Cost and Selling Price Calculations   76
- Sample Assignment Briefs   79
- Sample Questions for Student Research on
  'Finance and Business Controls'   81

3. Banking, Currencies, Visual Data and Insurance   82

- The Euro and the European Central Bank   82
- Functions and Services of the Central Bank
  of Ireland   85
- Functions and Services of Irish Commercial Banks   89
- ICT Technologies and Online Banking   90
- How Merchant Banks differ from Commercial Banks   94
- Foreign Exchange and Currency Conversions   95
- Business Information in Graphical Form   96
- Business Administration   103
- Insurance Against Common Business Risks   104
- Principles of Insurance   107
- Insurance Proposal Form   109
- Accident Claim Form   111
- Sample Assignment Briefs   114

4. Human Resources   116

- Manpower/Workforce Planning   116
- Recruitment Options   117
- Functions of The Human Resources Department   120
- Purpose of Maintaining Documents in the Human
  Resources Department   124
- Basic Rights of Employees as Protected under
  Current Legislation   128
- The Role of a Trade Union within the Workplace
  at Branch and National Level   133
- Different Employee, Employer Organisations
  and those Representing the Unemployed   134
- The Irish Congress of Trade Unions (ICTU)   137
- Features of Grievance Procedures   138
- Essential Ingredients of a Contract of Employment   140
- A Sample Contract of Employment   142

- The Services of the Irish Ombudsman   146
- The European Ombudsman   146
- A Sample Student Trade Union Assignment   149
- Sample Assignment Briefs – Human Resources/
  Trade Unions   155
- Sample Questions for Student Research on
  'A Trade Union'   156
- Sample Questions for Student Research on
  'The H.R. Department'   156

5. Preparing for Meetings   157
- Role of a Meeting within the Organisation   157
- Different Types of Meetings   157
- Roles, Powers and Duties of Officers at a Meeting   162
- Terms Associated with Meetings
  (including regulations governing meetings)   163
- Procedures for Voting at Meetings   165
- Purpose of an Agenda   166
- Purpose of the Minutes of a Meeting   169
- Purpose of Writing a Report of a Meeting   172
- A Sample Student Summary of Meetings   174
- How to Plan for a Meeting   176
- Sample Assignment Brief – Meetings   182
- Sample Student Assignment   182

6. Processing of Business Documents   187
- Definitions and Explanations of Documents and
  Business Terms including Discounts and VAT   187
- Choosing Suppliers, Pricing and Assessing Quotations 192
- Cheque, Bank Giro Form and Petty Cash Voucher   206
- Purchases Book, Sales Book and VAT Returns   209
- Sample Assignment   215
- Blank Documents that can be Duplicated   219

7. Retail Administration   224
- Different Types of Retail Outlets in Ireland   225
- The Impact of the Size and Type of
  a Retail Organisation   228
- Factors that Affect the Location of a Retail Outlet   229
- The Impact of Location on a Retail Outlet   230

- Legal Aspects of Retailing   232
- The Consumer Association of Ireland
  and Consumer Choice   235
- The Role of the Director of Consumer Affairs   237
- Retail Administration   238
- A Retail Case Study – A School Bookshop   238

8. Sample Exam Papers   246
- Two Papers for Business Administration   246
- Retail Administration Paper   251

Preface

- This book is designed to help students studying FETAC (formally NCVA) Business & Retail Administration.

- Chapter 1 focuses on the organisation and different organisational structures. There are actual company organisational profiles and charts included in order to back up the detail in the chapter as well as sample questionnaires and examples of S.W.O.T. and P.E.S.T. analyses that will help students to research information on organisations of their choice.

- Chapter 2 incorporates details on business controls, calculations of costs and selling prices, breakeven charts and cash flow forecasts.

- Chapter 3 focuses on banking, including online banking methods and ICT technologies in the finance and banking environment, display of business information, currency conversion, information on the Euro and insurance analysis.

- Chapter 4 contains details on human resource management and manpower/workforce planning, as well as legal features affecting the employee, and the roles of the Ombudsman.

- Chapter 5 explains how meetings are planned, the protocol connected with them, reasons for them and the usual terminology connected with meetings.

- Chapter 6 details procedures regarding business documentation, checking and matching dockets and documents, spotting overcharges or undercharges, pricing, dealing with queries, preparing documents for dispatch and payments procedures.

- Chapter 7 introduces the reader to features of different types and sizes of retail outlets, legal aspects of retailing with information on RGDATA, the Sale of Goods and Supply of Services Act, aspects of consumer rights, the Consumer Association of Ireland, Consumer Choice and the role of the Director of Consumer Affairs.

NOTE:
- Sample assignments are located at the end of each chapter.
- Practice questions appear at the end of every sub-section within the chapters.
- Student assignments, as appropriate, are given at the end of some chapters.
- Two Sample FETAC examination papers for Business Administration and one for Retail Administration appear near the end of the book.
- Appropriate source documents are located at the back of the book.

SUPPORT MATERIAL

For your support material check our website www.gillmacmillan.ie
Support material is available to lecturers only within a secure area of this website.
Support material for this book consists of solutions to questions.
To access support material for Business Administration, Second Edition:

1. Go to www.gillmacmillan.ie
2. Click on the 'logon' button and enter your username and password. (If you do not already have a username and password, you must register. To do this click the 'register' button and complete the online registration form. Your username and password will then be sent to you by email.)
3. Click on the link 'Support Material'.
4. Select the title Business Administration, Second Edition.

1. The Organisation

Organisations in Ireland – Citizen's Information

Organisations that matter to the business community, i.e. large organisations and small and medium enterprises (SMEs) are listed on the Internet. Some examples of state and semi-state organisations that business people look to are the Chambers of Commerce of Ireland, IDA Ireland (Industrial Development Authority), Enterprise Ireland, Shannon Development, Company Registrations Office (the CRO) and the Central Statistics Office (the CSO). Since Ireland has become a member of the European Union and has changed its currency to the Euro, it is of paramount importance that Irish citizens and businesses are familiar with the workings of European organisations. Some of these organisations have a say in or can impact on the operations of businesses within the Irish economy. Examples of such organisations include the European Central Bank, the European Commission, the European Parliament, the European Agency for Safety and Health at Work and the European Ombudsman. A comprehensive listing of European organisations and their Irish connections can be found at the Euro Info Centres web site –
www.eic.ie/links.html.

Types of Business Organisations

The main types of business organisation that exist today are:

1. *SOLE PROPRIETOR*: This is an unincorporated (does not have company status) business organisation owned by one person who receives the profits and incurs the liabilities personally.

2. *PARTNERSHIP*: In Ireland, the partnership form tends to be used for professional practice, such as solicitors or accountants. Partnerships are normally formed by a partnership deed setting out the agreement and conditions of the partnership. A less common form is the limited partnership, which allows one or more general partners who manage the daily affairs of the business and one or more limited partners who provide a fixed capital investment with financial liability limited to the capital investment.

3. *COMPANIES*: These fall into two categories:

PUBLIC LIMITED COMPANY

This is the main form of incorporation for firms issuing stocks or bonds, having stockholders, and directors that manage the company. The company is incorporated under a Memorandum of Association and Articles of Incorporation, providing the name, share capital, and commercial objectives. There must be seven or more stockholders. There must be a minimum of two directors that manage the daily affairs of the firm and who are usually selected by the shareholders. Annual meetings are required with 21 days advance notice provided. It is also necessary to disclose financial statements and meet statutory requirements for reporting.

PRIVATE LIMITED COMPANIES

The requirements for formation and reporting of private limited companies are generally the same as for the public limited companies. This form is the most popular type of commercial organisation in Ireland – a head office might be located abroad. There must be between two and fifty shareholders, no debentures or shares should be issued to the general public, and there is no minimum level of share capital.

4. FRIENDLY SOCIETIES: These are organisations registered with the Registrar of Friendly Societies such as credit unions, some co-operatives, some water schemes etc.

5. STATE BODIES – trading and non-trading.

6. SEMI-STATE BODIES – trading and non-trading

7. CHARITIES

8. CARING GROUPS

Virtual organisations and SMEs fit into one of the types of business organisation listed previously – usually private companies or partnerships.

- Virtual organisations such as virtual business schools, online tour operators, and Internet marketing companies, are some of the organisations that predominantly rely on Internet business and are called 'e-businesses'.
- SME's are small and medium enterprises that entrepreneurs develop when they find a niche in the market (where sufficient market demand exists) and with some state or semi-state help (e.g. IDA Grants, funding from City and County Enterprise Boards, or through Business Expansion Schemes, which are offered by financial institutions to help small businesses get up and running or expand). SME's interests are represented by the SFA (Small Firms Association) and by IBEC (Irish Business Employers Confederation) in some cases.

Note: The organisations mentioned here will be discussed in greater detail later.

What is an Organisation?

Barnard described an organisation as a 'system of co-operative human activities'. Organising involves the dividing up of tasks, the suitable allocation of these tasks to specialised personnel and the co-ordination and monitoring of the work in hand, to achieve agreed aims and objectives.

Sole Trader

- This business person is the only owner of the business. Pubs, newsagents, hair-dressers, restaurants, painters and decorators, bookshop owners etc. can all trade as sole traders.
- If he/she wishes to trade under a trade name other than their personal name, he/she must register in Dublin Castle under the Registration of Business Names Act 1963.
- The Safety, Health and Welfare at Work Act 1989 places responsibilities on all traders including the sole trader to ensure the health and safety of people at work and of the public affected by work activities. He/she must put into place appropriate safety measures, having carried out a safety evaluation of the risks involved and potential hazards to health and safety. A safety programme must be written down in the form of a Safety Statement.
- He/she must keep the books of the business in order and submit monthly and end of year tax returns and must only register for VAT if certain annual limits are exceeded.
- **Advantages of being a sole trader**
  (a) Speedy decision-making: no consultation required.
  (b) No profit-sharing.
  (c) Flexible hours.
  (d) No industrial relations problems.
  (e) Customer friendly personal service ensures consumer loyalty.
  (f) Suits family-run business.
- **Disadvantages of sole trader**
  (a) Unlimited liability: he/she is liable personally for all debts of the business. The business is not a separate legal entity.
  (b) Higher trade prices: since a small business does not buy in bulk as much as a larger one, not as many trade discounts can be gained. This causes a sole trader's costs to be higher and he/she passes on the cost to the consumer in the form of higher selling prices. Higher prices can cause decreased competitiveness and a loss of sales.
  (c) A larger capital requirement is necessary, funded only by the sole trader.
  (d) The business dies with the sole trader.
  (e) Complete competence in all areas of expertise is required, i.e. versatility, otherwise the business will not survive.
  (f) Administration overload can cause tax liabilities (owing money because books of the business are not in order).
- Sources of finance for the sole trader towards start-up:
  (a) Loans from banks and financial institutions.

(b) Personal savings.

(c) Hire purchase – getting assets like office equipment on loan.

(d) Good credit terms – being allowed time by suppliers before purchases must be paid for. (Sources of finance are discussed in detail in Chapter 2.)

Many sole traders evolve into Partnerships or Limited Companies. However, many sole traders prefer to remain with this structure because of full profit-taking and control. A good accountant is advisable to look after finances, tax returns and to implement changes in tax, VAT and employment legislation.

PRACTICE QUESTIONS

1. Outline *three* advantages of the Sole Trader/Proprietor.
2. Outline *three* disadvantages of the Sole Trader/Proprietor.
3. How does the Registration of Business Names Act 1963 apply to the Sole Trader?
4. Explain how the Safety, Health and Welfare at Work Act 1989 applies to the Sole Trader.
5. Why are Sole Traders' selling prices often higher than a larger trader?

Partnership

- This business operates on the basis of a minimum of two persons and a maximum of between twenty and fifty persons, depending on the business concerned.
- The partnership must register under the Registration of Business Names Act 1963 if the partners do not wish to trade under their own personal names.
- The Safety, Health and Welfare at Work Act applies also to the partnership (as it does to the sole trader).
- The books of the business must be kept in order. (VAT and other taxes must be paid regularly.)
- The partners usually draw up a Deed of Partnership to underpin the conditions of the agreement. Legally, if no written agreement like this is drawn up, the partners are covered under the Partnership Act 1890. Where the agreement is written up by the deed, the contents of the deed will overrule the conditions laid down by the Act.
- The Partnership Act 1890 states in general that profits and losses are to be shared equally. No new admissions are allowed without all the partners' consent. Disputes are settled by majority. Each partner can inspect the books and profits must be calculated before interest is paid to quasi-partners (partners that leave money in the business as a loan – explained below).
- There are four types of partner.
  (a) Active partner: one who participates fully in the running of the business.
  (b) Sleeping partner: one who contributes capital but does not take an active part in the running of the business.

(c) Quasi-partner: one who retires and leaves his/her money in the business as a loan and is paid interest on the loan once profits have been calculated.

(d) Limited partner: one whose liability or duty to pay debts is limited to the amount of capital which the partner invested – underpinned by the Limited Partnership Act 1907. With this type of partnership, one general partner with unlimited liability must exist. The Investment Limited Partnership Act 1994 was designed to encourage collective investment in businesses, and was aimed at attracting American investors to the Financial Services Centre in Dublin by providing them with a certain degree of financial protection.

- Unlimited liability means the partner/s, i.e. general partners, would have to cover their business debts by dipping into their own private funds if company monies could not meet the debt. One general partner might have to cover another general partner's debt because the partners are jointly and severally liable. The business is not a separate legal entity from the persons that own it and the partners are not protected by limited liability in a general partnership. Unlimited partnerships are risky and require a high level of trust to operate efficiently and survive.

- On the dissolution of a partnership due to the death, bankruptcy or retirement of a partner, or due to the partnership's completion (job finished), expiry time (which would be outlined in the deed), or court order to dissolve due to illegal activities, the procedure to dissolve is as follows:

(a) All assets are re-valued and sold (i.e. the realisation of the assets – liquidated – converted to cash).

(b) Creditors are paid off.

(c) Quasi-partners' loans are paid off.

(d) Capital is repaid to the partners.

(e) If there is any profit left over on the sale of the assets, it is divided according to profit-sharing ratios of partners. The dead partner's beneficiaries receive his portion.

(f) Beneficiaries have the option of becoming sleeping partners (leaving the money in the business, allowing it to continue to operate) or quasi-partners (leaving the money in the business as a loan where interest will be paid to them).

- **Advantages of a Partnership:**

(a) Greater Capital: greater possibility of expansion.

(b) Greater Specialisation – range of talents and expertise leads to improved productivity, speed and efficiency.

(c) Division of liability (sharing the debts).

(d) Consultation regarding decision-making.

(e) Accounts not published, so privacy maintained regarding transactions.

(f) Smaller scale partnership arrangements benefit from the ability to give personal service and gain consumer loyalty as a result, e.g. hairdressers, window companies.

- **Disadvantages of a Partnership:**
  (a) Unlimited liability (except in the case of limited partners): debts of company may have to be covered by dipping into personal funds.
  (b) The business is not a separate legal entity from the owners: owners can be sued personally for non-payment of debts.
  (c) Differences of opinion can cause inefficiencies.
  (d) Sharing of profits.
  (e) The death of a partner means the automatic dissolution of the partnership.
  (f) New partners cannot join without full agreement of all partners. This could deprive the business of new capital input.
- Examples of Partnerships:
  Doctors, solicitors, accountants, dentists, architects and many other regular businesses that trade either under their personal names or a trade name (in which case they must register under the Registration of Business Names Act 1963 in Dublin Castle).
- An example of limited partnerships that have grown is the amalgamation of the two largest accountancy bodies in the world, Coopers and Lybrand and Price Waterhouse, thus making a group of very powerful accountants.

PRACTICE QUESTIONS

1. Explain the differences between Active, Sleeping, and Quasi-partners.
2. What is the purpose of the Partnership Act 1890?
3. What is Unlimited Liability?
4. What is meant by 'The business is not a separate legal entity'?
5. Why would a Partnership dissolve?
6. What is the meaning of specialisation and how does it benefit a Partnership?
7. When a partner dies, explain the procedure that follows.
8. Outline *three* advantages of a Partnership.
9. Outline *three* disadvantages of a Partnership.

Companies

There are six main types of company:

1. State bodies: those totally funded by the government/state, e.g. the Army.
2. Semi-state bodies: those that are part funded by the government (public sector) and part funded by the private sector (firms and companies), e.g. the Electricity Supply Board (ESB).

State and semi-state bodies can be sub-categorised into trading and non-trading organisations as follows:

TRADING BODIES

Those which offer a service that you pay for.

Semi-state body examples are CIE (divided in three – Irish Rail, Bus Éireann (suburban) and Dublin Bus (city) transportation), ESB, Aer Lingus, Aer Rianta, and Bord na Móna (turf). Examples of state bodies are Health Boards. Many hospitals are part of the Health Board system and public patients and out-patients have to pay for services.

Some essential services would be loss-making services and are semi-state for this reason. The government subsidises CIE for unprofitable routes in order to provide a full service to the public.

NON-TRADING BODIES

A semi-state body like the IDA (Industrial Development Authority) is a non-trading body providing important grants and incentives for new investment. State bodies like the Army, Garda Siochana and the Blood Bank are non-trading bodies because they do not trade in goods or services for any fees, but they provide a free service to the public.

3. Unlimited companies: unlike partnerships, must register under the Companies Act 1983 but, similar to partnerships, do not enjoy the benefits of limited liability. Capital is provided by shareholders. Each individual amount is called a share.

4. Companies limited by guarantee: usually non-profit making like clubs registered under the Companies Act 1983 and liability is limited to the amount each individual member invests if the company gets into financial difficulty.

5. Private Limited Company: any business that applies to the CRO (Central Registrations Office) in order to gain limited liability and can place Ltd after the company name. Greater financial security is gained as the business is now a separate legal entity from the people that own it. Debts of the business are cleared by the business and money is not taken out of the owners' personal funds. The business, however, might be subject to Corporation Tax.

6. Public Limited Company: any well-established private limited company that has a good business track record and decides to float the shares of the business on the Stock Exchange, offering them to the public, and gaining a trading certificate allowing the business to place plc after their company name. The business is now a public company. More money or capital can be generated by going public through share capital. The company accounts have to be published and profit-sharing increases.

Formation of a Private Limited Company

(Converting from a Sole Trader, Partnership or Unlimited Company to a Private Limited Company)

You must decide on a company name. Look up the 'Frequently used numbers' section of the phone directory and find the Companies Registration Office –

Telephone (01) 8045200. You must check with the office that the company name you have decided on is not already in use and you must get three forms:

1. An A1 form will be sent to you on request by the Companies Registration Office, more formally known as the Registrar of Joint Stock Companies.
2. A 'Memorandum of Association' form.
3. An 'Articles of Association' form.
   Both the memorandum and articles are in booklet form and must be purchased from a law stationery office. Look up 'Stationery Offices' in the phone book.

PROCEDURE

1. When the legal documents have been drawn up by yourself or by a solicitor (Solicitor's Act 1954) they must be lodged with the Registrar of Joint Stock Companies. They are:
   (a) Memorandum of Association: containing information on the name and objectives of the company, a statement verifying that the company has limited liability, two signatures which are witnessed verifying the formation of the company, and the location of the registered legal office where all the legal documents are sent.
   (b) Articles of Association: containing the list of internal rules and regulations connected with the company such as voting rights, powers and duties of directors, and procedures regarding meetings.
   (c) A formal declaration of compliance with the Companies Act 1983.
   (d) A statement denoting the amount of Authorised or Nominal Share Capital of the company.
2. The documents are inspected by the Registrar and must comply with the Companies Act 1983.
3. When the documents are verified, the Registrar issues a 'Certificate of Incorporation', the birth certificate of a limited company.
4. The company can now commence business with the protection of limited liability and can place Ltd after its company name.
   Note: Limited liability indicates that the company is a legal entity separate from the owners. Regarding debts of the company, the company is sued, not the owners. Refer to **www.cro.ie** for further information.

Formation of a Public Limited Company

(Converting from a Private Limited Company to a Public Limited Company)

The Companies Registration Office must be contacted at Telephone (01) 8045200 to clarify the requirements regarding capital turnover and size of business.

1. The company wishing to become public must satisfy the following conditions:
   (a) have a stated minimum authorised capital where at least a quarter of it must be offered to the public.

(b) have a minimum market value.

(c) have a minimum number of shareholders.

(d) have a healthy track record – positive working capital.

(e) have a minimum profit level.

(f) accept full disclosure on its operations – salaries, profits and strategies. This is the reason why some businesses are reluctant to go public.

2. The legal documents that must be lodged with the Registrar of Joint Stock Companies are:

(a) Memorandum of Association – with at least seven signatures verifying the authenticity of the memo, as well as the other contents of the memo mentioned previously.

(b) Articles of Association – contents mentioned previously.

(c) A formal declaration of compliance with the Companies Act 1983.

(d) A statement denoting the amount of authorised or nominal share capital of the company.

(e) A list of agreed directors.

(f) Directors' written consent to become directors.

3. Company makes application to Stock Exchange Council through a stockbroker where shares are quoted.

4. The company employs a merchant banker, and the stockbroker and the merchant banker together inspect the books of the company:

(a) to verify that the books meet the Stock Exchange Council's requirements regarding the financial state of the company.

(b) to verify the healthy future prospects of the company.

5. When the Stock Exchange Council accepts the company's application to trade on the Stock Exchange, the Registrar of Companies issues the company with a trading certificate.

TRADING CERTIFICATE

A public limited company must not commence business or exercise any borrowing powers until the trading certificate entitling it to commence business has been issued by the Companies Registration Office (CRO). Before such a certificate can be issued, the company must file *Form 70* in accordance with section 6 of the Companies (Amendment) Act 1983.

6. Before shares are quoted on the Stock Exchange, the company must produce a prospectus after receiving the trading certificate (the birth cert. of the public limited company).

PROSPECTUS

The word 'Prospectus' is defined in the Act as 'any prospectus, notice, circular, advertisement or other invitation, offering to the public for subscription or purchase any shares or debentures of a company'.

An offer to existing holders of shares or debentures is also regarded as coming within the scope of this definition.

7. Once the Trading Certificate has been received and the Prospectus has been organised, the company can now commence trading on the Stock Exchange, quoting the shares of the company, and can place plc after its trade name. Refer to **www. cro.ie** for further information.

Friendly Societies

These societies are categorised in the Report of the Registrar of Friendly Societies 1994–1996 as follows:
1. Industrial and Provident Societies
2. Credit Unions
3. Friendly Societies registered under the Friendly Societies Acts.
4. Some trade unions.

1. Industrial and Provident Societies
These are divided in the following way:
Dairy societies, livestock breeding societies, meat-processing societies, livestock marketing societies, horticultural societies, egg and poultry societies, fishing societies, public utility societies. (Group water schemes and housing development are separate categories.)

Examples are Thurles Co-operative Creamery Ltd, Waterford Co-operative Society Ltd, Clover Meats Ltd, Donegal Potatoes Ltd, Goldenvale Co-operative Mart Ltd, Monaghan Poultry Growers Co-operative Society, Cappagh Group Water Scheme Society Ltd, Carlow Town Housing Co-operative Society Ltd, Clondalkin Community Enterprise Co-operative Society Ltd, and many others.

Most of the above-named industrial and provident societies are co-operative societies and have a co-operative organisational structure. The history of the co-op movement laid the foundation for the type of structures that exist today.

The co-operative movement had its origins in an English town in Lancashire called Rochdale. The father of the co-operative movement was a Welshman, Robert Owen (1771–1858). Together with a number of colleagues, they called themselves the Rochdale Pioneers and they drew up a set of rules called the Rochdale Principles which still govern the thinking and conduct of co-operatives:

1. Open membership – anyone can join.
2. Democratic rule – one vote per person.

3. Limited return on capital.
4. Surplus profit to be distributed according to number of purchases.
5. No credit – cash sales only.
6. Some profit is set aside for educational purposes.
7. Neutral on political and religious issues.

Characteristics of the Co-operative
1. Must register under the Industrial and Provident Societies Act 1893–1978 with the Registrar of Friendly Societies and if they convert to companies they must conform to the Companies Act 1990.
2. Can be formed by eight or more people.
3. One person, one vote, irrespective of number of shares held.
4. A member may not own more than an agreed number of shares.
5. As more capital is acquired, no further authorised share capital can be issued.
6. Shares are non-transferable and a member must sell back shares to the co-op and they are withdrawn.
7. Surplus on profits is distributed to members in proportion to their holding. Some is used for educational purposes.

Retail co-operatives, producer co-operatives and worker co-operatives exist; however, the co-operative movement has undergone dramatic change in recent years and must now compete to survive. Many have become public companies, having successfully adjusted to the competitive position required in the business world today. Examples of plcs like this are Kerry Group plc and Avonmore Waterford plc (who merged in September 1997 to form Glanbia). Activities like milk processing, dairy produce trading, pig farming and meat processing are carried on by the Kerry Group. Talks of mergers or take-overs of any remaining suitable co-ops have been common in recent times due to the benefits attached to this type of venture:

1. Extra finance from share issues.
2. Top-class management improving efficiency and productivity.
3. Benefits attached to large-scale operations (economies of scale). Examples of economies or benefits are bulk buying with large discounts, lower advertising costs per unit output, and top-class specialised workers.

Retail Co-operatives
Some co-operatives like Thurles Co-operative Creamery Ltd have had a retail outlet (shop attached to the co-op). In this they sell fresh produce as well as a range of household items to the public. Retail co-operatives like this are listed in the Registry of Friendly Societies under 'Industrial and Provident Societies – Dairy Section'. Other co-operatives like knitwear co-ops can have shops attached to them also. They are listed under the 'Other Productive Societies' section of the same publication.

2. Credit Unions

Characteristics

Credit unions were introduced to Ireland in 1958. The policy of self-help has proved popular and there are now 520 credit unions affiliated to the Irish League of Credit Unions in the 32 counties. There are over 1.8m members. The Irish League of Credit Unions is the representative and service body providing a wide range of services for affiliated credit unions. The league is administered by a board of directors elected at its annual general meeting by delegates from affiliated credit unions. Affiliated credit unions are organised into regional groupings called Chapters. Each credit union is a member of a particular chapter, which acts as a forum for the exchange of information, shared promotion and training programmes. There are 25 chapters, most of which meet on a regular basis.

1. Credit unions are formed under the Credit Union Act 1966 and the Industrial and Provident Societies (Amendment) Act 1978.
2. Individual credit unions are run by a voluntary board of directors elected by the members.
3. They are non-profit making organisations aimed at promoting thrift (savings) and making loans to members at a reasonable rate of interest. Members own the credit union and have a say in its running.
4. By law, all credit unions must register with the Registrar of Friendly Societies to which agreed rules and annual financial statements must be submitted, and a minimum of eight persons are required to form one.
5. One member, one vote, irrespective of the number of shares held.
6. The loans policy and conditions vary according to the size of the credit union, since every credit union is a separate autonomous organisation, managing its own affairs.
7. Loan applications are based on members' savings records and a member must be saving for at least three months before the first loan application will be considered.
8. The rate of interest is one per cent per month on a reducing balance basis.
9. Members cannot withdraw shares until an existing loan is paid off, and cannot avail of a top-up loan until one-quarter of an existing loan is cleared.
10. Life assurance covers a member in case of death to a certain maximum, according to savings, and life savings insurance allows savings to pass to the person nominated by the member. Loan protection cover can also be availed of on request in case of death, where the loan will be paid off by the insurance company of the credit union.

Nearly every town, village and organisation has a credit union and a few examples are Ballyfermot Credit Union, Blanchardstown and District Credit Union Ltd, CIE Staff (Cork) Credit Union Ltd, Teachers Union of Ireland Credit Union Ltd, and many more.

3. Friendly Societies registered under the Friendly Societies Acts

Examples are Arklow Pottery Welfare Society, the Prison Officers' Medical Aid Society, the Telecom Éireann Staff Friendly Society, Irish National Foresters, Stephen's Green Loan Fund Society, Kilkenny Archaeological Society and the Chinese Society of Ireland.

4. Some Trade Unions

Many trade unions register as friendly societies. (Refer to the section on the ICTU in Chapter 3.)

There are other friendly societies that are not registered with the Registrar, including charities and caring groups.

Charities

These are non-profit making organisations that are exempt from VAT which operate mostly on donations from fund-raising events, personal donations, as well as some government funding. Examples are St Vincent de Paul Society, Trócaire and Concern.

Caring Groups

Caring Groups give advice and counselling e.g. Cura, the Samaritans and Alcoholics Anonymous.

PRACTICE QUESTIONS

1. How do semi-state bodies and state-sponsored bodies differ?
2. Give *one* example *each* of:
    (i) a trading semi-state body
    (ii) a non-trading semi-state body
    (iii) a trading state body
    (iv) a non-trading state body.
3. Define the following:
    (i) Unlimited Company;
    (ii) Company limited by Guarantee;
    (iii) a Private Limited Company; and
    (iv) a Public Limited Company.
4. What are the procedures for unlimited companies to become private limited companies?
5. What are the procedures for a private limited company to become public?
6. Name *three* types of friendly societies. What characteristics are common to each?
7. How have Co-ops changed in status in recent years?
8. What are the Rochdale Principles?
9. What is a chapter with regard to credit unions?
10. Give a brief account of how Credit Unions operate.
11. How are Charities defined?

Features of Different Types of Organisational Structures

Factors Determining Organisational Design

1. **A Formal Organisation:** Functional divisions of labour that are based on the formal lines of authority affect the structure of an organisation.

   An organisation is structured to achieve specific goals with the formal functions of the organisation set out within a well-defined framework. Divisions of responsibilities are formally grouped to achieve specific tasks. Job specifications exist to make the individual's position in the organisation clear. There are chains of delegated authority used for different levels of decision-making and built-in channels of communication exist. Examples are banks, colleges, advertising agencies, software companies etc.

2. **An Informal Organisation:** This operates alongside the formal framework, where individuals within the organisation form social groupings and relationships and often use informal methods to get things done. It is flexible and spontaneous and often speeds up the completion of tasks based on informal teamwork. Newcomers sometimes have to 'get accepted' into informal groupings.

THE ORGANISATIONAL HIERARCHY AND ORGANISATIONAL CHART SHAPES (FLAT, TALL)

The lines of authority should be clearly defined in every organisation (i.e. every employee should be able to see clearly to whom he/she is responsible). Since the employee is answerable to somebody he/she is said to be, in the formal sense, a subordinate. The organisational structure is best displayed by constructing an Organisational Chart of the organisation in question. This chart represents a framework within which staff are designated to perform required activities.

The main factors that dictate the shape of such a chart are referred to as the 'Principles of Organisation':

1. Unity of command and unity of purpose: is ensured when employees know who exactly they are answerable to (ideally one person) and no conflicts arise regarding authority.

2. Span of control: generally means one superior at the head of the organisation and a varying number of subordinates. The wider the span, the fewer the levels of authority, the flatter the shape of the organisational chart. A narrow span of control will tend to create a tall structure (see Figure 1.1, above).

3. Amount of delegation: Delegation means the dividing up of responsibilities and spreading them out among subordinates. A high level of delegation results in a greater number of levels of authority.

4. Size of organisation: A greater division of work, specialisation and delegation is required in a larger organisation. The larger the organisation, the taller the shape of the chart; and the smaller the organisation, the flatter the shape of the chart.

5. Number and type of employees: The larger the organisation, the greater the labour force, and because of the need for greater departmentation and specialisation, there tends to be a greater number of levels of authority due to the workload and the need for delegation.

The horizontal and vertical dimensions of the pyramids are altered due to the factors above.

Question: Which in your opinion is more efficient?

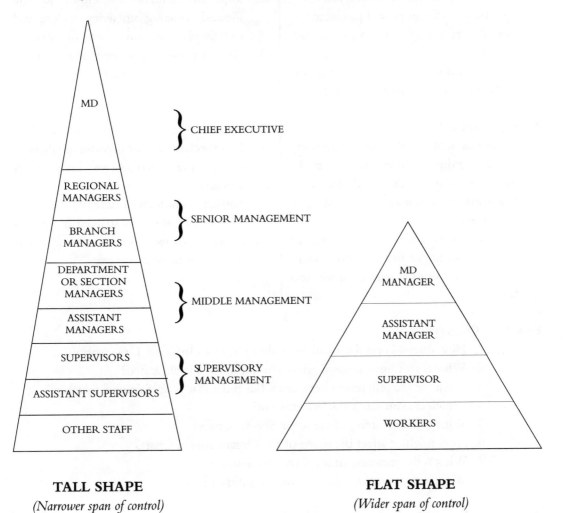

TALL SHAPE
(Narrower span of control)

FLAT SHAPE
(Wider span of control)

Figure 1.1 Organisational Pyramids

TALL SHAPE	*FLAT SHAPE*

CHARACTERISTICS: larger business with greater departmental divisions, specialisation and delegation; greater number and variation of type of employee; work involves more analysis research and development.

CHARACTERISTICS: smaller business with a small number of employees where work passes through fewer hands – few levels of authority.

ADVANTAGES:

1. Greater economies of scale i.e. benefits due to larger size, e.g. opportunities to specialise and divide up labour, increasing opportunities for improved productivity.
2. Greater efficiency in organisational methods.
3. Greater turnover – can afford to incorporate the most modern technology.

ADVANTAGES:

1. Information and decisions pass from top to bottom quickly via fewer levels.
2. Top management are closer to the ground ensuring efficiency – close and orderly planning and control of work.
3. Greater personal consumer attention and resulting consumer loyalty.

DISADVANTAGES:

1. Greater difficulty with maintaining unity of purpose due to communication problems – too many levels of authority.
2   Less consumer friendly – more informal due to size.
3. Decision-making may be slower due to time it takes to get from top to bottom and vital decisions might be made too late.

DISADVANTAGES:

1. Less specialisation or division of labour – usually lower wages for lower level workers.
2. Smaller economies of scale.
3. Lower turnover – restricted ability to invest in expensive modern technology as it may not be cost effective.

PRACTICE QUESTIONS

1. How does a Formal Organisation differ from an Informal Organisation?
2. What is an Organisational Hierarchy and how is it illustrated?
3. What are the differences between a Tall and a Flat Organisational structure?
4. Which do you think is more efficient?
5. What is the meaning of the term 'Specialisation'?
6. How might it affect the shape of the Organisational Chart?
7. What is the meaning of the term 'delegation'?
8. What is the meaning of the term 'subordinate'?

Departments within an Organisation

(Role of Departments in achieving the Objectives of an Organisation)

Nearly every organisation has five main functional areas, to which departments can be linked, depending on the type of enterprise in question. These functional areas are:

1. Technical: including production, manufacture, and adaptation of materials (Production Department).
2. Commercial: including buying, selling and exchange (Purchases and Sales Departments).
3. Financial: activities designed to obtain capital and to make the best use of it (Financial Department).
4. Accounting: including payroll, tax returns, stock-taking and the preparation of balance sheets, cost statements and business statistics (Accounting Department).
5. Managerial activities: dealing with staff incentives and documentation, manpower planning and selection and general administration regarding staff (Personnel Department).

The divisions above would represent departmentation by function – a logical and traditional method which allows the division of work into specialist areas and is especially evident in large organisations. Within each department workers are specifically skilled and are allowed to concentrate on one task or a group of linked tasks. This process is referred to as specialisation or the division of labour. The aim is to increase efficiency and productivity in the organisation. Departmentation involves the clarification and grouping of tasks allotted to groups of people. It allows the organisation to complete targeted tasks that it has set itself.

The various means of departmentation are

1. by function (functional)
2. by product (product – divisional)
3. by region (geographical or territorial)
4. by a mixture of the above (matrix).

DEPARTMENTATION BY FUNCTION
(with further sub-departmental divisions based on function)

DEPARTMENTATION BY PRODUCT

Managing Director (e.g. large supermarket)

sales	purchases	finance	production	personnel
home export	buying stores	costing records	assembly service	recruitment staff welfare

Figure 1.2 Functional Division of Organisation

Most companies have a mix of products at different stages of their life cycle. A single product might become outdated or unfashionable. Divisional managers might be given responsibility for a product or a brand line of products. It encourages expertise in sales and service areas.

Managing Director (e.g. a car, truck and aircraft components manufacturer like Volvo)

Divisional Manager Cars	Divisional Manager Trucks	Divisional Manager Aircraft Components

Figure 1.3 Product Division of Organisation

DEPARTMENTATION BY REGION OR TERRITORY (GEOGRAPHIC DIVISION)

Suitable for organisations where similar activities are carried out in widely different locations. On the spot decision-making would be required due to local knowledge and the duplication of accounting tasks could be costly, e.g. insurance companies or travel agencies.

Managing Director (e.g. Dunnes Stores Branches Ireland)

Regional Manager North-east Branch	Regional Manager North-west Branch	Regional Manager Midlands Branch	Regional Manager South-west Branch	Regional Manager South-east Branch

Figure 1.4 Regional Division of Organisation

DEPARTMENTATION BY MIXTURE (MATRIX)

Within functional departments staff might be organised by region or by product. Also within product departments the subdivision of functions might exist.

Functional departments organised by product:

Managing Director (e.g. Sales reps organised based on products) e.g. Roches Stores Ireland

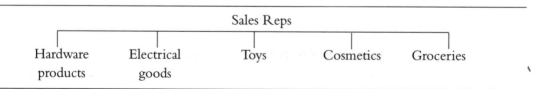

Figure 1.5 Matrix Division of Organisation – Function by Product

PRODUCT DEPARTMENTS SUBDIVIDED BY FUNCTION:

Managing Director (e.g. Bank servies organised based on staff functions)

e.g. AIB, Bank of Ireland or Ulster Bank

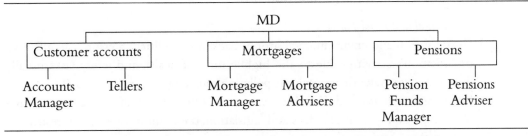

Figure 1.6 Matrix Division of Organisation – Product by Function

Departmental divisions are dictated by the size, type of business, nature of work involved, numbers, shifts, type of customer, and equipment specialisation.

Departmentation is the division of work into different areas. The division of people into groups within each department or sub-department and allocating a head of department will ensure a greater level of efficiency and specialisation, where the lines of authority and decision-making responsibilities are clearly defined.

Larger organisations find it cost effective to engage in this type of division of labour to increase sales and profits by utilising the expertise in each department, thereby linking the whole organisation in this way. Some of these organisations have a department specifically for research and development of product in order to out-manoeuvre their nearest competitors.

PRACTICE QUESTIONS

1. Define the term Departmentation.
2. Name and explain the *five* main functional areas to which departments may be linked.
3. Pick an organisation and outline and discuss the duties attached to each functional area (i.e. Departments).
4. Pick any business and make illustrated divisions based on the process of:
   (a) departmentation by function (i.e. departments in a business such as sales, personnel)
   (b) departmentation by product (i.e. products in a business)
   (c) departmentation by region (i.e. branches in the country).

Environmental Features affecting an Organisation

The factors that affect an organisation are:

1. *Political and Legal Factors*

Conservation and environmental groups backed by political pressure can affect an organisation's activities due to the highlighting of health and safety risks usually linked to noise, water or atmospheric pollution caused by the organisation. Regulations like registration, tax and VAT returns, as well as health and safety regulations, laws regarding employment practices and legislation, trade union laws etc. all restrict an organisation's activities.

Fiscal (tax and government spending changes and decisions) and monetary decisions, including changes in interest rates, sometimes have a profound effect on organisations.

2. *Economic*

The level of economic activity in an economy will dictate consumer income and purchasing power. The higher the level of disposable income (spendable), the greater the demand for goods. Price and changing interest rates will also affect consumers' decisions to purchase. Government fiscal (budget decisions on taxes and government spending) and monetary (interest rates and the availability of credit in banks) policies influence the cost of living and exchange rates, and therefore this also directly influences demand for goods and services from the organisation. The value of the domestic currency will influence investment in industry based on business confidence and the ability to borrow to invest, as well as confidence in future healthy economic activity. The number of competitors and their current success will also impact on an organisation from an economic point of view.

3. *Social and Cultural*

The ethical conduct of organisations is measured against legal and public standards. Organisations must carry out business in a responsible way that is both morally and legally acceptable. Attitudes, customs, beliefs and education, as well as behaviour and values, are generally adhered to by organisations. This will ensure that the business will remain a success or survive, whatever the case may be. Tribunals of inquiry are examples of the types of social factors that will affect an organisation's reputation (1998 Blood Bank Tribunal) in a positive or negative way, depending on the outcome.

4. *Technological*

New high tech equipment and computers have made work less time consuming and more capital intensive rather than labour intensive. Work patterns have changed totally as a result. The need for retraining and constant modernisation of product due to processes and products becoming obsolete (out of date) has been highlighted in recent times. This can incur extra costs for organisations. The development of the Internet is good from an educational point of view as well as being a medium for payment (for example by credit card), intercommunications and advertising for a business all over the world.

5. *Competitive Factors*

If a similar business becomes established locally, it may affect the business – depending on the nature of the business. Retail organisations are more likely to be affected than services like hairdressers or beauty salons, which tend to retain custom based on customer loyalty because of the hands-on nature of these businesses.

ECONOMIC ENVIRONMENT

SOCIAL/CULTURAL
ENVIRONMENT

THE
ORGANISATION

TECHNOLOGICAL
ENVIRONMENT

POLITICAL AND LEGAL
ENVIRONMENT

Figure 1.7 Environmental Factors impacting on an Organisation

Note: This analysis can be simply memorised by students, if they remember 'PEST plus C' (political, economic, social and technological factors that impact on an organisation, as well as competition factors).

Functions of Management

Henri Fayol (1841–1925) popularised the concept of the 'Universality of Management Principles', the idea that management should apply the same broad principles, no matter what sort of business is being managed. He is known as the 'father of modern operational management theory'. His work was published in 1949. He identified the following main functions of management:

1. Planning and Directing: to predetermine future action involving important areas like forecasting, objective-setting, decision-making and policy formation; also to direct events, as the organisation progresses towards achieving specific objectives. Planning is an essential element of good organisation and a manager must always be sure of goals.

2. Organising/Staffing: the activity of organising involves arranging and relating the

work (a structure of tasks) to be performed, so that it can be accomplished most effectively by staff. It involves progressing plans from the decision stage to the activity stage by grouping tasks into specialised jobs for each individual, where each individual's responsibilities are clearly defined. Organising also involves delegating authority (dividing up tasks) and clearly defining the lines of authority – where each person knows who is superior and who is subordinate. It also involves the co-ordination and supervision of performance at all times. Staffing involves finding and training suitable successors, as well as the responsibilities for hiring and firing where appropriate.

3. Communication: the key to good organisation where information flow is accurate and all inclusive with regard to staff. The manager will organise successfully by being open to change, by seeking new ideas and implementing them, and by incorporating new technology into the organisation.

Importance of Effective Communication within an Organisation

Communication is one of the factors of management which, when used appropriately, is the key to good organisation and which influences the efficiency and effectiveness of an organisation. Efficiency means 'doing things right'. Effectiveness means 'doing the right things'.

Effectiveness comes first and is the key to managerial success – as dictated by the style of management and how the functions of management are undertaken. All the other functions rely on the existence of a good information system within the organisation. If planning is to be effective, i.e. if there is to be an effective planning environment, the goals, strategies and policies of the organisation have to be communicated appropriately to those who need to know them. The single greatest cause of unco-ordinated planning is a manager's lack of understanding of his goals, company strategies and policies when he is endeavouring to make decisions. Otherwise, a planning gap is caused by a lack of communication: senior management understand goals and plans; workers know what they have to do; but middle management do not understand how their departmental goals and policies tie in with those of the organisation as a whole. Effective planning is fostered when proper communication is established and all levels of management are given the opportunities to contribute to plans which affect their areas of authority.

Efficiency can only be maintained when a high level of effectiveness is present and will be dictated by the individual skills, talents and styles of staff. Speed and efficiency with regard to work will gain the organisation a good reputation which will foster further future efficiency with results and productivity being based on good communication within the organisation.

4. Commanding: the activity of instructing subordinates, the demonstration of leadership skills. The roles regarding the 'Command' function can be subdivided into the following categories:

   (a) Interpersonal: the manager is the figurehead, leader and facilitator for liaison purposes.

   (b) Informational: the manager is a monitor, disseminator (sender of information in and out of the organisation), spokesperson (giving information to the organisation, having received it from either external or internal sources).

   (c) Decisional: the manager makes decisions about internal disturbances, and is the initiator of change and innovation.

   (d) Resource allocator: the manager takes charge of budgeting and the efficient management of time, money, materials, equipment and personnel.

   (e) Negotiator: the manager must deal directly with staff, customers and suppliers.

5. Co-ordinating and Motivating: the activity of co-ordinating involves harmonising activities of the different groups within the organisation; making sure each section and subsection operates efficiently and relates its efforts to the others. Motivating involves encouraging greater work effort aimed at achieving better results, the activity aimed at satisfying needs and drives within the work situation.

6. Controlling: activities and methods used by managers to ensure that previously agreed plans are in fact working (clarity of purpose, the awareness of objectives and targets). Henry Gantt, a specialist in scientific management, developed a type of bar chart which mapped actual and planned performances of the organisation based on agreed and established goals and standards. The chart provided a reviewing technique to compare target with actual performance over time. It allowed the effectiveness of the organisation to be judged in the light of specific targets. Based on mapping performance in this way, the organisation could take corrective action if a decline was detected.

GANTT CHART

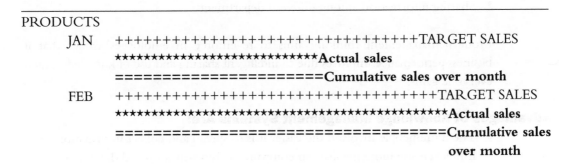

Figure 1.8 Gantt Chart

Explanation of Gantt chart:

- In January sales fell short of the target, so corrective action is required – either improvement of product or marketing improvements.
- In February sales exceeded the target. More money through higher profits might allow for spending on product diversification or spending on research and development of product.

PRACTICE QUESTIONS

1. List the environmental features that make an impact on an organisation and explain them briefly.
2. What are the *six* functions of management?
3. Briefly explain each.
4. Why is the function 'communication' linked with organisation?
5. How does Effectiveness differ from Efficiency?
6. Explain the roles of the manager with regard to the command function.
7. Why is motivation so significant?
8. What is a Gantt chart and which function is it connected with?

Knowledge Management

Knowledge management is the method used by employers and managers to leverage knowledge to improve overall performance. (The analysis of performance in an organisation is known as performance appraisal).

Knowledge Management Systems Involve:

1. Examining how an organisation's knowledge is maintained, accessed and exchanged. This knowledge comes from staff. Managers aim to encourage the sharing of knowledge and sometimes this requires a cultural change within the organisation.
2. Sharing information among different departments.

Modern management thinking aims to re-enforce in employees' minds that if business performance improves due to intelligent sharing and use of knowledge, then everyone gains.

Advantages of Knowledge Management Systems Are:

1. The more people involved the easier it is to spread and collect information.
2. Employees are more involved in company decision-making and the development of the business, which in turn stimulates greater work effort and productivity and leads to much lower staff turnover.
3. They keep the organisation ahead of the curve and cut costs.

Knowledge is power!

Information overload and increased
workforce mobility are highlighting the
need for knowledge management.
Sorcha Corcoran reports

Knowledge management is a
system that provides information
to employees to do their jobs
more effectively as well as preserving an
organisation's intellectual capital.

Information is everywhere, but finding
the information needed to take action,
make informed decisions and effectively
perform a job is still a challenge.

One of the key challenges of
introducing a knowledge management
system into an organisation is the cultural
change required. However, once
employees are convinced of the system's
merits, it should result in a more efficient
and better performing organisation.

Deloitte & Touch (D&L) was one of
the first companies in Ireland to
introduce a knowledge management
system, integrating it with the company's
human resources function two years ago.
Since then, this system has been
incorporated into the performance
appraisals of its 100 consultants, who are
assessed several times a year.

'As a professional services
organisation, we are overloaded with
information from all sources. We needed
to establish how to leverage our
knowledge to improve overall efficiency
and performance,' says Alan Whelan,
D&L's knowledge manager. 'Knowing
what you know and not reinventing the
wheel are the buzzwords of knowledge
management.'

Whelan explains that previously,
information and knowledge were
hoarded or segmented, supporting one
department or process. Often, company
culture did not support collaboration,
because employees were not required to
team together to identify customer—
focused solutions. Similarly, technology
links did not exist across organisations
and organisational systems usually only
supported one department or process.

The shift towards customer-focused,
cross-functional collaboration and
increased knowledge requirements is
driving the demand for better knowledge
management.

One of the lynchpins of D&L's
knowledge management system is its
corporate intranet, which is accessed by
the firm's 10,000 consulting staff
worldwide. The database contains a large
body of work, including proposals and
deliverables to clients and strategy
documents, and is searchable under
various headings.

Introducing procedures and
technology is a costly but straightforward
exercise, but Whelan believes getting
staff to use these systems is more
difficult.

'This is why we linked knowledge
management into performance appraisal.
It makes it clearer to staff that it is part of
our corporate culture that everyone gains
from. We are alleviating the issue of
individuals being the owners of
information, and trying to embed this
knowledge into the organisation.'

An important cultural element to the
success of D&L's knowledge
management system is that senior
management support it and, to keep
enthusiasm alive, D&L gives constant
reminders to consultants of the
importance of knowledge management.
On the third Friday of every month, it
communicates the message centrally to
all consultants, as they gather to discuss
the development of the business. Whelan
produces a knowledge management
newsletter every two months and also
runs occasional competitions, with prizes
for the best contribution to the system.
Knowledge management is part of
D&L's staff induction programme and is
also incorporated into ongoing staff
training.

Mobility of staff is a strong motivator
for introducing knowledge management.
Whelan cited the example of the building
manager at the Microsoft plant in Seattle,
who was the only person who has all the
building's blueprints. He left to work
elsewhere, but Bill Gates asked him to
come back as he has such exclusive
knowledge. Whelan says staff turnover
rates are not high at D&L, and believes
its internationally recognised as an
employer of choice.

Whelan fulfils a dual role at D&L, as
knowledge manager and consultant. He
heads a knowledge management
committee of six consultants, which has
a rolling membership. 'The more people
that are involved, the easier it is to get the
message across,' he says.

The advantage of running an effective
knowledge management system are
clear, but above all, it keeps an
organisation ahead of the curve and
reduces costs. Failure to examine how an
organisation's knowledge is maintained,
accessed and exchanged may expose
companies to revenue loss, increased
error, lost information, lack of customer
focus and the need to recreate processes
and information.

Sunday Independent, June 2002

The Need for Quality within an Organisation

Quality Control is part of an organisation's overall control mechanism used to maintain standards and to identify deviations that are unacceptable compared to an agreed standard of quality. It involves taking corrective action, if deviations are significant, to restore the agreed acceptable level of quality. The role of quality control is to ensure that appropriate standards of quality are set and that variances beyond the tolerances are rejected. It is, however, possible to mass produce items that are almost identical but are not defective and conform to quality standards.

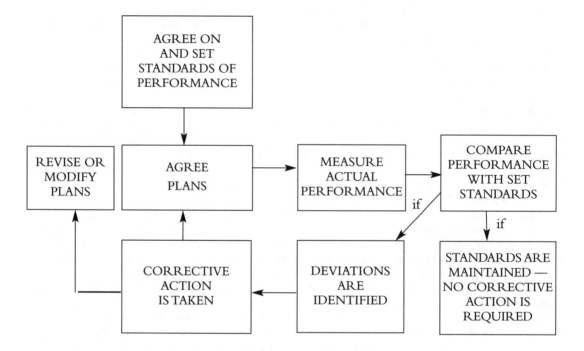

Figure 1.9   How Control is maintained

There is a need for quality control in an organisation because it is linked directly with such factors as:

1. Price: Businesses ascertain the quality of their products and charge selling prices which should correlate with these standards. Products such as highly priced porcelain will be subject to far higher quality controls than run of the mill household earthenware.

2. Consistency: Must be maintained to justify prices and for businesses to maintain competitiveness.

3. Safety: Products like pharmaceuticals and food require the highest standards of

quality to ensure the good health and safety of the community. Vehicles in general, e.g. public transport vehicles, cars etc. are also subject to intensive testing to ensure public safety.

4. Legal requirements: Pharmaceutical products are subject to health controls which are backed by legislation. The general public expect the highest quality with regard to products that they purchase. Legal action taken against businesses will affect their reputation and appropriate corrective action will be necessary to restore public confidence.

Quality Controls and Measures

THE MOST WIDELY USED TECHNIQUES ARE

1. 100 per cent inspection: this is used when perfect quality is required, e.g. in the construction of a nuclear reactor plant or pharmaceutical product.
2. Random Sampling: where batch production takes place, 100 per cent inspection is not always necessary, nor is it always effective, where inspectors' ability to concentrate might be affected by noisy or busy surroundings. (Up to 15 per cent of defective items pass unnoticed, recent studies have shown.) Better results can sometimes be achieved by random sampling. Random sampling means that a batch is accepted or rejected on the basis of the number of rejects found after taking a random sample from the batch.
3. Continuous Sampling: this is used in mass-production systems, and entails an initial 100 per cent inspection until a predetermined number of correct items have passed in succession; then random sampling begins and continues until a further reject appears; then 100 per cent inspection is recommended, and the cycle is repeated if necessary.
4. Quality Circles: a quality circle is a group of people within an organisation who meet together on a regular basis to identify, analyse and solve problems in relation to quality, productivity or other aspects of day-to-day working arrangements using problem-solving techniques. The idea of quality circles is based on the Japanese ethos of quality.

ESSENTIAL FEATURES OF QUALITY CIRCLES

1. Membership is voluntary.
2. Group usually between five and ten members.
3. Group selects the problems to be tackled and methods of operation.
4. Leader is usually the immediate supervisor.

EFFECTIVENESS DEPENDS ON

1. Commitment and support of top management.
2. Full consultation with staff.
3. A participative approach by management.
4. Delegation of decision-making.
5. Trust and goodwill on all sides.
6. An effective support structure of consultation and negotiation.

5. Group members will receive training in communication and problem-solving skills, quality control techniques and group processes.
6. The group recommends solutions to management and, where possible, has authority to implement agreed solutions.

7. Support of trade unions and/or staff representatives.
8. An effective training programme including development of quantitative skills.
9. Continuous monitoring and review of results.

BENEFITS OF QUALITY CONTROL

1. Reduction in costs of scrap or re-working.
2. Reduction in complaints from customers.
3. Enhanced reputation for company's products.
4. Feedback to designers and staff about performance of products and the machines required to produce them.

QUALITY CONTROL IN SERVICE TYPE ORGANISATIONS

This concerns staff and their approach to clients as well as their skills and professional performance in these organisations (efficient human resource management). Quality with regard to service will be maintained by:

1. Attention to monitoring staff performance and refresher retraining to update staff.
2. Management should be open to new innovative ideas and be willing to implement them.
3. Lines of communication should be kept open to avoid staff-management relationship problems.
4. Corrective action should be taken to restore damaged reputation due to bad client-handling techniques.
5. Prompt and efficient response to client enquiries or problems should take priority.
6. Efficient manpower planning and back-up mechanisms for handling absenteeism. Manpower planning is the activity of matching the labour need with suitably skilled labour and making appropriate projections with regard to future expected shortfalls of labour in order to ensure efficiency and quality of service.
7. Maintain a professional image at all times.

Quality Awards

THE MAIN QUALITY AWARDS PRESENTED TO ORGANISATIONS ARE:

1. Quality Mark: information available from the Irish Quality Association – 'Excellence Ireland'.
2. Hygiene Mark: information available from the Irish Quality Association – 'Excellence Ireland'.
3. ISO 9000: information available from the National Standards Association of Ireland (NSAI).

Smaller organisations whose market share is mainly in the domestic market would tend to apply for the Irish Quality Association Quality Mark and/or the Hygiene Mark. The IQA certification body is now renamed Excellence Ireland.

THE Q-MARK

The Q-Mark from Excellence Ireland has become one of the most sought-after trademarks in the Irish business world. To be awarded a Q-Mark an organisation is independently audited on key operational criteria and business results.

Benefits of the Q-Mark:
- widely known by consumers
- recognised as a reliable and trustworthy indicator of quality
- means significant operational efficiencies
- improves morale and teamwork
- will increase your bottom line.

The steps to achieving Q-Mark certification are simple. If you have not sought Q-Mark certification before, all you have to do is:
- fill in the application form
- submit it to Excellence Ireland
- wait for an audit to be scheduled
- have the audit completed and the result submitted to a board of independent assessors.

If your organisation passes the minimum threshold then it will be awarded the Q-Mark for a period of 12 months.

Many organisations, particularly first-time applicants, may need some practical assistance such as training, a mock audit or some direct in-company help. Excellence Ireland will be happy to provide any or all such assistance.

THE HYGIENE MARK

The National Hygiene Mark Programme is open to any company in the food or non-food sector. Companies are assessed under the following headings (with some variations depending on the company):
- Structural Hygiene
- Operational Hygiene
- Food Storage and Protection
- Staff Facilities and Personal Hygiene
- Hygiene Management System

A written report is issued and graded on a scale of A to F. A corrective action and surveillance system is in place.

Hygiene Mark (Assessment areas)

Structural hygiene	Operational hygiene	Food storage & protection	Staff facilities & personal hygiene	Hygiene management system
Size/Layout/ Design/Finish	General operational hygiene	Deliveries from suppliers	Sanitary (toilet) conveniences	Records
Water supply	Equipment & Utensils	Cold food storage	Handwash facilities	Hazard analysis
Lighting	Cleaning & Disinfecting	Temperature control	Locker areas	Hygiene training
Ventilation	Equipment requirements	Food storage	Eating facilities (canteen)	Other
Proofing	Storage of cleaning equipment	Defrosting of food	Protective clothing	
Grounds	Handling of money	Cooking	Jewellery	
	Sawdust	– hot food handling	Cosmetics	
	Internal waste control	– cooling of hot food	First aid	
	Food hygiene practices	Food display	Unhygienic habits	
	Cleanliness of grounds & premises	Returns area		
		Stock rotation		
		Pest control		

Source: Information leaflet from 'Excellence Ireland'

Recognition (The Hygiene Mark)

Successful applicants (typically grade C or above) are presented with **The Hygiene Mark**.

Companies who secure a consistently high score over a three year period are awarded **The Triple Hygiene Mark.**

Awards (The National Hygiene Awards)

The annual audits are used to select award winners in various industrial categories.

The overall best performance is recognised by **The Supreme Hygiene Award.**

ISO 9000

Companies with international links will tend to have a preference for ISO 9000. ISO 9000 registration is a logical move for a company demonstrably committed to quality, i.e. a company that already holds both or either of the other two awards. Some companies may consider ISO 9000 not relevant to their particular needs or too expensive, since generally speaking a small to medium-sized company can expect to pay €4,000–€5,000 plus expenses on consultation fees. Added to this is the staff time devoted to preparing the quality system and the cost of the audit of this system, as well as the production of a quality manual. The National Standards Association of Ireland (NSAI) is the certification body for ISO 9000.

The Michelin Guide – Star Ratings

The Michelin Guide awards restaurants between one and three stars based on the quality of the cuisine served: *three stars* indicate that food, wine, décor and service are exceptional; *two stars* indicate perfection; and *one star* means that food is very good and there is a pleasant environment.

The Guide warns readers not to compare the very fancy 'de luxe' restaurant that has *one star* to a simpler restaurant 'where you can appreciate fine food at a reasonable price'. (Refer to **www.cuisinenet.com**)

Bord Failte Quality Assurance

Tourism Accommodation Approval (B and B approval)
This organisation allocates Bord Failte approval to bed and breakfast accommodation. It is located in Donegal. (Tel: 072 52760)

Excellence in Tourism (Hotel, Guesthouse, Caravan and Camping Park Accommodation Approval)

This organisation awards different Bord Failte grades of excellence to accommodation within the tourist industry as indicated above. It is located in Dublin. (Tel: 01 676 8018)

Quality Training

Any entrepreneur wishing to enter the food and drinks industry (i.e. restaurants or hotels) should at the very minimum consider the FÁS Certificate Course in Foundation Hygiene for Food Handlers as it ties in very nicely with the requirements of the three quality marks.

The Irish Quality Association (Excellence Ireland) provides training and information on quality systems and FÁS may grant aid attendance on these training programmes by qualified applicants under the FÁS Training Support Scheme. The applicants would need to apply for grant aid to FÁS before attendance on the course.

PRACTICE QUESTIONS

1. How does the basic control mechanism in an organisation operate?
2. Briefly explain the factors that dictate the need for quality in an organisation.
3. Explain the *four* main techniques used to maintain quality in organisations.
4. What are Quality Circles and have they a good chance of being effective in your opinion?
5. What are the benefits of quality control in an organisation?
6. Why does quality control in service type organisations differ from quality control in manufacturing organisations?
7. Name the *three* main quality awards.
8. Why does ISO 9000 differ from the other two awards?
9. What are the Michelin Guide Awards?
10. How does Bord Failte guarantee quality with regard to accommodation in Ireland?

How Students can Research Organisations

Methods to Collect Data

A survey is a framework used to collect primary data (raw data). Surveys are usually carried out using the following methods:

1. Observation or Direct Measurement.
2. Enumeration.
3. The Personal Interview (face-to-face).
4. The Telephone Interview.
5. The Postal Interview.
6. The Internet Interview.

OBSERVATION AND DIRECT MEASUREMENT

This describes the counting or measuring of items of data. The Roads Authority often employs this type of survey technique when it is carrying out a traffic survey. The survey can involve counting the number of cars that pass a particular location in a given time period.

ENUMERATION

This involves the distributing of questionnaires and the follow up collection of them. An example is the Census of Population. Due to the length and detail required on the Census Questionnaires, households need time to complete them. The collectors are called enumerators.

THE PERSONAL INTERVIEW

This is a face-to-face interview where 'the interviewer' asks 'the respondent' (person being interviewed) a series of questions that are contained on the interviewers questionnaire. The interviewer records the responses. Example: Detergent and washing powder manufacturers often use this survey technique. They carry out door-to-door household surveys, the results of which can be used as part of their advertising campaigns.

THE TELEPHONE INTERVIEW

This is an interview by telephone where the interviewer asks the respondent a series of questions that are contained in the interviewer's questionnaire. The interviewer records the responses.

THE POSTAL INTERVIEW

This questionnaire is posted to the respondent when a survey is being conducted.

THE INTERNET INTERVIEW

Many marketing research agencies have web sites on the Internet and offer their services that include construction of questionnaires, fieldwork, collection of data, processing data and analysis of the results of research. Companies and businesses find that this is a useful way of analysing business performance and making comparisons with competitors. Email (Electronic Mail) allows questionnaires to be sent to respondents via computer and increasingly the Internet is being used to collect data and show results and the analysis of these results.

QUESTIONNAIRES & QUESTIONNAIRE DESIGN

A questionnaire is a group of questions compiled to do a survey. Types of questionnaires include:
1. The questionnaire for a Census
2. The questionnaire for the personal interview
3. The questionnaire for the telephone interview
4. The postal questionnaire
5. The Internet questionnaire

QUESTIONNAIRE DESIGN

In order to put a useful questionnaire together – where information can be easily collated and coded, the investigator must be aware of different type of questions that can be asked.

OPEN-ENDED QUESTIONS: These questions are questions that lead to opinionated answers and are difficult to code but inject a useful level of variety and variability into a survey when they are constructed correctly. For example:
*   Q What do you think of the performance of the current government?
*   Q How in your opinion can we improve this product?

MULTIPLE-CHOICE QUESTIONS: These questions allow the respondent to choose from a range of options:
*   Q What kind telephone manner has Mary got?
    (a) Fair
    (b) Good
    (c) Very Good
    (d) Excellent

*   Q What daily newspaper do you buy most often?
    Choose *one* only.
    Independent
    Times
    Evening Herald
    Examiner
    Belfast news
    Belfast Telegraph
    Irish Sun
    Irish Mirror

DICHOTOMOUS QUESTIONS: These questions allow the respondent to choose as an answer either yes or no.
*   Q Do you support Labour for the coming General Election?
    Yes   No

*   Q Did you shop on Grafton Street today?
    Yes   No

TYPES OF PROBLEM QUESTIONS: These are the type of questions that lead to unreliable answers and are best avoided.
*   Leading Questions: Is it not true that Mary speaks well on the telephone? (The question is suggesting the answer is 'yes'.)
*   Ambiguous Questions: Do you think that Mitsubishi Lancers are better than Volkswagon Jettas?
    (What does 'better' mean? – maybe cheaper or better quality – It is open to interpretation.)

- Irrelevant and Unnecessary Questions: Keep to the point and make sure that the survey only asks the questions that it needs to fulfil its purpose.
- Complicated Questions that involve other instructions: If the answer to this question is 'yes', enter a tick at the top of the form and move to question 53. If 'no' answer question 52.
- Unreasonable Calculations: How much do you clock up on your phone bill in a week?
- Multiple Questions: Do you travel to work by car or by bus or do you walk? Some people might use all three modes on different occasions.
- Questions containing difficult, not easily definable words: Do you think that President Clinton should be impeached?
- Offensive or Tactless Questions: Do you go to Mass every Sunday?
- Emotive Questions: Based on Catholic beliefs, do you think that contraception is acceptable?
- Questions based on Memory: How many times do you go to the supermarket in a year?

S.W.O.T. and P.E.S.T. Analyses

The S.W.O.T. and P.E.S.T. analyses should be carried out when the student has done all the fieldwork and all possible avenues of questioning have been exhausted. The student should then compile comprehensive analyses in these two areas based on both facts (data collected) and the student's own opinions of the organisation being examined.

S.W.O.T. ANALYSIS

SWOT stands for the Strengths and Weaknesses of the business as well as the Opportunities afforded to the organisation and the Threats that endanger its performance or continued existence.

Examples of questions useful for analysis:

Strengths:
1. Are management structures well organised Are there good communication structures between management and staff?
2. Is technology future focused and of help to staff?
3. Is the organisation well located?
4. Does infrastructure (road, rail transportation) benefit the organisation?
5. Are social conveniences for customers like car parking, creche facilities etc. available to customers?
6. What type of pricing policy exists?

P.E.S.T. ANALYSIS

PEST means the Political, Economic, Social and Technological factors that affect the business in its own right, as well as in the context of the industry it is part of.

Examples of questions useful for analysis:

Political:
1. Have new political decisions had beneficial or non-beneficial effects on the business?
2. Has the business applied for and/or received any government grants?
3. Has the business had to register with particular bodies connected with the industry itself and/or connected with health, hygiene and safety. For example, leisure centres may look for grants from the Irish Sports Council.
4. Have the owners had to look for planning permission?

S.W.O.T. ANALYSIS continued

Weaknesses:
1. Does bad management exist? How can it be improved?
2. Is there a problem with personal hygiene?
3. Does poor customer service exist?

Opportunities:
1. What future plans have the business? — New ideas/possibilities/product or service diversification/more cost-efficient and higher quality operations.

Threats:
1. Has the conversion to the Euro currency affected the business?
2. Have new European regulations affected the business?
3. Are new or existing competitors a problem?
4. Are the cost of new technology and the pace of business innovation causing products or services to be obsolete (out of date)?

P.E.S.T. ANALYSIS continued

5. Has the government had to intervene to settle disputes and what effects has this had on the business?
6. Does the business play a part or benefit from the industry being placed high on the political agenda?

Economic:
1. Has the boom/recession in the economy affected the business/sales? Has new business developed? Has there been a positive or negative impact on the business?
2. Has expansion of product/service and/or premises taken place?
3. Have product and/or service diversification and/or change taken place?
4. Has new technology been employed due to the economic boom?
5. Have closures/job losses taken place due to the recession or are there more employed due to the boom? Is there a shortage of appropriately skilled labour?
(A Business Employment Profile in the form of a Chart would be useful and impressive — Line Graph, Bar Chart, Pie Chart — refer to 'Simple ways to illustrate results of research.')

Social:
1. Has there been a change of ownership resulting in a new work ethos (competitive urge) which is more customer orientated (more consumer friendly atmosphere)?
2. Have new infra-structural developments (improved roads and rail accessibility) and better customer facilities like car parks and creches made a direct impact on the business — by making it easier for people to avail of the service or to visit and purchase?
3. Have pollution and/or noise controls made it more difficult for the business to operate?
4. Have changes in fashion and popularity of certain products forced the business to change or lose money?

Technology:
1. Has the purchase of more modern equipment given the business the 'competitive edge' or have competitors won out in this way?
2. Has new technology meant redundancy or job losses (labour saving for management)?

Sample Assignment Brief

You are required to investigate and analyse topics appropriate to the structure and functions of any organisation of your choice. Please explore:

1. Internal organisational structures and functions.
2. External organisational structures.
3. The impact of these structures/functions on the performance of the organisation. Choose either the company where you have completed your work experience or any other organisation of your choice.

Sample Questions for Student Research on 'The Organisation'

These questions or a sample thereof may prove useful to students when carrying out a personal interview (face to face) for any assignment on *The Organisation*.

HISTORY & SIZE OF ORGANISATION

1. When was the business established?
2. Did it relocate and or change its name? (Is the business name registered in Dublin Castle?)
3. How many staff are employed male/female?
4. What goods/services does the business offer?
5. How large (square footage/no of floors etc.) is this branch of the Organisation. Could I sketch a plan of the building? Or use or take a photo of it?
6. Are there branches nationally/internationally? Please specify.

ORGANISATIONAL STRUCTURE

7. Could you provide me with an Organisational Chart of the staff and departments displaying regional, functional and product and or service divisions?
8. Are there many lines of authority (middle managers)? (Is there a flat or tall hierarchy?)
9. What are the functions of the staff mentioned on the Organisational Chart and/or other staff?

OWNERSHIP, INSURANCE AND BUSINESS CONTROLS

10. Who owns the business? Tick which category the business falls into:
    - Sole Trader
    - Partnership
    - Private Company

- Public Company
- Friendly Society
- State Body
- Semi-State Body
  - Other – please specify.
11. Is there a Board of Directors?
12. How is shareholding split?
13. Has the business got a:
    - Certificate of Incorporation.
    - Trading Certificate.
    - Other.

    Can I include a copy in my project?
14. What general category of finance was used to set up the business? E.g. Bank Loan, Overdraft, Venture capital.
15. How is the business insured?
16. How are the following controls handled in the Organisation?
    - Financial Control (Cash flow etc.)
    - Credit Control (Debt Collection and Payment/Credit terms).
    - Stock Control (EPOS, Stock-takes etc.)
    - Quality Control (quality testing, quality circles, etc.)
17. Does the business possess a quality mark? E.g. Q Mark, Hygiene Mark, ISO 9000, Star Ratings etc. If yes, is this beneficial?

INTERNAL ORGANISATIONAL STRUCTIRES (COMMUNICATION AND STAFFING):
18. Is the business represented by any lobby group, e.g. ISME, SFA, IBEC?
19. How is the formal organisational structure arranged? E.g. timetable, roster, rota, shifts.
20. How do staff complete tasks informally? E.g. swooping shifts.
21. How are staff interest and motivation maintained? E.g. Staff days, bonuses, commission.
22. Tick which communication systems are used to make the business operate well rate whether they are effective or not:

	Not Effective	Fairly effective	Very Effective
Intercom	❑	❑	❑
Meetings	❑	❑	❑
Notice boards	❑	❑	❑
Networked computer systems (e.g. staff email/ ICT access and usage)	❑	❑	❑
Internal phones	❑	❑	❑
Staff knowledge management	❑	❑	❑
Other	❑	❑	❑

23. Have recent global events affected the organisation? In what ways?
24. Has the change to the currency and European Union affected the business? In what ways?
25. Have recent political decisions affected the business?
26. What types of advertising, marketing and PR methods are used by the business to gain exposure?

FUTURE FOCUS

27. Has the Organisation got a five-year plan? What main plans are envisaged?

Student Analysis
(Impact of internal and external organisational structures/functions on the performance of the organisation)

Note: The student should carry out S.W.O.T. and P.E.S.T. ANALYSES (check previous information on this) and conclude by summarising what impact they think the functions and structures of the organisation have on its performance.

The student could take the following structure for this section:

My opinions on how effective and efficient the organisation is. (Being Effective means making the right choices. Being Efficient means a tight and well-run organisation.)

The following are examples of how students could analyse the impact different structures or functions have on the performance of the organisation:

Efficiencies	How these efficiencies affect the Organisation	Inefficiencies	How these inefficiencies affect the Organisation
Good Staff Management Interaction	Means for Good Productivity and a Happy Working Environment	Problem with Customer Service	Bad for Company Image
Up-to-date ICT Technology and nicely Constructed Website	Higher Sales than Nearest Competitor	Frequent Office Equipment Breakdown (Photocopier)	Slows Down Completion of Work and Causes Staff Irritation.

Simple Ways to Illustrate the Results of Research

Please refer to information on graphs and charts and the display of business information in Chapter 3. The following is a simple explanation and example of how to show the results of research in graphical form. The Chart Wizard in Microsoft Excel could be used to create these graphs.

Q1. How many staff are employed? Male/female?

Answer: 250 in total – 100 female and remainder male broken down into 20 females in sales, 10 females in production and remaining females in administration. There are 50 males in sales and the remainder in production.

Summary Figures:

	Sales	Production	Administration	Total
Males	50	100	0	150
Females	20	10	70	100
				250

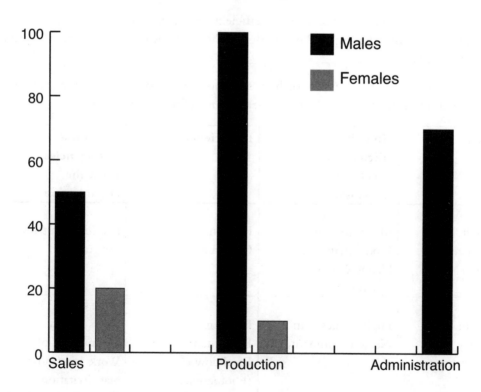

Staff Numbers

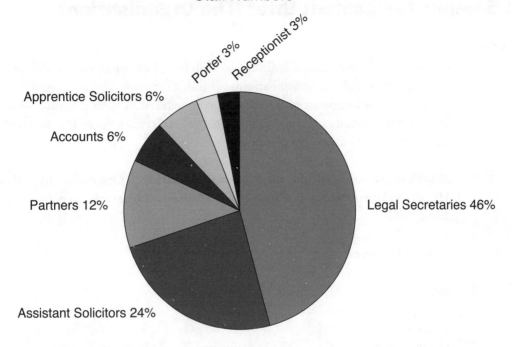

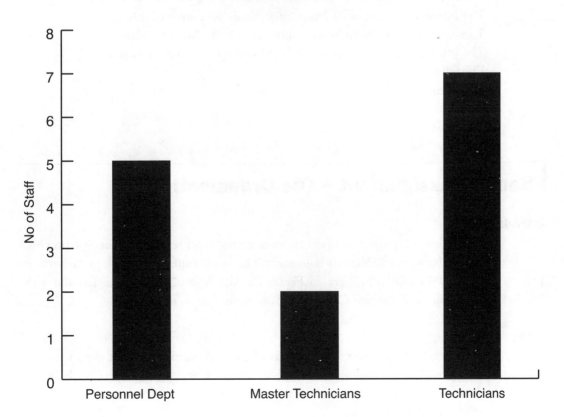

Sample Assignment Brief 'The Organisation'

Brief

Candidates are required to investigate and analyse topic(s) appropriate to the structure and functions of an organisation of the candidates' vocational area: e.g. internal/external organisational structures, communication, quality, human resources. Evidence will include reference to the impact of such structures and/or functions on the performance of the organisation.

Business Administration on 'The Organisation'. Compiled by Miriam Hirad – Business and Computer Student, Limerick Senior College 2002/2003

Table of Contents

Introduction
Aim
Objectives and Methodology
History, size and location of the St Munchin's Family Resource Centre
The internal structure of St Munchin's Family Resource Centre
The external structure of St Munchin's Family Resource Centre
The impact of the structure on the performance of the organisation
Efficiencies
Inefficiencies
Conclusion
Appendix

Sample Assignment – The Organisation

Introduction

The following project is based on two weeks' work experience at St Munchin's Family Resource Centre in Ballynanty. The work experience took place between Monday 11 March and ended Friday 22 March 2002. This project outlines the history of the Resource Centre and how equipment is financed.

Aim

My aim is to do a case study of the area I covered during my work experience and to explore the internal and external workings of St Munchin's Family Resource Centre. Ultimately, I wish to make the reader more aware of how much the centre is needed by the community.

Objectives and Methodology

I completed this project by compiling a questionnaire to be answered at the centre. I asked my supervisor to check the questions and then carried out this project. The questionnaire can be found in the appendix to this project. I also received leaflets from my supervisor; these leaflets are included here.

The history, size and location of St Munchin's Family Resource Centre

Unlike many other centres, St Munchin's Family Resource Centre is non-profit making. It is here to serve the people of the community. It was established by Sr Ursula in 1987 and was first set up in a normal three-bedroomed house. It has now dramatically expanded to three houses. The centre has always been housed in Ballynanty at Cloncocnnane Road.

The property is not owned by the people who run the centre, but by Limerick Corporation. The people in the centre could not afford to purchase these buildings as they do not have sufficient funds.

In the following pages I will include a copy of the centre's three-year plan. So you can see for yourself what the centre does before you continue reading this project.

Press Pack June 2001

Established in 1987 as an initiative of Limerick Social Services, St Munchin's Family Resource Centre in Ballynanty has a fourteen-year history of serving the people of its community. Over the years the work and profile of the centre has changed in many ways, but the centre's commitment to the local community, to all the community, stands firm.

The extent of St Munchin's Family Resource Centre's work has grown according to the local community's needs. At present it has five main broad areas of work:

1. Crèche
2. After-school Support
3. Work with Women's Groups and Families in the Area
4. Community Education
5. Senior Citizens Support.

As a Limited Company with Charitable Status the Management Committee of the centre is also the Board of Directors of the company. This committee of eleven members is comprised of people from the local community, a worker nominee, a tutor and a member of Limerick Social Service Council. All activities in the centre are overseen and managed by this committee along with the following:

- Sunshine Crèche Committee
- After-school Club Committee

- After-school Support Training Group
- Personnel Group
- Public Relations Committee
- Education Committee
- Senior Citizens Committee
- Bereavement Group Committee
- Finance Committee

All of these committees are fully functioning and assume responsibility for its particular project.

Mission Statement

Our mission is to support, give information, respond to learning needs, develop leisure and social activities for all in a friendly and welcoming atmosphere.

This statement is to be found underpinning all the work and activities of St Munchin's Family Resource Centre.

A three-year plan for 2000–2002 has been devised for St Munchin's Family Resource Centre. The objectives of this plan are:

1. To continue to develop existing and new structures which will support the family at all stages in partnership with other relevant bodies.
2. To develop the Community Education Programme by responding to the identified needs of the community at all levels from basic learning needs to further certification.
3. To make our building more accessible and user-friendly for all and to put it to best use.
4. To develop ongoing training and good employment practice so that the gifts and talents of the staff, committee members and volunteers are developed to their full capacity.
5. To develop channels of communication between the centre and the local and wider community by the establishment of a PR system.
6. To set up an ongoing process of monitoring and evaluation of all services and structures.

As well as ten full-time staff employed at the centre a range of FÁS initiatives provide a number of staff for the centre. At present there are twenty-one workers employed in the centre, Crèche and Community Hall under the Community Employment Scheme. Their work includes childcare, secretarial, youth work, receptionist, housekeeping and maintenance, outreach etc.

Two Job Initiative Schemes are in operation in Ballynanty which provide eight full-time staff at the centre. These projects are under the auspices of St Munchin's Action Centre and The Bridge, St Mary's Action Centre respectively.

Staff Structure at St Munchin's Family Resource Centre

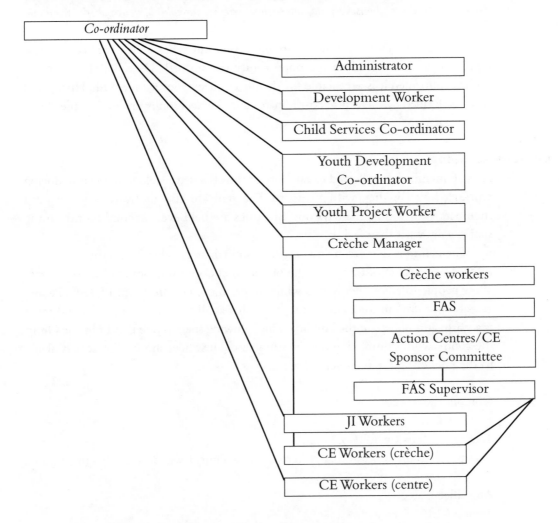

Co-ordinator (*responsible the Board of Management for all aspects of centre*)

Administrator (*responsible for administrative aspects of centre which includes wages, course enrolment and management, etc.*)

Development Worker (*responsible for certain projects at the centre, e.g. women's groups, community education, PR etc.*)

Child Services Co-ordinator (*responsible for all services to children under seven years*)

Youth Development Co-ordinator (*responsible for all services to young people over seven years*)

Youth Project Worker (*responsible for Follow Your Dream Project, a special project for a small group of young people*)

Crèche Manger (*responsible for all aspects of day-to-day running of crèche*)

Crèche Workers

FÁS JI Workers (*maintenance, housekeeping, outreach to senior citizens, crèche*)
FÁS CE Workers (*housekeeping, after-school, crèche, caretaking, youth work, reception, secretarial*)

No staff member is at present in any union but when staff members are first employed they are all given the opportunity to join SIPTU or BAPTA. As these unions confirmed it is acceptable for them to join whenever they wish. Hiring and firing is decided by the centre co-ordinator and the decision is finalised by the Board of Management.

Courses Available

All staff members are allowed to take any of the classes available in the centre during working hours if they wish to do so. The staff are also motivated by the head members as they organise days out. Meetings are held every second month so the staff can say what they feel.

The centre is there to help everyone as much as possible. To do this the centre offers a wide range of things for the public to choose from. Some of these courses allow people to enjoy themselves while they achieve certificates in FETAC. People can also just drop in for a cup of tea and a chat as all the staff are friendly and there is a warm atmosphere in the building. The following sheet is one that I obtained from the centre while completing my questionnaire. The Sheet shows all that is available to the public and the members of staff.

Computer Centre
ECDL Classes
Teenagers Thursday 4.30–5.30 p.m.
Computers available for e-mail, Internet access Thursday and Friday 9 a.m.–1 p.m.

An Office Career
Typing (RSA) Tuesday
Office Procedures Friday
Computers Monday, Tuesday, Wednesday

Confidential Information Service
Queries regarding your rights, entitlements, etc. will be answered on a one-to-one basis

Library Now Open
For children and adults

Childcare Course – FETAC
Level 1 and Level 2

Learn to make and design
Children's Irish dancing Costumes in our
Sewing and Embroidery Classes
Why not make something for your home in our new
Sewing and Soft Furnishings Class?

After-school Skills Support Training Course
At FETAC Level 2

You can get FETAC qualifications in
- English/Communications
- Office Procedures
- Childcare
- Cookery
- Personal Effectiveness
- Computers
- Crafts
- Maths

The Internal Structure of St Munchin's Family Resource Centre

The internal functions of the centre depend on the funding received. As the centre is known by the government as a company limited by guarantee and also as a charity, whatever money the centre makes for charging people for attending classes, they cannot make a profit as they have a Chargeable Status Certificate.

The staff's functions are allocated to them either by their supervisors or by FÁS. At present a total of thirty-six staff are employed at the centre.
- Eighteen part-time workers are employed under the community employment scheme (FÁS).
- Eight full-time staff are employed under the Job Initiative Scheme (FÁS)
- Ten full-time workers, employed directly by the centre, include a crèche manager, an after-school club co-ordinator etc.

The management structure of the centre is shown below. Each of these groups shown is answerable to the Board of Management. If the managers in the centre wish to purchase technology equipment they must ask the Board of Management for their permission.

The Board of Management consists of a total of ten people from the community. Everyone employed in the centre is answerable to the Board. They make all the major decisions affecting the centre.

MANAGEMENT STRUCTURE OF THE FAMILY RESOURCE CENTRE

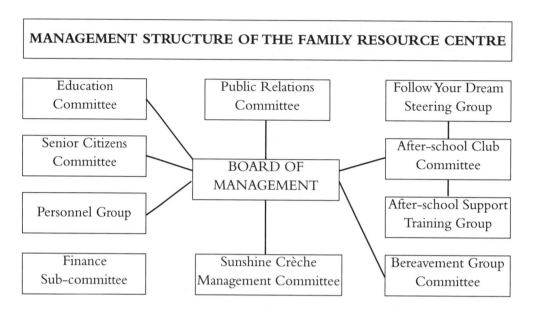

Resources at St Munchin's Family Resource Centre

The communication systems in the centre are very high-tech in most areas. A computer room connects you to the Internet. The new Dell Dimension Computer is one of the newest additions to this room. There is a notice board in the main entrance to the building. Of the four telephones, three are for internal use only, in the reception, the crèche and kitchen. The telephone with the external line is located in the head office on the second floor of the building. Leaflets, the newspaper and sometimes the radio are also used to communicate with the public.

The centre is not recognised by any Quality mark, but as there is a kitchen and crèche in the building there are occasional visits from health inspectors. They are always satisfied with the standards upheld by St Munchin's Family Resource Centre. The family resource centre has a Safety Statement that I was not allowed to include in this project.

The external structure of St Munchin's Family Resource Centre

The external structures of St Munchin's Family Resource Centre are what happen outside the building. The tutors who take the education classes are all from outside the centre. Some are from primary schools or colleges and teach at the centre in the evening also.

As the centre cannot make a profit, they have to depend on grants and donations from people outside. Those who make such donations include the VEC, PAUL Partnership and also the Mid-Western Health Board. Without these donations the centre would not survive.

There are many visits from outside inspectors to ensure the centre maintains high standards for the public. All those unemployed who attend classes or visit the centre are from the community.

The impact of the structure on the performance of the organisation

This section is divided into the following headings:

- Efficiencies
- Inefficiencies.

The following information will show in my opinion the efficiencies and the inefficiencies of St Munchin's Family Resource Centre.

EFFICIENCIES

1. *Security*

The security system in the centre was very good. A camera in the main reception area is connected to a TV system showing everything that was happening in the reception area.

2. *The Centre's good image*

When on my work experience I found that the centre had a good image which attracted people there.

3. *Interaction of staff*

All staff members interacted well with each other and with all members of the public.

INEFFICIENCIES

1. *Building facilities*

The centre is held in three houses. It would be better if more space was available.

2. *The use of only one external telephone*

The use of a telephone with an external line in the reception area would make the work in head office a lot easier.

3. *Depending on funds*

The dependence on funding means there is no job security in the centre. If funding stopped, staff would lose their jobs.

Conclusion

While completing my work experience and this project, my knowledge of St Munchin's Family Resource Centre has grown dramatically. I hope that some day the centre will not have to depend so much on grants as it does now.

Appendix

Questionnaire for work experience

1. When was the business established?

2. Did it relocate or change its name at any time?
3. How many staff are employed?
4. What goods/services does the business offer?
5. Have you an organisational chart of staff and departments?
6. Is there a Board of Directors?
7. What are the functions of staff?
8. Has the business got a:
   - Certificate of Incorporation
   - Trading Certificate
   - Other
9. Who owns the business?
10. Does any lobby group represent the business?
11. How is the formal organisational structure arranged?
12. How do staff complete tasks informally?
13. In your opinion how is the business
    - efficient
    - inefficient?
14. How are staff motivated?
15. What communication systems are used to make the business operate well?
16. Has the organisation got a five-year plan?
17. Is the business insured?
18. What general category of finance was used to set up the business?
19. What are the main factors that affect the business (negative/positive)?
20. How is finance controlled?
21. What types of advertising, marketing and PR techniques does the business have?
22. Has the business gained a Quality Mark?
23. Does the business have a Safety Statement?

2. Finance, Business Controls and Ratios

Why is Control So Important in Business?

It is a managerial task aimed at:

1. Setting standards.
2. Measuring performance against standards.
3. Feedback of results.
4. Correcting deviations that stray away from set standards.

(Refer to Figure 1.8 Gantt chart and Figure 1.9 How Control is maintained in Chapter 1.)

Control is one of the functions of management. The different types of control necessary in business are:

1. *PLANNING CONTROLS:* This involves the determination of instructions to be used as directives for activities within the company and to determine standards that are to be used for comparison. There must be clear, unambiguous plans to enable managers to carry them out efficiently and effectively. (Refer to the functions of Management in Chapter 1.)

2. *FINANCIAL CONTROL:* This involves budgeting – the formulation of plans for a given future period, expressed in quantitative terms; money management using cost and revenue controls.

   The following are the different types of financial controls that are used, depending on the nature of the business in question:

   1. Non-budgetary Controls
      Marginal Costing and Breakeven Charts:
      Marginal costing involves monitoring any extra costs incurred in a business and can help with price-fixing. Breakeven analysis is an extension of marginal costing. The breakeven chart maps total costs and total sales revenue and where the two lines intersect is the company's breakeven point. Below this line the company will see what output is making a loss, and above it what profit is being made on the other output. Total Costs are made up of Fixed Costs and Variable Costs.

      Fixed costs are for example rent, rates, permanent wages, insurance of premises – the type of costs that do not change as output or production increases.

Variable costs are for example part-time wages, raw material costs and overhead expenses like heat and light, telephone and general day-to-day bills that increase as output or production increases.

It is also important to note that there is a difference between direct and indirect costs.

Direct costs, like direct labour, are those costs that contribute directly to production. Production cannot take place without them.

Indirect costs, like indirect wages, selling expenses, administration and insurance, do not contribute directly to the physical production process. They are costs that are difficult to attribute to specific products or cost units. A good understanding of the terms mentioned will help students to answer the questions on breakeven charts, which will appear later in the section.

2. Budgetary Controls:

   This involves Standard Costing, which is costing out a job in terms of labour, materials and overheads. This is done together with monitoring total costs. Higher profits are gained by minimising costs.

   Departmental Budgets are an integral part of the functional budget which forms part of the Master Budget of a business – the departmental expenditures being generally sales, production, stocks, administration, capital expenditure, R & D (research and development), cash and credit control (debtors and creditors), purchasing, and profit & loss and balance sheet forecasting.

   A clearly defined financial policy allows management to authorise specific expenditures. The tight monitoring of costs using comparisons between actual and budgeted costs can allow the mismanagement of costs to be traced to a particular department. The correction of such deviations can then take place in order to minimise costs and maximise profit levels.

3. Financial Ratios

   Liquidity, primary, current, sales, expense and operating ratios are used to measure efficiency and to summarise and assess overtrading, solvency and profitability in a business. Financial control can be maintained by observing the resulting ratios and making improvements where necessary.

4. PPBS – Planning, Programming and Budgeting Systems

   This is a method used by government to control expenditure and to make decisions based on choices regarding money allocation for planned public expenditure. Calculations and benefit analyses are carried out by the programme.

3. *CREDIT CONTROL:* This involves the monitoring of debtors' and creditors' records – a system to ensure payment (into and out of the business): the means employed by a business to control the amount of credit it allows to its customers/debtors (the people that owe the business money) and to negotiate the amount of credit it is allowed to take from its creditors (the people to whom the business owes money).

The term 'credit terms' is the amount of time allowed to pay a bill. Suppliers can give 30 days (one month's credit) 60 days (two months' credit) or 90 days (three months' credit). Trade discount and settlement discount agreements are usually built into the terms of credit (discussed further in Chapter 6, 'Processing Business Documents').

4. *QUALITY CONTROL:* This involves the establishment of appropriate standards of quality. Variances beyond certain tolerances are rejected. The main methods used to control quality are 100 per cent inspection, random sampling inspection, continuous sampling, quality circles, and the application for quality awards (refer to the latter half of Chapter 1 for an explanation of these methods). Control charts are also often used and represent a graphical method to identify tolerance limits within which an item produced is acceptable and is not a reject. These charts have 95 per cent and 99 per cent tolerance limits.

5. *STOCK CONTROL:* Businesses must strive to maintain the optimum level of stock. This, however, depends on the following factors and the relationship between them:

1. The cost of holding stock – dictated by the type of goods in question – perishable/non-perishable, deterioration period, how long before the good becomes obsolete (out of date), and the cost of warehouse space.
2. Discounts available through bulk buying (warehouse space needed).
3. The variability of consumer demand.
4. On time, scheduled production supply to meet the demand: the shortage of materials or late delivery of materials can lead to major decreases in profits.

Keeping these factors in mind, a happy medium (optimum level) regarding stock levels must be reached, where a maximum and a minimum level of stock is set per item.

Minimum Stock: There exists the problem of holding the minimum amount of stock necessary to satisfy production (supply) and consumer demand, but at the same time not understocking. *Understocking* can lead to shortages of materials, with consumers switching to the nearest competitor (a loss of business and damaged reputation) – supply not keeping up with demand.

Maximum Stock: *Overstocking* can lead to excess supply (goods that do not sell) and the price must be reduced to dispose of the excess, like a sale (a loss-making venture).

Purchasing managers often make use of the Economic Order Quantity formula (EOQ) to estimate acceptable levels of stock per annum:

$$EOQ = \sqrt{\frac{2DS}{IC}}$$

D = Annual demand
S = Ordering costs (storage & delivery)
IC = Annual cost of holding stock (like the cost of the administration of stock (documentation etc.) and the cost of the security of stock)

QUESTION

The annual demand (D) for a product is 3,000 units and the cost of placing an order is €8 (S).

The annual cost of carrying a unit of stock of 10% is (IC).

Using the EOQ formula, work out:

(a) How many units should be ordered each time.

(b) How many times during the year the order should be placed.

ANSWER

$$\text{EOQ} = \sqrt{\frac{2DS}{IC}}$$

$$\sqrt{\frac{2 \times 3,000 \times 8}{10\%}}$$

$$\sqrt{\frac{2 \times 3,000 \times 8}{\frac{1}{10}}}$$

- Turn the divisor upside down and multiply – divisor is the fraction under the line in the case above.

$$\sqrt{\frac{48,000 \times 10}{1}}$$

Answer to Part (a)   692.82 = 693 units
Annual Demand = 3,000
Each Order = 693

Answer to Part (b)   4.3 = 4 times

- 693 units should be ordered each time – 4 times a year.

Average Cost is estimated as follows $\dfrac{\text{Total Cost}}{\text{Output (number of items produced)}}$

Weighted average cost is total cost weighted against proportion of income spent on goods.

REPLACEMENT COST OF STOCK: any stock that does not sell or is damaged in transit or in the process of selling is calculated as wastage (e.g. perishable items or stock that goes off easily like vegetables, fruit and bread). In these cases consumers like these goods to be very fresh. The stock must be replaced. Sales agents that deliver bread, in particular, must bear the loss of bread that does not sell and the amount taken out is the replacement cost. Systems have been developed in recent times to minimise waste, helping to achieve low stock levels without causing shortages.

PRACTICE QUESTIONS

1. Why is control so important?
2. Revise how Control is maintained (Fig. 1.9) and link it with the Gantt Chart (Fig. 1.8).
3. Name the *five* main controls that managers have to maintain in day-to-day business.
4. Distinguish between Fixed Costs and Variable Costs.
5. Distinguish between Direct Costs and Indirect Costs.
6. Explain how financial controls apply to business.
7. What is Credit Control?
8. Distinguish between a Debtor and a Creditor.
9. What is Quality Control? Link Fig. 1.9 with Quality Control.
10. With reference to Stock Control, what factors will affect a business that is looking to maintain an Optimum level of Stock? Explain these implications in your own words.
11. Differentiate between Minimum Stock and Maximum Stock and the problems with both.
12. What is the purpose of the Economic Order Quantity formula?
13. When trying to estimate the cost of stock, distinguish between Average Cost, Weighted Average Cost and Replacement Cost.

Ordering Stock – Re-order Levels and Quantities

Re-order level: indicates when to purchase more stock.
Re-order quantity: indicates how much to purchase.

When shelf space is freed up, it indicates the speed at which stock is being bought up by consumers. This will dictate the need to re-order stock. Trained personnel in retail outlets carry out stock-takes on a regular basis, to make sure that the appropriate levels of stock are being maintained. In large retail outlets like supermarkets, it is usually the responsibility of individual sales distributors and agents to keep their shelf space well stocked and to contact their suppliers and make further deliveries based on the retail outlet's requirements. From time to time, based on changing consumer choice, seasonal factors and other factors, shortages occur and either the retail outlet manager, department manager or the stores supervisor will inform the sales distributor/agent of the extra requirements. Some unsold stocks, like bread and perishables, are taken back by the suppliers. However, this is not always the case.

How the Retail Outlet Monitors Incoming and Outgoing Stock

In some supermarkets, deliveries are checked in through the stores area at the back of the supermarket. This is usually the responsibility of the stores supervisor.

1. *COMPUTERISED STOCK CONTROL AND THE ROLE OF ELECTRONIC POINT OF SALE IN STOCK CONTROL (EPOS):* In some supermarkets, a stock scanner is used to check in each individual delivery and to check out any returns (unsold/out of date stock) – last in, first out. A separate printout of the check–in and check–out is given to the agent/distributor. The number of goods sold is estimated by taking the number of goods delivered *minus* the returns.

Some supermarkets do not have stock scanners and in this case each agent has a separate stock card. The number of goods sold per day is noted on the stock card. The agent can estimate how many goods he/she should put on the shelves by looking at last week's sales column. An example of a stock card follows on page 58.

Stock control computer programs incorporate stock ratios to indicate the efficiency of stock control in a business. Examples of these ratios are:

(a) Raw material/Total sales turnover
(b) Work in progress/Total turnover
   Both of these ratios show stock-holding in relation to amount sold – detects level of overstocking or understocking.
(c) Raw materials/Purchases, i.e. total purchases/average stock – shows how many times stock is turned over or replaced – indicating the frequency of restocking.

New computerised stock control systems can monitor and track orders and balances and can indicate to the stock controller that stock renewal is required and 'best before' dates can also be estimated.

Other advanced stock control systems have good forecasting techniques incorporated into them in order to evaluate certain degrees of errors, i.e. degrees of overstocking or understocking. The mistakes are noted and adjusted using statistical methods like 'exponential smoothing'. Using this method, stock levels are adjusted by a proportion of the most recent errors in stock numbers and a new forecast of stock requirements results. The Box-Jenkins statistical method is based on the adjustments of errors themselves, based on past errors. Both methods are accurate and satisfy the requirements of larger organisations and those that deal in stock that could be a risk to the health and safety of the community. Examples are pharmaceutical products and nuclear products.

EPOS means Electronic Point of Sale. The point of sale occurs at the check-out when the product has just been sold to the customer. Goods are checked through an electronic check-out scanner system where bar codes automatically program prices into the cash register. The till receipt is the proof of purchase and proof of the point of sale of goods to the customer. Using till details on how much stock is left, the outlet is a means of controlling stocks.

EPOS Systems: New Solutions for the Retailer and the Consumer

From the smallest huckster shop to video stores to supermarkets, electronic point-of-sale (EPOS) and scanning systems are in operation. What used to be seen as a high tech novelty are now part of the norm, but instead of functioning purely as a counting system (goods sold, stock received, stock remaining etc.), today's EPOS systems are focusing more and more on the consumer, for the mutual benefit of retailer and customer alike. Modern retailers are becoming ever more aware that information is everything, and the more they know about the erratic spending habits of modern society, the better they will be able to cater for its needs. Today's retailing wars are being fought with technology in the quest for understanding the customer, tracking their purchasing habits, adding systems that help them decide on a purchase, speeding up service and literally trying to take the hassle out of shopping.

What is becoming increasingly clear is that information technology systems are essential in helping solve the riddles of what people want to buy, why they buy it and what makes a happy shopping experience. Software is being created and updated for PC-based EPOS tills, which include a vast range of functions including bar code scanning, card readers, receipt printing, dockets, loyalty schemes and communications. The advantage this technology gives to the retailer is instant information on what products they're selling, which are the more popular and, most importantly, who they're selling it to. Proper use of

this information has led to the success of loyalty schemes introduced by retail chains over the last few years. Basic loyalty schemes offer the customer price reductions tantamount to the frequency of their visits to the outlet. Alongside, products can be given a boost in exposure to the consumer by the addition of extra points; for example, "Buy a bottle of Yankee Cheez-in-a-Can today and receive 300 points!" This allows the popularity of the product to be gauged by the EPOS system; it will suggest whether Cheez-in-a-Can should be replenished and advise what time of year it sells best. Affinity schemes involve a wider network of companies based on the same premise (such as the "SuperClub" card) and similarly give retailers a mutual boost, while attracting the same demographic of customers.

EPOS systems have also developed to account for theft or "shrinkage", with compatible software being introduced to combat it. Most retailers have an idea as to when suspicious dealings are most likely to occur at the service till, such as the refund or exchange of goods, excessive voiding of transactions, and multiple manual entries of credit card details after the initial swipe. Although instinct is an advantage to any retailer, what EPOS systems offer is an effective means of detection. All of these events are identifiable while they take place, and the data can be processed quickly and efficiently. With EPOS systems in place with the relevant software, retailers have solutions that enable them to detect "shrinkage" patterns and prevent theft before it occurs.

For the consumer, information technology in stores and shops adds a vibrant new element to the way they spend money. The introduction of easy to use touch-screen kiosks give customers access to services, from locating the deli counter to what wine might suit the lasagne they just bought. In Britain, some car showrooms allow the prospective buyer to create the car of their choice on-screen, while music stores give the customer a chance to browse through CDs, check the prices, listen to selected tracks and print a list of what they've chosen. With interactive kiosks in place, the next step is integrating them with the advantages of loyalty cards, allowing retailers access to a very comprehensive profile of what their customers want.

The attention being focused on the individual has led to concern from some consumers. There are those who think that personal information stored by retailers can be construed as intrusive. What people gain from the developments in EPOS technology is accurate pricing, a much higher level of service, and discount advantages through loyalty schemes. The customer's involvement in loyalty schemes is voluntary, and any information held by the retail company is available to the customer. On the subject of credit card confidentiality, the retailer cannot hold on to any credit information after the transaction has been completed. So with the initial fears of EPOS systems having been allayed, one can truly say that both retailer and consumer are helping each other into the next millennium.

2. *CONTINUOUS WRITTEN RECORD:* This is based on the same idea as above. However, the account of goods coming in and taken out is handwritten on Stock Cards. The supervisor takes account only of the difference between the goods that come in and returns taken out.

3. *PERIODIC WRITTEN RECORD AND OBSERVATION:* Trained personnel that work in the supermarkets/stores might do a check on the stock position at the end of every month. This would act as a double check on agents. Discrepancies possibly due to theft or numerical mistakes would be noted when Sales Volume is compared to Till Takings.

4. *BIN CARDS:* An account is also kept of changes in stock, in item order. For example, a bin card might exist detailing the change in the stock of jars of jam. The balance of the remaining stock of jam is recorded on the card (example of a bin card below).

BIN CARD No. . . . .

ITEM Flour   UNIT   1.5 KG

DATE	RECEIVED	ISSUED	BALANCE
1 Mar	12	3	9
5 Mar	–	4	5
8 Mar	12	4	13

It would probably not be cost effective for other smaller retail outlets like boutiques, jewellers and small shops to have a computerised stock control system. However, it is becoming the norm in most businesses in recent times.

Note: Not all suppliers allow returns to be taken back. In most cases sales agents for bread and other perishable goods have to bear the cost of overstocking. To avoid this, they streamline stocks to a minimum level. Most shops like clothes shops only return items when they are damaged or when too many were delivered compared to what was ordered.

STOCK AND ORDER CARD

Department 16 Bread & Cakes

Sales from :
Order from:

Store
Supplier
Phone

Product Description

MONDAY		TUESDAY		WEDNESDAY			THURSDAY			FRIDAY			SATURDAY			SUNDAY	
Stock Floor		Stock Floor		Stock Floor			Stock Floor			Stock Floor			Stock Floor			Stock Floor	
Sales	Order	Sales	Order	Sales	Order	Order	Sales	Order	Order	Sales	Order	Order	Sales	Order	Order	Sales	Order
3		2		3	3		1	3		3	4		4			0	
1		1		2	2		4	3		3	5		3			0	
2		1		2	3		5	3		6	4		6			0	
3		5		7	8		11	6		20	16		18			0	
3		4		7	16		7	-		15	9		10			0	
5		7		13	-		7	8		18	15		12			2	
0		0		0	-		0	-		0	-		0			0	
1		7		7	2		8	10		14	5		8			0	
4		7		5	9		7	-		13	9		9			0	
2		0		2	6		2	-		2	6		3			4	
3		1		2	5		6	7		3	5		8			0	
0		1		5	-		5	10		8	10		11			0	
0		2		3	-		9	10		2	5		4			0	

Total: ___ ___   ___ ___   ___ ___   ___ ___   ___ ___   ___ ___

Signed for . . . .   by: . . . .

Supplier: . . . .

Stock Card example (agents and sales distributors fill these cards in on a daily basis in some retail outlets).

- Stock Sales column – indicates the quantity sold the previous week.
- Floor Order column – the aim is to match or improve on the quantity sold the same day the previous week. This will, however, depend on the amount still on the shelves from the previous day.

For example on Friday, where 20/16 appears, this indicates that 20 items were sold that day last week. Only 16 items are replaced because 4 must have been left unsold on the shelf from the previous day. The previous week's sales (Stock Sales column) provide a guideline as to how many items should be put on the shelf to avoid shortages occurring.

Stock Turnover is measured using the following formula

$$\frac{\text{Cost of Sales}}{\text{Average Stock}}$$

Average Stock: is Opening Stock *plus* Closing Stock divided by 2.

Stock turnover describes the number of times stock is replaced. Jewellers generally have low levels of stock turnover because the goods for sale are expensive. Shops, supermarkets and pubs would have high levels of stock turnover, with perishable (milk, fresh cream) and fresh goods (bread, some vegetables like carrots and broccoli) having a very short shelf life. The deterioration period, together with the fluctuation of consumer demand, will dictate the profitability of the retail outlet. The level of stock turnover will be indicated by the stock re-order levels.

Factors that Influence the Levels of Profits and Stock Turnover of a Retail Outlet

The following factors have beneficial influences on the levels of stock turnover and profitability:

1. More competitive prices.
2. Supplier advertising via television, radio, papers, direct mail, leaflet drops, personal selling (like cooking food in a supermarket), public relations exercises (creating an image that the public relates to the product) and special offers will usually increase consumer demand. Publicity in the form of the short sharp shock method is a marketing technique that can increase sales also.
3. Sunday and late opening hours will increase stock turnover.
4. Customer Service: consumer friendly shop layout, self-service with helpful and friendly back-up customer service and free home delivery.

5. Material Service: safety and hygiene, as well as the assurance that the outlet is always well stocked, with a wide and varied choice of stock which is always fresh. If the lines of authority are clearly defined when problems arise, prompt and efficient service should be provided in response to customer complaints, returns and replacement of damaged goods.

The following factors have undesirable effects on the levels of stock turnover and profitability:

1. High prices in relation to competitors can discourage demand.
2. The deterioration period together with the fluctuation of consumer demand, which can sometimes be unpredictable and perhaps seasonal, will dictate levels of wastage and unanticipated losses.
3. When supply falls short of demand due to badly managed re-ordering, failure to deliver or late delivery, the nearest competitor could win out (the substitution effect). This depends greatly on individual suppliers' relationships with their sales distributors and sales agents.
4. If stock returns are not taken back by suppliers, sales agents will streamline stock which is likely to cause understocking and shortages from time to time.
5. The cost of holding stock and warehouse space will dictate stock re-order levels and quantities.

Breakeven Charts

PRACTICE QUESTION

Morton and Murphy Ltd project sales for the next twelve months at 100,000 units sold at €10 per unit.

The firm expects the following expenses:

Direct material cost	€3 per unit
Direct wages cost	€2 per unit
Administration expenses	€150,000
Rent of the premises for the year	€100,000
Advertising fixed budget (yearly)	€10,000

Based on the 12 monthly financial information given:

A. Make the appropriate pre-calculations to prepare to draw a Breakeven chart.
B. Draw a Breakeven chart and include the following detail on it:
   (a) The Breakeven point.
   (b) The 100% Present Capacity position.

(c) The Profit or Loss when 20,000 units are produced.

(d) The Profit or Loss when 60,000 units are produced.

(e) Comment on your findings.

SOLUTION

In order to draw the chart, Variable Costs must be grouped together and then Fixed Costs must also be totalled. Sales *less* Variable Costs = Contribution (an amount that is contributed to the business – a type of profit figure). When Fixed Costs are then deducted, depending on how high these fixed costs are, an overall loss could result. If Fixed Costs are lower than Contribution, then a profit will result.

QUESTION (A) PRE-CALCULATIONS:

	€	€
Sales (100,000 x €10 per unit)		1,000,000
Less VARIABLE COSTS		
Direct Material costs	300,000	
Direct Wage costs	200,000	
Administration expenses	150,000	
TOTAL VARIABLE COSTS		650,000
CONTRIBUTION		350,000
Less FIXED COSTS		
Rent of premises for year	100,000	
Budgeted advertising	10,000	
TOTAL FIXED COSTS		110,000
Net profit		240,000

PROCEDURE TO DRAW THE CHART

1. Graph paper must *always* be used to ensure accuracy.
2. 'Output or number of units produced' is plotted on the X axis and Sales revenue is plotted on the Y axis.
3. The 100 per cent Capacity line should be drawn in first – vertical line
4. Then the Fixed Costs line should be drawn in – horizontal line.
5. The Sales line should extend from the Origin to the Present Capacity Sales revenue level.
6. The Variable Costs line should extend from the Fixed Costs line to the level of Variable Costs. It should intersect the sales line at the Breakeven point which can now be read from the graph, above which there is a profit and below which there is a loss made.
7. To read the profit figure or the loss figure from the graph, draw a straight dotted line from the given output level intersecting both the Sales line and the Variable Costs line.

8. If a Loss is detected, the output level will be below the breakeven output level and the straight dotted line will hit the Sales line first. The Loss is the DIFFERENCE between the two intersections and is read from the Y axis.

9. If a Profit is shown, the output level will be above the breakeven output level and the straight dotted line will hit the Variable Costs line first. The Profit is the DIFFERENCE between the two intersections and is read from the Y axis.

QUESTION (B) (a) TO (d) Breakeven Chart Morton & Murphy Ltd

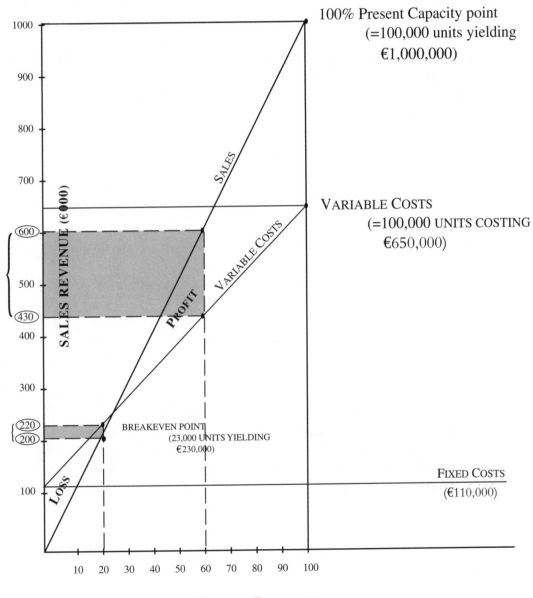

100% Present Capacity point
(=100,000 units yielding
€1,000,000)

VARIABLE COSTS
(=100,000 UNITS COSTING
€650,000)

BREAKEVEN POINT
(23,000 UNITS YIELDING
€230,000)

FIXED COSTS
(€110,000)

SALES REVENUE (€000)

OUTPUT PRODUCED
(000s UNITS)

QUESTION 1B (e) COMMENT

The Breakeven point indicated on the chart is where 23,000 units of production yield €230,000 in Sales revenue. Any output/production level below this will show a Loss, and above it will generate a Profit.

The 100% present or current capacity line indicates the maximum point of production to which the business can go, given present resources available. This business is capable therefore of generating a maximum of €1,000,000 (€1m) in Sales revenue by producing 100,000 units. This would always be difficult to achieve due to problems that occur, like employee absenteeism, shortages or damaged materials, machinery breakdown and other unpredictable occurrences.

The first small shaded area represents the Loss that would be incurred if the business only produced 20,000 units. This amount (€220,000 *minus* €200,000 = €20,000 loss made) 20,000 units is too low a level of production and indicates an under-utilisation and wastage of resources. This means that resources like labour and materials would not be used to the fullest capacity at this level of output.

The large shaded area represents the Profit that would be generated if the business produced 60,000 units. This profit (€600,000 *minus* €430,000 = €170,000 profit made) indicates good productivity (output per person) and the level of production is above breakeven point. Resources are being well employed to generate a good profit. The business is, however, a good distance away from optimum capacity.

The Fixed Costs line indicates costs that remain the same irrespective of any other activities in the business. In this case a set figure for rent and also for advertising has been agreed and will not change over the year.

PRACTICE QUESTIONS

1. What are Re-order Levels and Quantities?
2. How are stock levels monitored in retail outlets?
3. What are Stock Ratios?
4. What is EPOS?
5. How is a Stock Card written up?
6. How is Stock Turnover calculated? What does it indicate?
7. Explain *five* factors that have a good effect on Stock Turnover and Profitability.
8. Explain *five* factors that have a bad effect on Stock Turnover and Profitability.
9. The financial breakdown of the business owned by James and Sons Ltd is as follows:

		€	€
Sales (3,000 units at €120 each)			360,000
Direct labour		100,000	
Direct materials		50,000	
Factory overheads	– variable	12,000	
	– fixed	18,000	180,000
			180,000
Selling expenses	– variable	30,000	
	– fixed	16,000	
Other fixed overheads		12,000	58,000
Net profit			122,000

From the information provided:

(A) Make appropriate pre-calculations to draw a Breakeven chart.

(B) Draw a Breakeven chart and include the following details on it
   (a) The Breakeven Point.
   (b) The 100% Present Capacity position.
   (c) The Profit or Loss when 250 units are produced.
   (d) The Profit or Loss when 1,250 units are produced.

(C) Comment on your findings.

Sources of Finance for Business

The acquisition of money, often called capital, is the first step necessary to set up or develop businesses. Different interpretations of capital exist but it usually means money either in a liquid (cash) or non-liquid form (in the form of an asset). Together with the other three factors of production – Land (premises), Labour (workers), Enterprise (the entrepreneur co-ordinates activities) – Capital is the basis of successful business start-up or expansion. The four factors are known as the Factors of Production.

Business people usually avail of the following possible Sources of Finance to commence or develop businesses:

1. Bank or financial institution loans.
2. Personal savings.
3. Loans from family or friends.
4. Grants and incentives from public bodies (like the IDA, Forbairt).
5. Investment by promoters, partners or shareholders.

Capital can be defined as follows:

FIXED CAPITAL: the non-liquid form of capital – money in the form of land, buildings, machinery, equipment – usually not for resale and used as part of the running of the business.

WORKING CAPITAL: the difference between Current Assets and Current Liabilities of a business. Current liabilities generally consist of creditors (the people to whom the business owes money) and short-term loans. The lesser the current liabilities of a business the better because it allows for more working capital or current accessible money for immediate use in the business. Current assets are generally stock, debtors (the people that owe the business money) – there is money out there to be collected. The more debtors there are, the better. A healthy working capital figure ensures that the business has sufficient funds in the form of current assets to cover its current liabilities.

VENTURE CAPITAL: This is investment received from an investor who wishes to take a high risk, keeping in mind the possibility of making a higher than average positive return, as well as the possibility of making a negative return. An example of a venture capitalist is Richard Branson. Some promoters would also fall into this category.

SOCIAL CAPITAL: This refers to the infrastructure of the state i.e. roads, state schools, hospitals, public libraries. The basis for this public capital is through government spending of public monies

Short-Term, Medium-Term and Long-Term Finance

The sources of finance mentioned previously can be broken down into the following categories.

SHORT-TERM FINANCE (DURATION = UP TO ONE YEAR)
1. Bank overdraft: involves permission to overdraw an account in a bank to a specific amount, as sanctioned by the bank manager. It is a cheap source of finance, only available to customers who have a satisfactory record. Interest charged is allowable against profits or taxes. The facility can, however, be withdrawn at any time.
2. Bill of Exchange: could be described as similar to a post-dated cheque of sorts which is given in exchange for goods delivered. A bill may be discounted by the holder, should they require finance immediately, and the level of discount is normally agreed at the outset. The basic criterion applied to a bill transaction is that it should be self-financing by the date of maturity – this is usually thirty, sixty or ninety days, but can be arranged for longer periods. It is an unconditional order requiring the person to whom it is addressed to pay on demand a certain sum of money at an agreed fixed future date (an IOU).

3. Amounts due to be paid by Debtors still outstanding, but yet to be collected: these amounts can be used by a business as finance. Debtors are current assets to a business in this way.

4. Credit terms agreed by Creditors (people to whom the business owes money): When a business purchases goods on credit, rather than demanding payment up front, creditors allow either thirty or sixty days before the payment is due. This time lapse allows the business to use the money it has to finance the business until creditors' payments fall due. Businesses like Dunnes Stores can sell goods for cash (cash up front) and purchase their materials on credit, sometimes availing of ninety days' credit. During this time they can bank their takings and earn interest, thus benefiting. This method of financing, involving rapid turnover generating small profits, is often called 'Leaning on the Trade' or Trade Credit Taken.

5. Letters of Credit: requests from the issuing bank to its foreign agent to honour all cheques presented by the holder only up to the limit specified in the letter of credit. It is an undertaking of a bank to honour demands for payment and is usually the means under which trade is carried out between companies in different countries.

6. Factoring: the sale of debtors for less than their actual value to a finance company – this company being called 'the factor'. The debtors are no longer the debtors of the supplier but the debtors of the factor. It means immediate cash to finance the business. A loss is made, however, where the value of the debtors might have been €100,000 and sold to the factor for €94,000.

7. Taxation and Expenses Due: There is a period of time, i.e. six to twelve months, before interest is levied on unpaid business taxes. A business can allow the money that is to be used for payment to accumulate interest. It is sometimes used for something else and in this way acts as a short-term loan to the business. Unpaid VAT and taxation on profits are often used as finance for businesses in this way. The same criterion can be applied to overheads and short-term expenses like ESB bills, rent and rates and advertising bills. If payment can be delayed, the money acts as short-term finance.

MEDIUM-TERM FINANCE (DURATION 1 TO 5 YEARS)

1. Term Loan: These are usually designed to finance the purchase of fixed assets. Repayments are made by agreed stated amounts as negotiated. Repayments are usually paid monthly or quarterly and the borrower knows exactly what his commitment is. Term loans are usually more expensive than overdrafts.

2. Hire Purchase: Also called Instalment Credit, it is a method of paying for equipment in instalments, while gaining possession of the equipment immediately. An example is payment for televisions, fridges etc. as part of the household ESB bill. An initial contract is signed on receipt of the article purchased and the repayment might be six payments over a year, every two months, included on the

ESB bill. The purchaser does not own the article, however, until the final instalment is paid. A computer might be purchased over five years in the same way.

3. Leasing: This gives a business the opportunity to use an asset, without ever owning it, for a specified number of years for set payments. The ownership of the article will never pass from the leasing company. This is availing of non-liquid capital to advance a business.

LONG-TERM FINANCE: (DURATION 5 YEARS AND OVER)

1. Investment/Owner Capital: Promoters, partners, shareholders, venture capitalists can all be owners of a business and are responsible for investing and contributing long-term capital to the business. The more the investment, the greater the ability for a business to grow and expand and to become more competitive by being able to purchase the most modern equipment and to employ highly skilled staff and pay them accordingly.

   Ordinary shareholders, preference shareholders and debenture holders contribute the capital to the business. These shares are said to be the Equity Share Capital of the business – this means the holders are entitled to the equity or balance of profits.

   Ordinary shareholders are the risk-takers because there is no guaranteed dividend (money paid out of profits, not out of the original capital). They are the last people to get money. (Generally they have voting rights.)

   Preference shareholders carry a fixed dividend and must be paid before ordinary shareholders. (Generally they have less or no voting rights compared to ordinary shareholders.)

   Debenture holders contribute the capital in the form of a long-term loan, carrying a fixed rate of interest and a specified repayment date (maturity date). Debenture holders are paid before the other shareholders, even if profits are inadequate to cover the repayment. The risk of court action exists if a business defaults on the interest payments, and this could force receivership. (Generally they have no vote.)

2. Sale and Lease Back: Large companies often run short of ready finance and may decide to sell their premises to an investment institution. These companies then lease the same buildings or offices (a long-term lease – usually twenty years) from the investment institution Business continues as before, but on a rental basis. The rent is reviewed every few years. Ready finance is received up front on the sale of the premises, allowing the business to become liquid again, despite having to pay rent in exchange.

3. Government and semi-state grants: New domestic small businesses as well as export orientated businesses tend to gain finance in the form of grants because these producers help to improve the Balance of Trade situation through import substitution and capital inflow.

PRACTICE QUESTIONS

1. What are the *four* Factors of Production?
2. What are the differences between Fixed capital and Social capital?
3. What are the differences between Working Capital and Venture Capital?
4. What are the differences between a Bank Overdraft and a Term Loan?
5. What is a Bill of Exchange?
6. How do Letters of Credit and Credit Terms differ?
7. Why are Debtors regarded as sources of short-term finance and how is Factoring connected with debtors?
8. Why is Taxation regarded as a source of short-term finance?
9. Are Leasing and Sale and Lease Back one and the same?
10. Define Hire Purchase giving a current example.
11. How do Ordinary, Preference Shareholders and Debentures differ with regard to ownership of a business?
12. What is Equity Share Capital?
13. Explain the following: Dividend, Sale and Lease Back, and Government/semi-state grants.
14. Why are domestic entrepreneurs given grants?

Commencement and Development Finance

Commencement Finance: start-up finance for new entrepreneurs, who have no track record. It is also referred to as Seed Capital.

Development Finance: This is the type of finance required by existing businesses when they wish to expand. It is also referred to as Expansion Capital. Expansion capital is regarded as being less risky than seed capital by most financial institutions. Businesses with a healthy track record will be given expansion capital readily by these institutions.

EXAMPLES OF SCHEMES AND BODIES THAT PROVIDE COMMENCEMENT FINANCE ARE:

Allied Irish Bank Enterprise Development Bureau, Enterprise Ireland, Bank of Ireland Enterprise Support Scheme, Shannon Development, IDA, FÁS and Area Partnerships (government-financed organisations geared mainly towards financial support for the long-term unemployed who wish to train or retrain with the view to starting their own businesses), and the Arts Council (where a cultural aspect of enterprise must be displayed).

EXAMPLES of a scheme that deals with development finance is the Business Expansion Scheme (BES) which was introduced in 1984. It encourages the general public to invest money in the shares of approved companies where the money can be written off against taxes. Also incentives on dividends exist for investors. The companies availing of the finance must not be quoted on the Stock Exchange. Investment duration is five years minimum.

Matching the Sources of Finance with Particular Needs of the Organisation or the Individual

Long-term finance is usually sought by businesses who run short of finance or wish to commence or expand businesses, where the amount of capital required is large. The decisions and commitments are long term and costly and require serious consideration before they are undertaken.

Medium-term finance need not necessarily apply to a business. Someone might want to buy a home computer for their children or change a car by availing of a term loan. They might wish to lease a photocopier or buy the computer paying in instalments availing of hire purchase.

Short-term finance is usually required by businesses. A bank overdraft, however, can be sought by ordinary individuals who have a good track record with their bank. It will be reviewed after a year, whereas a term loan (medium-term finance) might have a repayment deadline of up to five years. Other sources like credit terms and taxation and expenses due represent short-term ways of maintaining the use of money, that would otherwise be used to pay creditors, to finance the business. (This concept is explained under 'Short-term Finance' in the previous section.) Also, quick money can be acquired by factoring, but a loss is made in the short term.

Cash Flow Forecasts

These are charts which analyse a business's inflows of money compared with outflows of money in order to predict whether a business will have enough money coming in to adequately cover outgoing expense payments due. Every business should compile a cash flow prediction chart or forecast each year or half yearly depending on the business. Typical inflows are sales, loans, investment capital raised, grants and refunds.

Typical outflows are interest on loans, purchases, wages, commission, advertising, rent and rates, light and heat, telephone, administration expenses, general expenses, personal drawings, and any capital expenditure like spending on fixed assets (office equipment/furniture, premises, plant, motor vehicles for the business).

THINGS TO BE KEPT IN MIND WHEN COMPILING A CASH FLOW CHART

1. Debtors' and Creditors' Credit Terms: For example, if we allow our debtors (people that owe us money) one month's credit, this means that if we bill them in January, the inflow will not occur until February (February entry into chart).

If our creditors (people we owe money to) allow us two months' credit, this means that if they bill us in January, we will not have to pay until March – outflow will not occur until March (March entry into chart).

Important: It is only at the moment that the inflows and outflows occur that the figures are lodged into the Cashflow chart and **not when the bills are dated.** This appears to be the most common mistake made by students.

2. Terms like 'month in arrears' and 'in the month incurred': Wages paid out by us a month in arrears (often referred to as a lag in the payment of wages by a month) means, for example, work done by employees in July will not be paid out by us until August (August entry into chart).

   Expenses paid out by us per month or in the month incurred means, for example, in June itself (June entry into the chart).

3. If a wage increase of 15% is due from June onwards, the increased figure will appear in the months from June onwards (including June). Note: the wages figure *never* reverts back to the original amount.

4. Terms like 'quarterly in arrears': Bills due for payment quarterly in arrears means at the end of every three months. Sometimes the first payment date due will be given, for example, a light and heat bill of €2,000 payable quarterly in arrears beginning on 1 February. Entries into the chart would be €500 in February, €500 in May, €500 in August and €500 in November. If no first payment date is given, and the chart is a twelve monthly forecast starting in January, the entries into the chart would be €500 in March, €500 in June, €500 in September and €500 in December.

5. A cash purchase of goods: This is recorded in the chart as stock – an amount bought and paid for on the same day. March cash purchases of goods for stock, paid for immediately, is entered into the chart as an outflow in March only.

6. Calculation of Commission: (This exercise is probably the one that students find the most difficult.) If staff are to receive a 5 per cent commission of total sales, it means that the calculations should be worked on the question given and not the chart the student is compiling. Cash and Credit Sales will be listed in the question and these are added per month to get each month's Total Sales.

   For example: if the sales information in the question is

SALES	Cash	Credit
January	2,000	3,000
February	5,000	2,500

and the commission is to be calculated at 5 per cent of Total Sales, payable to staff each month one month in arrears, then 5 per cent of €5,000 = €250 is entered into the chart in February. (This represents January wages not paid out until

February.) Five per cent of €7,500 = €375 is entered into the chart in March. (This represents February wages not paid out until March.)

7. If new equipment or machinery is purchased, it is entered once in the month that it is purchased. The equipment is assumed to be purchased and paid for immediately, unless other information is provided where a lease exists. If this is the case, it becomes an ongoing bill that is either paid monthly or perhaps quarterly.

Note: Depreciation has *nothing to do with cash flow*, so it is ignored in this regard.

PRACTICE QUESTION

Frank Smith is expected to have the following inflows and outflows of money from 1 January to 30 June 1998. The cash balance at 1 January was €1,000.

1. Expected Sales

Month	Cash €	Credit €
January	2,300	1,000
February	2,000	1,500
March	3,000	1,800
April	2,800	1,400
May	3,300	1,500
June	3,500	1,900

2. Expected Expenses

	Jan	Feb	Mar	Apr	May	June
Purchases (credit)	700	1,500	1,300	1,000	1,000	1,000
Cash purchases	300	2,000	800	1,000	1,100	1,400
Wages	1,000	1,000	1,000	1,000	1,500	1,500
Purchase of office equipment		7,000				
Rent and rates	300	300	350	350	350	350
Administration	70	60	60	60	60	65

3. Purchases are on credit, where one month's credit is taken from suppliers.
4. Debtors are allowed two months' credit.
5. Commission is 2% of total sales and is paid to employees one month in arrears.
6. A yearly light and heat bill of €2,000 is payable quarterly in arrears, with the first payment starting in February.
7. The lag in the payment of wages is one month.
8. Administration expenses are payable a month in arrears.
9. Any other expenses are paid out in the month incurred.

Based on the information given, you are required to:

(a) Compile a Cash Flow Forecast for Frank Smith for the period 1 January to 30 June 1998.

(b) Identify the sources of shortfall of cash.

(c) Recommend any provisions that should be put in place to avoid shortfalls of cash.

SOLUTION TO PRACTICE QUESTION

(a) Cash Flow Forecast for Frank Smith for the six months ending 30 June 1998

CASH INFLOWS	Jan €	Feb €	Mar €	Apr €	May €	Jun €
Cash sales	2,300	2,000	3,000	2,800	3,300	3,500
Credit sales	–	–	1,000	1,500	1,800	1,400
TOTAL INFLOWS	2,300	2,000	4,000	4,300	5,100	4,900
CASH OUTFLOWS						
Cash purchases	300	2,000	800	1,000	1,100	1,400
Credit Purchases	–	700	1,500	1,300	1,000	1,000
Wages	–	1,000	1,000	1,000	1,000	1,500
Commission		66	70	96	84	96
Office equipment		7,000	–	–	–	–
Rent and rates	300	300	350	350	350	350
Admin. expenses	–	70	60	60	60	60
Light and heat	–	500	–	–	500	–
TOTAL OUTFLOWS	600	11,636	3,780	3,806	4,094	4,406
NET (inflows – outflows)	1,700	–9,636	220	494	1,006	494
BALANCE 1/1/xx	1,000	2,700	–6,936	–6,716	–6,222	–5,216
BALANCE 30/6/xx	2,700	–6,936	–6,716	–6,222	–5,216	–4,722

(b) Mr Smith will experience a shortfall of cash in February. This is due to the proposed purchase of office equipment. Cash inflows for credit sales are not due in until March and this is also a major cause of the shortfall.

(c) The following provisions should be put in place to avoid the cash shortfall:

1. Either postpone the purchase of the office equipment or acquire a loan to cover it in January.

2. The length of payment time allowed to debtors needs to be reviewed and reduced to one month's credit. Money from credit sales would come in in February if this could be agreed.

PRACTICE QUESTIONS

1. Distinguish between Commencement and Development Finance and what bodies provide these monies?
2. What are Area Partnerships?
3. What is the purpose of the Business Expansion Scheme?
4. Does a Term Loan represent a form of short, medium, or long-term finance?
5. Why are Cash Flow Forecasts so vital to organisations?
6. Is Depreciation part of a cash flow chart?

Note: In order to understand fully the detail in the following section, the student should be able to prepare a cash flow forecast as has been explained.

Credit Control and Cash Flow/Liquidity

The frequency of cash inflows and outflows will be regulated by the credit terms agreed between purchaser and seller. Control on credit allowed means, in simple terms, chasing up money that is due to you. It is in the interest of all retail outlets to have a tight credit control policy.

Liquidity Ratio

Accountants measure liquidity using the Liquidity Ratio which ideally should be

1:1.   Formula: $\dfrac{\text{Current Assets } less \text{ Closing Stock}}{\text{Current Liabilities}}$

Answer will be CA *less* CS: CL

Current assets consist of valuable items in a business that can be easily converted into cash. Debtors (people that owe you money) are an example – money due to come in. Current liabilities consist of debts that we owe like creditors (people to whom we owe money). Closing stock is excluded because it is regarded as the current asset that is the most difficult to convert into cash. A business's current assets must be able to cover its current liabilities. In other words, the money it has must be able to cover the money it owes.

If a business shows a Liquidity Ratio of 2.5:1 this indicates a bad credit control policy and an under-utilisation of resources (meaning credit control personnel are not doing their job properly and debts are not being collected on time). There is a danger in this case that outstanding debts could turn into bad debts and would have to be written off – causing unnecessary losses that could be avoided.

If a business shows a liquidity ratio of 5:1 this indicates that its current assets are unable to cover its current liabilities, so even if the debtor payments due are collected on time, there would not be enough money generated to allow current liabilities to be paid off. The business in this case has a very serious liquidity problem and must substantially increase sales and profitability in order to break even.

Cash flow charts were discussed in the previous section. Since they are a means of measuring future requirements with regard to money needs, they therefore help a business to avoid shortfalls of cash and allow for appropriate future cash planning.

Impact of Credit Control Policy on the Liquidity and Profitability of a Business

A tight and regulated credit control policy is essential to ensure *on time* cash inflow and outflow.

DEBT COLLECTION: making sure that debts are collected and money is received when it is supposed to be received will:

1. Reduce the liquidity ratio and bring it nearer to the ideal 1:1 ratio.
2. Allow accurate cash flow forecasting, with planned spending being postponed if a shortfall occurs. If spending is essential, loan arrangements can be put in place.
3. Skilled credit control personnel will be able to estimate monies that are likely to be paid late, as well as possible bad debts. Money can then be put aside to cover these eventualities.
4. Future investments can be confidently planned, e.g. the purchase of new premises or equipment.
5. Costs can be minimised once sufficient monies are collected to pay off debts. This, combined with appropriate price competitiveness, advertising mechanisms, materials and customer service, will ensure a higher level of sales and will increase profit margins.

DEBT PAYMENT: making sure that money owed by the business is paid out to creditors on time will:

1. Avoid unnecessary interest accruing on loans, overdraft facilities and credit cards.
2. Ensure a good reputation with regard to debt payment and will help to gain new customers/sales through goodwill (reputation).
3. Allow an accurate picture to be drawn with regard to how much money is available to either put aside or invest.
4. Uphold good reputation with regard to business management and profitability and attract new investors. Greater capital investment means business expansion and further profitability.

Once a business remains within the credit term agreed (payment within a month or two months) and once this degree of flexibility is respected, creditors will usually be thankful for the business and may put more business in the direction of the company.

When a business has:

1. a satisfactory level of stock turnover, as indicated by how many times stock is replaced (empty shelves that are efficiently restocked) – discussed previously under the heading 'Stock Control';
2. an effective and efficient Credit Control Policy, indicating a well managed cash flow record; and
3. a 1:1 Liquidity Ratio (or as near to this as possible), indicating that the business has enough money in current assets to cover its current liabilities;

this will imply that the retail outlet is operating at a high level of efficiency and profitability and it has a healthy turnover per annum.

PRACTICE QUESTIONS

1. What is Credit Control?
2. How might a business know that there is a problem with its credit control policy?
3. What does a Liquidity Ratio of 3:1 indicate?
4. What does a Liquidity Ratio of 8:1 indicate?
5. How are Cash Flow Forecasts linked to Credit Control policy?
6. Explain *five* benefits of prompt debt collection.
7. Explain *four* benefits of prompt debt payment.
8. Why might efficient cash flow and credit control policies indicate profitability?

Unit Cost and Selling Price Calculations

The easiest way to understand Cost Analysis and how Selling Prices are arrived at, is to take a question as follows:

PRACTICE QUESTION

You are the administrator of a restaurant and in the business of monitoring costs. The following information is made available to you:

Ingredients to produce ten portions of Irish stew.

1 kg lamb	@ €1.35 per kg
1 kg potatoes	@ 4c per kg
1 kg onion	@ 13c per kg
2 leeks	@ 5c each
1 head celery	@ 10c
1 kg button onions	@ 18c per kg
1 bunch parsley	@ 5c

You are required to:
(a) Calculate the Total Cost of the ingredients used.
(b) Find the Average Cost per portion.
(c) Work out the Selling Price so that the business can achieve a 40% profit on materials.
(d) Calculate the Profit in money terms.

SOLUTION

(a) Cost of ingredients Total = €1.95

(b) Average Cost per portion = $\dfrac{€1.95}{10}$ = 20 cent

(c) Selling Price = Cost *plus* Profit (the Selling Price formula is a formula that must be learned)

Selling Price is always 100%

Therefore 100% = Cost *plus* Profit

Related to question:

$$100\% = \text{Cost} + 40\%$$

therefore   Cost = 60%

from (a)   Cost = €1.95

$$60\% = €1.95$$

What are we looking for? Answer 100% Selling Price

So $1\% = \dfrac{€1.95}{60}$

$$100\% = \dfrac{€1.95 \times 100}{60}$$

Answer = €3.25

The Selling Price that would be charged for the dish is €3.25

(i.e. $\dfrac{€3.25}{10}$ = 33 pence per portion based on 10 portions, which was not asked).

(d) The Profit in money terms is found in the following way:

Apply the Selling Price formula again but this time in money terms rather than in percentage terms.

Selling Price = Cost + Profit
€3.25   = €1.95 + Profit

Answer: therefore Profit = €1.30

It is important to note that different businesses have different profit margins and therefore the percentage profit levels will vary. Larger businesses can afford to charge lower selling prices because they can avail of large trade discounts through bulk buying or buying raw materials cheaper abroad. They create unmatchable price levels (too price competitive) that have contributed to smaller traders having to close their businesses.

Specialised businesses often have to charge higher prices because it is more expensive for them in terms of their costs and they combat their cost problems by passing on the cost to the consumer in the form of higher prices.

Warning! The last practice question only deals with Material costs in the catering industry.

There are three main costs in every business.
1. Materials (like shampoos and conditioners for hairdressers and food and drink for chefs).
2. Labour (payment for labour is wages – a rising cost in business).
3. Overheads (like electricity bills, telephone bills, insurance, advertising, stationery).

All three costs have to be taken into account when a business is setting selling prices.

Competitors' prices also have to be considered. It must be remembered that unless a business can secure a solid market share, it cannot charge extraordinarily high prices, because consumers generally look for a mixture of 'value for money' and 'quality'. Some consumers will continue to buy a good or avail of a service based on consumer loyalty.

Securing a good reputation (through advertising and a good marketing strategy) and resulting consumer loyalty will allow greater flexibility regarding selling prices.

PRACTICE QUESTIONS
1. What *three* types of costs are connected with every business?
2. How is Selling Price defined?
3. Why can larger businesses afford to charge lower prices?
4. List *four* factors that will have an influence on Selling Prices set by business people.
5. You are a chef and owner of a business and the cost of the ingredients of an Irish stew (which is divided into four portions) is as follows:

425 g stewing lamb	@ €2.20 per kg
400 g potatoes	@ 70c per kg
100 g celery	@ 50c per kg
100 g button onions	@ 50c per kg
10 onions	@ 10c each
100 g leeks	@ 55c per kg

(a) Calculate the Total Cost of the ingredients.
(b) Find the Average Cost per portion.
(c) Work out the Selling Price so that the business can achieve a 40% profit on materials.
(d) Calculate the profit (on materials only) of the dish as a whole, in money terms.

Note: Be careful to calculate the cost based on 1,000 g = 1 kg.
    In the case of drink 1,000 ml = 1 litre.

Sample Assignment Briefs

1. You have decided to start your own business. You are required to prepare a cash flow chart for the first six months of trading and a breakeven chart to present to your bank as you require an overdraft facility.

2. Candidates should investigate finance and business controls within an organisation of their choice under the following headings:
   • Brief History, Size, Ownership and Staff Structure.
   • Management Controls which include Planning Controls, Stock Controls, Quality Control, Financial Control, Credit Control.
   • Overall Performance Appraisal.

CHOOSE QUESTION A OR B BUT NOT BOTH

A. Downey and Sons Incorporated produce goods and have recently received worrying cost information.
   One product exists within the range of goods that is making a loss. Financial Cost and Sales information on this product is as follows:

Sales (2,500 units at €120 each)		€300,000
Direct Labour	€200,000	
Direct Materials	€40,000	
Factory Overheads – variable	€10,000	
–fixed	€30,000	€280,000
		€20,000
Selling Expenses – variable	€15,000	
– fixed	€8,000	
Other Fixed Overheads	€6,000	€29,000
Net Loss		€9,000

(i) Make the appropriate pre-calculations to prepare to draw the Breakeven chart.

(ii) Draw the Breakeven chart and include the following details on it:

    (a) The Breakeven point.

    (b) The 100% Present Capacity position.

    (c) The Profit or Loss when 500 units are produced.

    (d) The Profit or Loss when 2,000 units are produced.

    Comment on your findings.

(iii) What recommendations would you suggest that would improve the Breakeven level and convert the Net Loss to a Net Profit?

B. Based on your knowledge of stock control, analyse the stock control procedures that are operated by a supermarket or superstore in your home locality or wherever is most convenient. (The student should prepare well by summarising the appropriate parts of the text material in Chapter 2.)

3. Freebird Ltd manufactures rail engines and carriages. The business expects cash shortages to occur. The following details apply to the business:

1. Sales are expected to be €2 million in January 1998 and are expected to grow at 3% per month until December 1998. Debtors are allowed one month's credit.

2. The business has €300,000 in the bank in January 1998.

3. The issuing of company shares is expected to raise €600,000 in July.

4. Redundancy payments of €400,000 have to be paid out in May.

5. Purchases are calculated at 20% of sales. The company avails of one month's credit.

6. Wages are calculated at 30% of sales, and paid to employees one month in arrears.

7. Administration costs are expected to amount to €550 per month.

8. The outright purchase of premises is expected in February at a cost of €7.2 million.

9. Government grants of €40,000 will be received every quarter, beginning in March.

10. A tax refund of €3,000 will be received in April.

    (a) Prepare a Cash flow forecast for Freebird Ltd, for the 12 month period 1 January to 31 December 1998.

    (b) Identify the location of and reasons for any shortfall of cash.

    (c) Make appropriate suggestions to Management of Freebird Ltd as to how to avoid shortages of cash, based on this 12 monthly projection.

Sample Questions for Student Research on 'Finance and Business Controls'

1. Can you provide me with a little information about the history, size, ownership and staff structure of the organisation?
2. What types of planning controls are used by the business?
3. Are 'Knowledge Management Systems' used?
4. Is performance appraisal part of the business?
5. What financial controls are used in the business? E.g. breakeven analysis, budgeting, cash flow forecasting, cost analysis (income and expenditure analysis).
6. Are any specific types of computer software used for financial control within the business?
7. What are the main sources of finance in the business? Loans, overdrafts, investor capital, grants, savings – please specify?
8. How is debt collection managed?
9. How is debt payment managed?
10. What terms of trade (credit terms, discounts) are:
    - Offered to debtors.
    - Taken from creditors.
11. How does the business control quality and maintain standards of excellence? E.g. 100% inspection, random sampling, quality circles, observation.
12. Who mainly supplies the business with:
    - Goods.
    - Services.
    (Include office stock)
13. How are stock levels monitored? E.g. EPOS System, stock cards, indexing, MBWA – management by walk around, ordering/reordering.
14. Have understocking or overstocking ever posed a problem for the business? If so, why?

3. Banking, Currencies, Visual Data and Insurance

The Euro and the European Central Bank

There were 15 EU countries in the EEA (European Economic Area) – Germany, Belgium, Spain, France, Ireland, Italy, Luxembourg, The Netherlands, Austria, Portugal, Finland and Greece, Denmark, Sweden and the United Kingdom. More recently Norway, Iceland and Liechtenstein have come into the EEA with further enlargement anticipated in the future.

1 January 2002 marked the launch of Euro bank notes and coins. The introduction of the Euro as the single currency for around 300 million European citizens was a truly historic event.

The European Central Bank (ECB) has been at the centre of this development. The ECB was first established on 1 June 1998. The German Bundesbank in Frankfurt is the nerve centre of the ECB. It is the governing bank that covers the 12 different countries in the Eurozone (approximately 304 million men, women and children).

The ESCB or European System of Central Banks consists of the ECB and the National Central Banks (NCBs) of each individual member state. Three member states Denmark, Sweden and the United Kingdom are part of the ESCB but have opted not to adopt the Euro currency.

the euro

On 1 January 2002 the euro banknotes and coins were put into circulation.

...banknotes, coins and more...

The decision-making bodies of the Eurosystem are part of the ECB namely:

1. The Governing Council – the central decision-making body in charge of monetary policy for the euro area. The Governors of each NCB are members of the Council.
2. The Executive Board.
3. The General Council — for those member states that have not adopted the Euro.

Transition to European integration began with the Maastricht Treaty in 1997. Countries wishing to adopt the single European currency had to strive to meet the following economic criteria known as the Maastricht criteria:

*   Low inflation.
*   Sound public finances.
*   Low interest rates.
*   Stable exchange rates.
*   Political independence of its NCB.

These criteria laid a solid foundation for the new currency and a single monetary policy.

In January 1999, the locking of EMU (European Monetary Union) currencies against 'The Euro' marked the official beginning of EMU.

IRREVOCABLY FIXED EXCHANGE RATES

1 euro =	40.3399	Belgian Francs
	1.95583	Deutsche Mark
	340.750	Greek Drachmas
	166.386	Spanish Pesetas
	6.55957	French Francs
	0.787564	Irish Pounds
	1,936.27	Italian Lira
	40.3399	Luxembourg Francs
	2.20371	Deutch Guilders
	13,7603	Austrian Schillings
	200,482	Portuguese Escudos
	5,94573	Finish Markkas

Eleven print works were set up all over the Euro Area and the first Euro coins were produced in August 1999. Approximately 14.5 billion Euro bank notes were produced. The Irish mint (Currency Centre) producing Euro notes and coins is located in Sandyford, Dublin.

The Euro Currency was introduced on 1 January 2002. In Ireland both the Irish currency and the Euro were legal tender (acceptable in exchange for goods and services) until 9 February 2002. Since then, the Euro has replaced the Irish currency.

AN ORGANISATIONAL CHART OF THE EXECUTIVE BOARD
OF THE EUROPEAN CENTRAL BANK

EUROPEAN CENTRAL BANK

Executive Board

Willem F. Duisenberg, President

Communications
Counsel to the Executive Board
Internal Audit
Secretariat and Language Services

Lucas Papademos, Vice President

Administration
Legal Services
Planning and Controlling

Eugenio Domingo Solans

Banknotes
Information Systems
Statistics

Sirkka Hämäläinen

Operations
Payment Systems
Risk Management

Otmar Issing

Economics
Research

Tommaso Padoa-Schioppa

ECB Permanent Representation in Washington D.C.
International and European Relations
Prudential Supervision

FUNCTIONS OF THE ECB
(IN CO-OPERATION WITH THE NCBS JOINTLY KNOWN AS THE ESCB – EUROPEAN
SYSTEM OF CENTRAL BANKS)

1. To support and contribute to the general economic policies in the Community with the main objective of price stability.
2. Open Market Operations in general – to steer interest rates, manage the liquidity (cash) situation in the market and signal the monetary policy stance within the euro area – the decision on which OMO instrument is to be used lies with the ECB. The executing of the instrument is carried out by individual NCBs. (OMO instruments are listed later.)
3. Standing Facilities – The ECB determines the effect of overnight liquidity on market interest rates and signals the general monetary policy stance following these events. The administering of standing facilities are dealt with by NCBs. (Types of standing facilities are listed later.)
4. Minimum Reserves – the application of minimum reserves by the ECB is intended to stabilise money market interest rates and to control monetary expansion that can cause inflation.
5. Counterparties – a broad range of counterparties participate in the eurosystem ensuring healthy foreign exchange swaps.
6. Eligible Assets – counterparties may borrow from their own NCB by using eligible assets located in another member-state as collateral. This eligibility is controlled by the ECB.

Functions and Services of the Central Bank of Ireland

The Central Bank of Ireland became established in 1943 following the passing of the Central Bank Act 1942. It replaced the Currency Commission, which functioned as the national currency issuing authority up to then.

The Bank is now an NCB – part of the ESCB (European System of Central Banks). It shares a main objective of price stability with the other NCBs. This is backed up by the Central Bank Act 1998.

Functions of the Central Bank

1. The implementation of monetary policy acting as part of the ESCB (in co-operation with the ECB and other NCBs) to execute the main **instruments of the Eurosystem as follows**:

OPEN MARKET OPERATIONS

(a) The main Refinancing Operations – concerning refinancing to the financial sector (short-term).

(b) The longer-term Refinancing Operations.

(c) Fine-tuning Operations – this involves managing liquidity in the market and steering interest rates to smooth them following unexpected liquidity changes. Occasionally the ECB will decide whether fine-tuning bilateral operations (two or more countries) are necessary and it will execute the instrument itself.

(d) Structural operations – when the ECB wishes to adjust the structural position of the Euro System via the financial sector. The issuance of debt instruments are carried out by the NCBs.

STANDING FACILITIES

To provide overnight liquidity to counterparties backed by eligible assets. These can be broken down into:

(a) The marginal lending facility – counterparties can get overnight liquidity from NCBs against eligible assets.

(b) The deposit facility – counterparties can make overnight deposits with the NCBs.

MINIMUM RESERVES

NCBs must hold only minimum reserves of cash to avoid too much money being given out – contributing to inflation.

ELIGIBLE ASSETS

The types of suitable assets to act as collateral for counterparties loans and the eligibility criteria are established by NCBs, subject to the ECB's approval.

2. Acting as agent for and banker to the government.

3. It is legally responsible for the supervision of most financial institutions in Ireland including banks, building societies and a broad range of non-bank firms, exchanges and collective investment schemes.

4. Its Currency Centre prints Euro bank notes and mints Euro coins which are issued into circulation through the banking system. The Central Bank will accept all Irish bank notes and coins for years to come. (Note: other Euro area foreign bank notes and coins cannot be accepted and must be exchanged for euros in their own NCB.)

5. The bank reports to the Minister for Finance annually (audited accounts) – its statement on annual accounts is published and is a primary source of financial statistics on the Irish economy. The Governor of the CB appears before the Oireachtas when asked to do so.

6. The vast majority of the Central Bank's net profit is paid to the Irish exchequer (Government).

AN ORGANISATIONAL CHART OF THE CENTRAL BANK OF IRELAND

BANC CEANNAIS NA HÉIREANN
CENTRAL BANK OF IRELAND

Statement of Accounts   Organisation Chart   Departments

Organisation Chart as of 11th March 2002

THE BOARD OF DIRECTORS

JOHN HURLEY, *Governor*

DAVID BEGG	DONAL BYRNE	TOM CONSIDINE
GERARD DANAHER	FRIEDHELM DANZ	ROY DONOVAN
MICHAEL McBENNETT	JIM NUGENT	MARTIN O'DONOGHUE

MANAGEMENT AND ORGANISATION

	Function	*Head of Function*	*Deputy Head of Function*
Director General			
Liam Barron	-European Monetary Affairs and International Relations	John O'Leary	John Flynn, John Kelly
Deputy Director General and Secretary			
Brian Halpin	-Financial Control	Pat Treanor	Mary Sheehy
	-Financial Markets	Tony Grimes	Robert O'Hara
	-Payment and Securities Settlements	Dermot Maher	Paul O'Brien
Assistant Director General			
Gerry McGrath	-Corporate Services	Hugh O'Donnell	Joe Doherty, Brenda O'Sullivan
	-Human Resources and Planning	Jim Cummins	Lucy O'Donoghue
	-Information Systems	Padraig O Conaill	Clare Byrne, Michael Enright
	-Internal Audit	Peter Charleton	
Assistant Director General			
Louis O'Byrne	-Currency Issue	Michael Farren	Michael Bushe, Brian Murphy, Frank Porter
	-Currency Production	Daragh Cronin	
	-Engineering	Declan O'Brien	

Assistant Director General

Michael Casey			
	-Economic Analysis, Research and Publications	Tom O'Connell	John Frain, Maurice McGuire
	-Monetary Policy and Statistics	Frank Browne	John O'Neill

Assistant Director General

Liam O'Reilly			
	-Banking Supervision	Adrian Byrne	Billy Clarke
	-Securities and Exchanges Supervision	Pat Neary	Mary Burke
	-IFSC and Funds Supervision	Michael Deasy	George Treacy
	-Retail Investment and Insurance	Con Horan	Bernard Sheridan
	-Regulatory Enforcement and Development	Mary O'Dea	Terry Donovan

BANC CEANNAIS NA H ÉIREANN
CENTRAL BANK OF IRELAND

Statement of Accounts   Organisation Chart   Departments

Departments

The Central Bank
Notes and Coins
Supervision
Publications
Statistics
Consultation Papers
Exchange Rates and TWCI
The Euro
Off-site Links
Site Map
Document Search
Job Opportunities
Contact Us
Terms and Conditions

- Banking Supervision

- Corporate Services

- Currency

- Economic Analysis, Research and Publications

- European Monetary Affairs and International Relations

- Financial Control

- Financial Markets

- Human Resources and Planning

- IFSC and Funds Supervision

- Information Systems

- Internal Audit

- Monetary Policy and Statistics

- Payments and Securities Settlements

- Regulatory Enforcement and Development

- Retail Investments and Insurance Supervision

- Securities and Exchanges Supervision

Functions and Services of Irish Commerci

The most prominent commercial banks in Ireland are Allied Iris
Ireland, Ulster Bank, Permanent TSB, National Irish Bank, Agr
Corporation (ACC), and Industrial Credit Corporation (ICC).

Other foreign banks that have branches in Ireland are Barclay's Bank, Banque
Nationale de Paris, Chase Manhattan, Bank of America and Citibank.

Some of the functions of commercial banks consist of
1. Savings and Payment Facilities – deposit and current accounts (chequebook and cheque card), Special Saving Accounts (SSAs).
2. Giving out loans – bank overdrafts, term loans, credit cards.
3. Changing currencies, travel documents and mediums of payment abroad – foreign exchange, traveller's cheques, Euro cheques.
4. Providing internal and external mechanisms to transfer money from account to account.
   (a) Internal – direct debits, standing orders, Bank Giro (credit transfer)
   (b) Bank drafts, money orders.
5. Certain insurances – life assurance and pensions.
6. Payment of bills through commercial banks – electricity bills, telephone and mobile phone bills and student college fees – CAO etc.
7. Issuing credit cards and laser cards.

Refer to Chapter 6, 'Payment Methods', for full explanations of the payment methods mentioned and also refer to 'Sources of Finance' in Chapter 2.

OTHER BANKS
1. Industrial and Corporate Banks – AIB Finance and Leasing, Smurfit Finance and Leasing, Ulster Bank Commercial Services.
2. Merchant Banks – AIB Capital Markets, Ansbacher Bankers, Bank of Ireland Asset Management, Guinness & Mahon (Ire) Ltd, Smurfit Paribas Bank (Ltd).

Industrial, corporate and merchant banks provide financial and banking services for the business sector and are regarded as Wholesale banks.

ICT Technologies and Online Banking

The term 'ICT technologies' means Information and Communication technologies. In the current information age, advances in world communication have helped to increase globalisation and to make the world a smaller, more accessible place. The main types of ICT technologies that exist today include:

1. The Internet – a worldwide network of computers joined by telecommunication lines.
2. The email facility – both a computer and mobile phone medium allowing us to send and receive electronic information.
3. Video Conferencing – a mode of communication that cuts out the need to travel where a video link can facilitate the participant e.g. the 'poshare' video conferencing program.
4. Video Phones – used extensively by journalists to relate news to a newsroom at the touch of a mobile phone button.

What is E-Business?

E-business refers to all business processes that take place across electronic networks. This includes everything from buying and selling of goods and services through the world wide web, to interactive television, to advertising on the net.

Examples are: e-research, e-security, e-property, e-travel and tourism, e-education, e-working (telecommuting – working from home using ICT technologies), e-government, e-health, e-transport and **e-commerce** (an interchange of goods, services or property of any kind through an electronic medium which can be the Internet, or over intranets (websites that can only be accessed within a company or group of companies), using interactive kiosks, using telephones or mobile phones or WAP phones (WAP means Wireless Applications Protocol). The interchange of goods, services or property via WAP phones is known as m-commerce.

B2C Transactions (Business to Consumer)

Online shopping involves the selecting of products from a virtual shopping area and putting them into a virtual shopping basket, paying by credit card and conveniently availing of home delivery of the goods. The provision of new product information to existing and future customers through the electronic medium has indeed revolutionised business to customer transactions.

B2B Transactions (Business to Business)

E-business transactions **between businesses** include the sourcing of new partners and materials helping to open up new markets and provide better customer support.

Taking ADSL for a speed test

Broadband internet access via ADSL is finally
here for Irish internet users.
Dick O'Brien gives it a test drive

If you're a heavy internet user, one of your main bugbears may well be the speed at which you can access it. Most users in Ireland go online via a 56kbps (kilobits per second) dial-up modem. While this may be adequate for browsing ordinary web pages, trying to do anything more ambitious, such as downloading large files or viewing multi-media content, is often time consuming.

As a result, the arrival of broadband, or high-speed, internet access has long been anticipated. One such broadband technology is ADSL (asymmetric digital subscriber line), which is basically an upgrade of existing copper telephone lines.

Technology for living has been using Eircom's new i-stream ADSL service for the past two weeks. There are three packages on offer. The option we chose, i-stream solo, is probably the most suitable for home users. It offers data speeds of up to 512kbps downstream and 128kbps upstream. The connections fee is 199.65 (including VAT). Users will then have to pay a monthly fee of 107.69. The other additional installation cost is that an ADSL modem will have to be acquired. Customers have the option of purchasing an ADSL USB modem for 175.45 or an ADSL Ethernet modem for 242.

The first think one notices when using ADSL is the speed of web browsing. Almost every web page loads instantly. Similarly, email comes and goes extremely quickly. Even emails with large attachments took less than a minute to download. Another advantage to the service is that it provides a permanent connection to the internet. This means that you can set your email program to check your mail every 10 minutes, saving you the trouble of going online to check it at regular intervals. Because i-stream is a flat-rate service you can stay online as long as you like.

Another advantage is that you can still use your phone line for voice calls while you're surfing. That being said, a monthly download limit of 3GB applies to the i-stream solo service. Eircom charges 3c per megabyte for material downloaded over and above the allowance. However, 3GB is a quite a large amount and most users will probably come nowhere near this limit. In order to put ADSL through its paces we tried out a few common tasks. First of all we went to CNET Download (www.download.com) to download some software. The file we chose was 9MB in size. It took just under three minutes to download. Usually this would take at least half an hour over a dial-up connection. Downloading music

is another popular activity for internet users. We visited Irish music site Cluas (www.cluas.com) and a 3MB MP3 file took just under a minute to download. Again, this was roughly 10 times faster than it would have been over a dial-up connection.

The next stage of our trial was multimedia. We visited the QuickTime site (www.quicktime.com) that features a large amount of movie trailers. We managed to view a trailer for the upcoming Lord of the Rings movie without any interruption, something that would have been nigh on impossible before. The RTÉ site (www.rte.ie) was also accessed successfully and we were able to listen to radio broadcasts without interruption.

There's no doubting that ADSL is a far superior service to dial-up access. However, its price may prove restrictive for many users. While it may make sense for business users and those who work from home, 107.69 is a lot for the average home user to pay for internet access every month. While Eircom has indicated that it may introduce a service designed for the residential market at a later stage, this is at present the cheapest ADSL option offered by the company.

Sunday Independent July 2002

Arranging travel tops the poll among internet users

Twenty eight percent of all online shopping in Ireland is related to travel, according to a new survey by market research company Taylor Nelson Sofres MRBI (TNS MRBI). It is the highest proportion of spending on travel in any of the 37 countries surveyed. The survey also found that 19% of internet users in Ireland have shopped online in the four weeks prior to the survey.

The research was part of TNS MRBI's third global e-commerce report, which involved interviews with 42,238 people in 37 countries earlier this year. The report found that 46% of Irish people have used the internet in the four weeks previous to the survey, an increase of 7% on last year's survey. That growth was mostly in home users

as more home PCs are being bought and used for web surfing.

Globally, CDs and books are, as they have been in the past, the most popular online purchases. But in Ireland it was travel, and no country spent more, proportionately, on travel than the Irish.

'The growth in low cost airlines appears to be clearly represented in this survey,' said Luke Reaper, a director of TNS MRBI. Books and CDs came second (15% of purchases) while tickets, at third, made up 12% of purchases.

The survey discovered that the proportion of internet users doing shopping had stayed static but that the number of internet users had risen, increasing the actual number of shoppers. It is also discovered a

surprisingly high common spend on the web.

Online retailers will be encouraged by the average spend on the internet. In Ireland, the average amount spent was 364 in the four-week period, despite findings that security is still the main barrier for users.

If there is going to be an improvement in the numbers of online shoppers then they have to deal with security,' said Reaper. 'One in four users who didn't buy said it was because they didn't want to put their credit card on the internet.'

Also encouraging is the age profile of shoppers: 77% are under 20, meaning that internet shopping is likely to grow as that demographic grows up.

Online Banking/Transactions/Investment

Online banking today allows the customer:

1. To access his or her account, to view balances, to print out online statements – a 24-hour service.
2. To see transaction history.
3. To pay bills.
4. To search for or track a cheque.
5. To top up mobile phones online.
6. To make transfers of money from account to account or out and into an account.
7. To invest in stocks and shares online.
8. To apply for a loan, a mortgage or a credit card online or to get an insurance quote (life policies etc).
9. To avail of foreign exchange facilities online.
10. To establish an Internet merchant account in order to set up a credit card payment system on a customer's (businesses) web site – transferring credit card details between the bank and customer web site and providing a secure certificate to

AN INTERNET BANKING DEMO

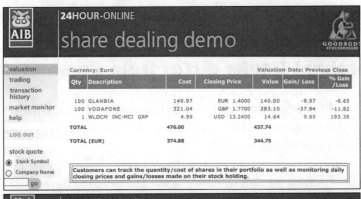

24HOUR-ONLINE
share dealing demo

GOODBODY STOCKBROKERS

valuation
trading
transaction history
market monitor
help

LOG OUT

stock quote
◉ Stock Symbol
○ Company Name
go

Currency: Euro   Valuation Date: Previous Close

Qty	Description	Cost	Closing Price		Value	Gain/ Loss	% Gain /Loss
100	GLANBIA	149.97	EUR	1.4000	140.00	-9.97	-6.65
100	VODAFONE	321.04	GBP	1.7700	283.10	-37.94	-11.82
1	WLDCM INC-MCI GRP	4.99	USD	13.2400	14.64	9.65	193.39
TOTAL		**476.00**			**437.74**		
TOTAL (EUR)		**374.88**			**344.75**		

Customers can track the quantity/cost of shares in their portfolio as well as monitoring daily closing prices and gains/losses made on their stock holding.

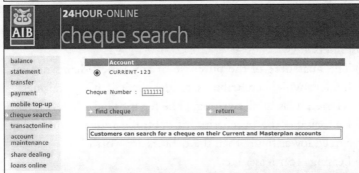

24HOUR-ONLINE
cheque search

balance
statement
transfer
payment
mobile top-up
cheque search
transactonline
account maintenance
share dealing
loans online

Account
◉ CURRENT-123

Cheque Number : 111111

→ find cheque   → return

Customers can search for a cheque on their Current and Masterplan accounts

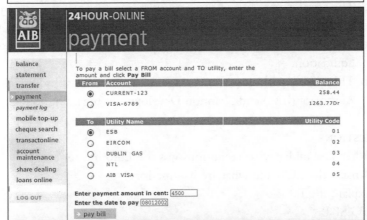

24HOUR-ONLINE
payment

balance
statement
transfer
payment
payment log
mobile top-up
cheque search
transactonline
account maintenance
share dealing
loans online

LOG OUT

To pay a bill select a FROM account and TO utility, enter the amount and click **Pay Bill**

From	Account	Balance
◉	CURRENT-123	258.44
○	VISA-6789	1263.77Dr

To	Utility Name	Utility Code
◉	ESB	01
○	EIRCOM	02
○	DUBLIN GAS	03
○	NTL	04
○	AIB VISA	05

Enter payment amount in cent: 4500
Enter the date to pay 08012002
→ pay bill

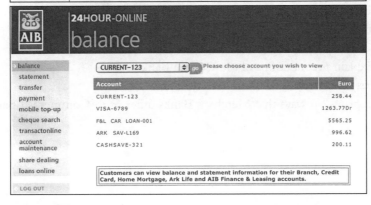

24HOUR-ONLINE
balance

balance
statement
transfer
payment
mobile top-up
cheque search
transactonline
account maintenance
share dealing
loans online

LOG OUT

CURRENT-123 ⇕ go   Please choose account you wish to view

Account	Euro
CURRENT-123	258.44
VISA-6789	1263.77Dr
F&L CAR LOAN-001	5565.25
ARK SAV-L169	996.62
CASHSAVE-321	200.11

Customers can view balance and statement information for their Branch, Credit Card, Home Mortgage, Ark Life and AIB Finance & Leasing accounts.

encrypt and protect the credit card details. (The bank and ISP – Internet service provider will help determine the types of software needed to carry out secure transactions.)

How Merchant Banks differ from Commercial Banks

1. They do not deal with the public in general and are therefore wholesale banks.
2. Their services are for investors, large-scale business activities (private sector) and government (public sector).
3. No short-term loans are offered. These banks are only located in prominent city areas – they do not have a network of branches like commercial banks.
4. Some of the notable services, other than the regular range of financial and banking services that are offered to large investors, private sector and public sector customers are:
   (a) The guarantee of the purchase of any issued shares not taken up by shareholders which contributes to the capital of the business – this service is referred to as Underwriting. (The fee is called a Spread.)
   (b) Factoring – the purchasing of debtors to give businesses ready cash for an agreed lower figure than the debtors are worth.
   (c) Leasing – car leases etc.
   (d) They give expert advice and consultation to the private sector, e. g. firms who want to go public, and they liaise with the Stock Exchange on their behalf.
   (e) They take active parts in mergers, take-overs and company rationalisation and liquidation.
   (f) They liaise with government agencies like Forfas, Industrial Development Authority (IDA) and Shannon Development regarding foreign investors.

PRACTICE QUESTIONS
1. When and under what conditions was the Euro introduced?
2. What is the ECB and what are its functions?
3. Explain the Terms:
   (a) ESCB.
   (b) OMO Instrument.
   (c) NCB.
   (d) EMU.
4. Explain *five* functions of the Central Bank.
5. List *six* functions of Commercial Banks.
6. Explain *four* ways that Merchant Banks differ from Commercial Banks.

Foreign Exchange and Currency Conversion

EMU – European Monetary Union has meant that Europeans can now travel within the European Community and exchange Euros for Euros. (Refer to the beginning of this chapter.) Member states that have signed up for EMU and have converted to the Euro currency no longer have the inconvenience of watching changing foreign exchange rates in order to figure out different costs of living and value for money in exchange for goods and services. There is now a greater ease of movement of money in EMU countries in particular in relation to travel and among European holiday-makers.

However, the currencies listed in the foreign exchange paper clip are not part of EMU and are denominated against the Euro e.g. 1 Euro = .9665 Dollars and 1 Euro = .629 Sterling. So for every Euro the tourist would only get about 62 British pence.

FOREIGN EXCHANGE

Market euro
(previous close in parentheses)

			Tourist euro Country	Buying	Selling
Dollar	0.9665	(0.9673)	UK	0.612	0.6505
Sterling	0.629	(0.625)	US	0.9405	0.9945
D Krone	7.4247	(7.4218)	Canada	1.501	1.563
Jap Yen	118.55	(118.2)	Sweden	8.915	9.255
Sw Franc	1.4713	(1.4666)	Denmark	7.265	7.695
Sw Krona	9.075	(9.1075)	Switzerland	1.4213	1.5513
Nor Krone	7.35	(7.329)	Malta	0.391	0.431
HK Dlr	7.538	(7.5425)	Cyprus	0.5575	0.5975
Can Dlr	1.528	(1.5271)	Australia	1.7077	1.8227
Aus Dlr	1.7627	(1.7635)	Japan	113.85	123.05
NZ Dlr	2.0533	(2.0515)	Norway	7.15	7.6
Sing Dlr	1.7205	(1.7211)	N Zealand	1.9783	2.1283
Czech Kr	30.401	(30.356)	S Africa	10.1791	10.6591
Pol Zl	4.0386	(4.0599)	Thailand	39.405	45.405
Hng For	242.85	(243.50)	Hong Kong	7.188	7.908
Turk Lira	1647378	(1641268)	Singapore	1.6405	1.9405

Financial Information **Ulster Bank**

COMMODITIES

Copper	$1495.5	($1501.5)	Nickel	$6550	($6770)
Lead	$417	($422)	Platinum	$547.5	($553)
Zinc	$769	($773)	Silver	$4.57	($4.57)
Tin	$3925	($3895)	Gold	$316.30	($316.25)
Aluminium	$3101.5	($1311)	Oil	$27.68	($28.28)

Factors Affecting the Value of a Currency

Many factors have an effect on the value of a country's currency.

1. Economic boom or recession – trade cycle – investors speculate and if there is an upswing in the economic performance of the economy, investors are attracted (together with government grant incentives) to set up and offer jobs. If this trend continues, it signals a rise in the value of the currency.

2. Rising interest rates make it more difficult for people to spend as much because their loans (like mortgages) are higher and they find it difficult to save. This leads to depressed demand for goods and services, closures and unemployment. Investors look unfavourably on this type of economy and the value of the currency falls.

3. Inflation: Sometimes governments find it necessary to devalue a currency when inflation (rising prices) and interest rates are unmanageably high.

Business Information in Graphical Form

1. Tables

Tabulation is the procedure used to organise raw data (unorganised data usually in note or prose formation) into a table. In order to understand the data that is contained in a table, we must differentiate between data and statistics as well as primary and secondary forms of the latter.

(a) Primary Data: is data that has been collected by the investigator personally. He/she knows under what conditions the data was collected and its limitations, e.g. a spending pattern survey carried out by using a questionnaire in a busy street in Dublin.

(b) Secondary Data: is data that already exists and is used by someone else. The conditions under which it was collected or its limitations are not known.

(c) Primary Statistics: are figures that are put into a table and have been collected as part of primary data.

(d) Secondary Statistics: are simply percentages or averages that appear beside the primary statistics in the table – a useful way of analysing primary statistics.

PRACTICE TABULATION QUESTION

Employees in Marshall Company numbered 1,500. The company was organised into three departments, Production, Sales and Administration. 400 people were employed in Production and 630 in Administration. There were 460 young females, 200 young males and 420 senior females employed with the company.

Of those working in the Production Department, 130 were young males, 90 were young females and 100 were senior females. The remaining employees in the department were senior males.

Administration was made up of 220 senior males, 200 senior females and 40 young males, with the remainder young females.

Sales was made up of 120 senior males, 120 senior females and 30 young males, with the remainder young females.

1. Compile a suitable table of information from this raw data detailing
   (a) Primary statistics – the information above in an organised fashion and easy to read.
   (b) Secondary statistics to analyse the employment distribution.
2. Comment on your findings.

Steps to tabulate raw data:
1. Decide on the number of rows and columns and whether a total column is needed (not always).
2. The independent variables (males and females categorised) should appear vertically and the dependant variable should appear horizontally (the numbers of employees, categories in production, in sales and in administration, generally are categorised based on being dependant on whether they are male or female).

   Other examples are 'The Profits of Companies' – the companies categorised would be the Independent variables, and profits would be the Dependant variable.

   'Sales over time' – time (in years, months, weeks or days) would be the Independent variable, and sales would change over time (sales = dependant variable).
3. Clarity and neatness is essential with headings and subheadings clearly labelled. A key should be used if wording is too extensive and it overloads and clutters the table.

SOLUTION TO PRACTICE QUESTION

1. Employee Details of Marshall Company

	Production		Sales		Administration		Total	
	No.	%	No.	%	No.	%	No.	%
Sen. F	100	25	120	26	200	32	420	28
Sen. M	80	20	120	26	220	35	420	28
Young M	130	32	30	6	40	6	200	13.3
Young F	90	23	200	42	170	27	460	30.7
	400	100	470	100	630	100	1,500	100

KEY:

Sen.   Senior

M   Males

F   Females

2. Comment

The same number of senior males are employed in the company as females. The largest concentration of senior males appears to be in Administration (35%) with 26% of senior males employed in Sales. The percentage numbers of young males and senior females in Production are 32% and 25% respectively. There is an unusually large number of young females employed in Sales, 42%. The small percentages of young males in Sales and Administration, 6% each, is also noteworthy.

It appears that young females are chosen to promote the business creating a young company image. Possibly the reason for a large number of young males in Production is extra physical strength or other factors like qualifications. Senior staff are concentrated in all areas, Administration figuring largest in proportion.

More information on company background, products produced or services offered would be necessary to make an accurate comment on the statistics in the Table.

Bar Charts

The most common bar charts are:

1. Component Bar Charts
   (a) They show the breakdown of the total amount into its component parts.
   (b) They show how components of a total change from year to year.
   (c) They isolate the component parts of each year's total.
2. Percentage Component Bar Charts:
   (a) They are similar to pie charts but are in the shape of a bar.
   (b) The parts of the total are shown as a proportionate block of the bar.
   (c) The length (magnitude) of the bar is not relevant because each bar is 100 per cent high.
   (d) Variations only occur in relative proportional sizes of percentage parts of the bar.
3. Multiple Bar Charts
   (a) The parts of the component bar are displayed side by side rather than all in the one bar as is the case for a component bar chart.
   (b) No Grand Total is shown – all the individual parts would have to be added up.
   (c) Comparative heights of each part of the total can be seen at a glance.

Most information can be depicted in one form or another by bar charts.

PRACTICE QUESTION

Given the following information draw:

1. A Component Bar Chart
2. Three Percentage Component Bar Charts – one for each year.
3. A Multiple Bar Chart.
4. Explore the reasons why one might be more useful than another.

Note: graph paper should be used to ensure a high level of accuracy.

The breakdown of company X's staff numbers was as follows:

Year 1: Production staff = 180, 75 Sales staff and 45 Administration staff.
Year 2: Production staff = 200, 80 Sales staff, 60 Administration staff.
Year 3: Production staff = 150, 60 Sales staff, 40 Administration staff.

Workings for Percentage Bar Chart, Company X

Year 1 P = 180/300 x 100 = 60%   S = 75/300 x 100 = 25%   A = 45/300 x 100 = 15%
Year 2 P = 200/340 x 100 = 58.8% S = 80/340 x 100 = 23.5%   A = 60/340 x 100 = 17.7%
Year 3 P = 150/250 x 100 = 60%   S = 60/250 x 100 = 24%   A = 40/250 x 100 = 16%

COMPONENT BAR CHART
STAFF BREAKDOWN
COMPANY X

MULTIPLE BAR CHART
STAFF BREAKDOWN
COMPANY X

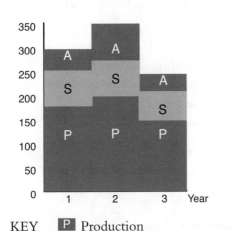

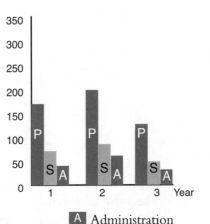

KEY   P Production   S Sales   A Administration

% COMPONENT BAR
CHART COMPANY X

% COMPONENT BAR
CHART COMPANY X

% COMPONENT BAR
CHART COMPANY X

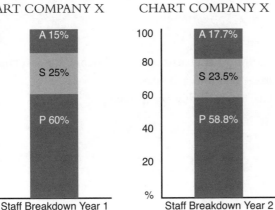

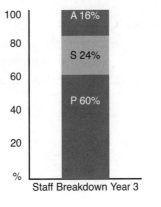

KEY   P Production   S Sales   A Administration

Pie Charts

Circular diagrams used to show the relative sizes of component elements of a total.
- Use a compass to draw circle
- Use a protractor to draw the segments of the circle when estimated.

How to calculate measurements to obtain the sizes of the segments of the circle:

(a) If information is given in figures (rather than percentages) use the following formula to obtain the degrees of the circle:

$$\frac{\text{No. of degrees}}{\text{Total Cost or Sales figure}} \qquad \frac{360}{2,000 \text{ (say)}} = .18 \text{ (multiply this by each individual Cost or Sale value to obtain the degrees of the circle)}$$

(b) If information is given in percentages use the following formula to obtain the degrees of the circle:

$$\frac{\text{No. of degrees}}{\text{Total percentage}} \qquad \frac{360}{100\%} = 3.6 \text{ (multiply this by each percentage value to obtain the degrees of the circle).}$$

(c) To get back from degrees of a circle to percentages, divide each degree figure by 3.6.
- Once the pie chart is drawn, usually percentages are indicated in each separate segment of the circle.
- Pie charts are similar to percentage component bar charts in content. However, it is usually easier to see differences in component parts of a pie chart compared with the bar chart.

PRACTICE QUESTION

(a) Look at the practice question on bar charts. For part 2 depict the information in the form of three pie charts – one for each year.

(b) Why are these three pie charts not readily comparable?

WORKINGS

To get the degrees of the circle

$$\frac{360°}{300} = 1.2 \text{ (multiply this by each part for year 1)}$$

$$1.2 \times 180 = 216°$$
$$1.2 \times 75 = 90°$$
$$1.2 \times 45 = \underline{54°}$$
$$\underline{\underline{360°}}$$

$$\frac{360°}{340} = 1.06 \text{ (multiply this by each part for year 2)}$$

$$1.06 \times 200 = 212°$$
$$1.06 \times 80 = 85°$$
$$1.06 \times 60 = \underline{63°}$$
$$\underline{\underline{360°}}$$

$$\frac{360}{250} = 1.44 \text{ (multiply this by each part for year 3)}$$

$$1.44 \times 150 = 216°$$
$$1.44 \times 60 = 86°$$
$$1.44 \times 40 = \underline{58°}$$
$$\underline{\underline{360°}}$$

STAFF BREAKDOWN COMPANY X Year 1

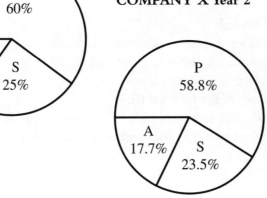

STAFF BREAKDOWN COMPANY X Year 2

STAFF BREAKDOWN COMPANY X Year 3

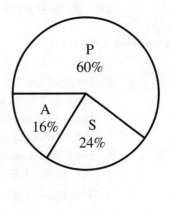

Line Graphs

Many businesses wish to keep track of sales or costs and find the use of a line graph a suitable way of doing this. The following example depicts sales over six months. Line graphs can be linked with Gantt charts (discussed under the 'Functions of Management' in Chapter 1). They both depict either sales or cost changes over time. If a target level of sales is anticipated, one can see at a glance whether this level has been reached or not.

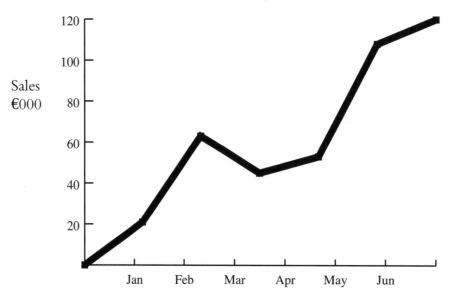

Visual display instruments like tables, bar charts, pie charts and line graphs are regularly used by, for example, survey agencies like MRBI or Irish Marketing Surveys to show results of opinion polls or voting trends at election time. Business television programmes and television news use them to show results of information that viewers find easy to interpret at a glance.

PRACTICE QUESTIONS

1. What is Tabulation?
2. How is Raw Data defined?
3. How do Primary Data and Primary Statistics differ?
4. How do Secondary Data and Secondary Statistics differ?
5. What steps are involved in drawing a table?
6. How do the *three* types of Bar Charts differ?
7. Which Bar Chart is similar in content (but not in shape) to a Pie Chart?
8. The Breakdown of Company Y's Staff numbers was as follows:

Year	Sales Dept	Production Dept	Administration Dept
Year 1	200	600	150
Year 2	210	500	120
Year 3	205	480	105

You are required to draw:

(a) A Component Bar Chart of the total information.

(b) A Pie Chart for 20XX only. Show full workings.

(c) A Multiple Bar Chart of the total information.

Business Administration

Portfolio of Coursework (Sample Assignment)

Subjects taken by the students at St Margaret's College are as follows:

Subject	No. of Students 20XX
LANGUAGES	
French	850
German	240
Spanish	200
	1,290
INFORMATION TECHNOLOGY	
Comp. Programme	300
Computer Applications	250
	550
PROFESSIONAL	
Management	380
Banking	120
Accountancy	190
	690
ACADEMIC	
Leaving Cert	150
Junior Cert	80
Transition Year	31
	261
Total no. students	**2,791**

1. Depict the above data in the following forms:
   (a) A Pie Chart – show full workings
   (b) A Multiple Bar Chart.
2. Comment on each visual display instrument used to display the data and the trend in the data.

Insurance Against Common Business Risks

The Irish Insurance Federation is the umbrella organisation for the insurance industry and is used by insurers (insurance companies) to check on the credit rating and solvency of brokers and intermediaries.

Insurance companies and brokers must register with the Irish Brokers' Association (IBA) before they are allowed to operate. Registering with the Irish Insurance Compliance Bureau allows them to be fully bonded and recognised. A brokerage cast outside the IBA fold could not operate unless it was registered with the bureau. Insurance companies are obliged to operate in accordance with the provisions of the Insurance Act 1989 and the regulations that are attached to the Act. Matters relating to non-disclosure of commercial fees and inappropriate business activities can lead to expulsion from the IBA.

An insurer can either be an insurance company, a financial institution or a broker that charges a fee called a Premium to insure private individuals and businesses against the risk of accident or theft. Insurers also offer life policies (life assurance) to protect against the risk of serious injury, disability and death.

A Broker is an individual or group of individuals like the Automobile Association (AA) whose business it is to search around for the best available quote – in this case for motor insurance – and they take a portion of the premium that they quote for themselves (like a middleman).

The Insured, the person or business being insured, can get the value of the lost item back and replace it. A life policy will provide the insurer with peace of mind and will compensate his or her dependants in the case of his or her death. (*Note*: Life policies differ in value.)

An Insurance Policy is the agreement drawn up between the Insurer and the Insured that is presented by the Insurer (like AXA) in the form of a document listing the conditions underpinning the agreement.

Underwriting a Risk is the guarantee given by the insurer to pay compensation to the insured (the extent of compensation is limited by the Principle of Indemnity – discussed later).

The most common insurance policies are

1. Motor insurance

2. House and contents insurance
3. Business insurance
4. Health insurance
5. Travel insurance
6. Life assurance
7. Other miscellaneous insurances

Motor insurance is compulsory by law (Road Traffic Act 1933) and is broken down into

(a) Third Party: The insurance company only pays out compensation for the damage to the other vehicle and/or person, but not for damage to your own vehicle.
(b) Third Party, Fire and Theft: Compensation is paid out for third party damage and for burn damage or theft of the vehicle and other appropriate compensation.
(c) Fully Comprehensive: The insurance company will pay compensation for the repair of all vehicles involved in any accident including your own as well as personal compensation. If you buy an expensive car, it is likely that parts for it will be expensive and it is best to avail of this type of insurance in this case.

- *Note:* The premiums – payments for motor insurance – will be higher if the driver is younger and regarded as being more risky. Premiums will also be 'loaded' (increased) for larger vehicles and if previous claims have been made.

No Claims Bonus: If a driver continues driving and is lucky enough never to have had an accident, he/she is rewarded with a no claims bonus which rises every subsequent year that the driver has a clear record.

- *Note*: Most insurances have increased substantially due to the high incidents of claims in recent times.

HOUSE AND CONTENTS INSURANCE

Usually when someone decides to buy a house, the house and contents insurance premium is included in the amount repayable to the financial institution that they take out their mortgage (house loan) with. People also have the option of insuring their house and contents with separate insurance companies if they prefer. The insurance is usually in case of burglary, fire etc.

BUSINESS INSURANCE

The most common insurance that businesses in general avail of is Full Public Liability Insurance. This covers them for accidents occurring on or in the vicinity of their premises. Crèches might have high premiums to pay due to the higher risk of children having accidents. Businesses involved in deliveries of any sort, where drivers are frequently parked in busy public areas, are subject to large premiums also.

HEALTH INSURANCE

The Voluntary Health Insurance Company (VHI) and BUPA (British) are the two main health insurance companies operating in Ireland. Up to the time BUPA established itself in Ireland, the VHI had a virtual monopoly (dominating the market). There are different Health Plans – Plan A, Plan B, Plan C, etc. that people avail of in case of accident or illness, to cover maternity needs etc. so that the cost of care is covered by the insurance.

Public hospital services themselves are free (doctors and nurses' services). In some cases, public charges exist for emergency services and for hospital accommodation, but maternity accommodation in a public ward of a maternity hospital is free.

TRAVEL INSURANCE

Usually tour operators and travel agencies organise baggage and medical insurance when people decide to go abroad on holiday. Banks now provide insurance that covers these types of risk which incorporate holiday cancellation, medical and hospital expenses, personal accident, legal expenses, lost baggage, or the cost of getting a person home in case of emergency. Other cover might include winter sports equipment, twenty-four hour medical emergency assistance, missed departure/connection, and loss of passport.

EMU IMPLICATIONS ON TRAVEL INSURANCE – WHAT TO DO IF YOU NEED HELP IN ANOTHER EU COUNTRY

Before leaving the country get an E1 11 (E one eleven) form from your local Social Welfare office, Health Board or doctor.

Emergency Care: In case of emergency only (defined by the doctor) it avoids the need to pay up front. The Social Welfare Department will pay the bill under its own system of payment. This is accepted throughout most of the European economic area.

Non-emergency Care: Complications arise for care that is not urgent where the traveller may have to pay for the cost of care abroad but can later claim this money back through the Social Welfare system. Get informed before you go!

LIFE ASSURANCE

This insures a person and his/her family in the event of his/her death or serious injury and it can also provide life savings if the person is willing to pay a higher premium for this provision. A lump sum of money will be paid out to dependants in the event of a person's death.

Many different policies are offered by different insurance companies and brokers and people in general usually avail of the type of policy that suits their own needs.

OTHER MISCELLANEOUS INSURANCES

Most business people that deal in assets will insure their equipment. For example, a hardware equipment hire business would have invested a lot of capital in the assets (equipment) and will insure them because they are the basis of their livelihood, e.g. lawnmowers or diggers for hire etc. Car hire would be another business that would probably pay large premiums. Farmers insure their stocks and animals against fire and theft, employers insure their premises against the risk of employee theft or dishonesty (Fidelity Guarantee). Examples would be banks, post offices etc. Marine insurance covers losses which might be suffered while transporting goods by sea.

INSURANCE PROTECTIONS AND RISK

- Most insurance policies are concerned with the risk of fire, theft, illness or death, and flooding in some cases.
- *Note*: **It is important to enquire into the exact amount of cover that a policy stipulates. In some cases the small print reads – cover except when loss is due to war or natural disaster etc.**
- Insurance means that the possibility exists that loss will be incurred and compensation is for the value of that amount only.
- Assurance means a guarantee of a lump sum of money on the death or confirmation of terminal injury of the insured or the maturity of a savings policy after a set number of years.
- Premiums rise as the perceived risks rise. Young people are particularly penalised in the case of motor insurance for drivers under 25 years. Public liability insurance for crèches is high and drivers involved in deliveries have also high insurance premiums to pay.

Principles of Insurance

The Principles of Insurance are concerned with the conditions which must exist that create the need to insure, allow for items to be insured and allow for appropriate compensation to be gained, having placed a claim with the insurer.

1. INSURABLE INTEREST

You wouldn't insure something unless you had an interest in doing so! The insured must benefit from the existence of what he/she is getting insured and must suffer if it is lost. In short, a value is attached to whatever is being insured. Legal ownership is a prerequisite to this principle.

2. UTMOST GOOD FAITH

Trust must exist between the insurer and the insured. If all facts are not disclosed it would lead to a void contract of insurance.

3. *INDEMNITY (SUBROGATION, CONTRIBUTION AND PROXIMATE CLAUSE ARE FOLLOW-ON CONDITIONS TO INDEMNITY).*

Only the loss incurred is compensated – no more. The insured is no better off (no profit gained) than they were prior to the incident that triggered the claim. Life assurance is an exception to this principle.

4. *SUBROGATION*

After the insurance company has paid out the compensation to the insured, the company is entitled to claim against any third party and can take legal action against the person who was responsible (inbuilt in the policy, the insured gives the company permission to do this by signature).

5. *CONTRIBUTION*

If two different insurance companies are employed, i.e. if the insured is overinsured, the principle of indemnity still applies, and the insured only gets back the loss and no more. A loss is calculated as follows:

Hibernian Insurance and GRE (Guardian Royal Exchange) are both insuring stock in a premises. Hibernian insures €12,000 worth of stock and GRE insures €6,000 worth of stock. €4,000 worth of stock is taken in a burglary.

Hibernian pay out $\dfrac{12,000}{18,000}$ x 4,000 = €2,667

GRE pay out $\dfrac{6,000}{18,000}$ x 4,000 = €1,333

TOTAL €4,000

6. *PROXIMATE CLAUSE*

This refers to the nature of the risk that an item is being insured against. The insurance company always checks the policy to make sure that the risk was insured against before they pay out the compensation.

Insurance Proposal Form

Request a Quote

If you are an existing policyholder click here.

Household quotation details required:

Title   Mr ▼

Full Name:

Full Postal Address:

Full Address of property to be
insured:

Is this your permanent residence?   Yes ⊙   No ○
If no please state details:

Telephone Numbers:

Daytime:

Evening:

Your e-mail address:

Your Date of Birth:

What is your occupation: (including
part time occupations)

Please select which type of cover   Buildings Only ▼
you need:

What is your buildings value?

What is your contents value?

Do you want accidental damage
cover?   Yes ○   No ⊙

Do you require cover for your personal belongings and valuables
outside your home?

Yes ⊂ No ⊙

If yes please state the sum insured and include details of any individual items worth more than €1,270 (£1,000)

Do you need cover for pedal cycles? *(please tell us how many and the total value)*

Do you have any of the following:

☐ Approved alarm to IS 199 standards

☐ Do you have any mortice locks on your outside doors

☐ Do you have smoke detectors fitted?

☐ Are you in a neighbourhood watch area?

Previous claims/losses during the last 5 years:

Date of claim:

Full description of claim/loss:

What is the amount of the payments made to date:

Is the claim settled?   Yes ⊂ No ⊙

If there are any other details you feel are relevant, please fill in the following section:

Your home is a Private Residence of standard construction and you have been free of convictions for the last 5 years.

Thank you for taking the time to complete this form, we will reply to you by e-mail with a quotation.

☐ Please tick here if you wish us to post a quotation out to you.

Accident Claim Form

Damage to Both Your's and Another Vehicle

Your Details:

Your Insurance Policy
Number:

Your Name:

E Mail address:

If you are registered for VAT please enter your VAT number here:

Home telephone Number:

Work telephone Number:

Your Vehicle Details:

Registration Number:

Make & Model :
e.g. Ford Escort 1.31

Is the vehicle registered in
your name?

Yes: ⊙

No: ○

Name of any financial institution or hire purchase company with an
interest in the vehicle?

Vehicle Damage...Inspection & Repair Instruction

Please check our approved repairer list before continuing.

Contact name and number to arrange a vehicle inspection:

What is the estimated cost of
repair?

Driver or person last in charge of vehicle

Full name:

Address:

E Mail address:

Date of Birth:

Home telephone Number:

Work telephone Number:

Driving Licence:

Full: ○

Provisional: ●

Category of Licence:

Did the driver have your permission to drive the vehicle:

Yes: ●

No: ○

Has the driver ever been convicted of a motoring offence or had any previous accidents?

Yes: ●

No: ○

Accident details:

In what location did the accident happen:

Please enter the date and time of the accident:

In your view, how did the accident happen:

By how much do you consider yourself to blame?

Select one ▼

Please enter the name/s of any persons (including yourself) who admitted liability verbally or in writing at the scene of the accident:

Name of Garda and station to whom the incident was reported to or investigated by:

Has notice of intention to
prosecute been given or
summons received?

Yes: ○

No: ●

If 'yes' give details:

Witness details:

Name:

Address:

Approximate age:

Phone Number:

Witness category: Select one   ▼

Details of other vehicles/property involved:

Name of owner:

Name of driver:

Address:

Registration Number of
vehicle:

Vehicle Make/Model:
e.g. Ford Escort 1.31

Please describe the damage
to this vehicle:

Name of other person's Insurance Company:

Other Person's Policy
Number:

SUBMIT

PRACTICE QUESTIONS

1. Write notes on
   (a) The Irish Insurance Federation.
   (b) The IBA.
   (c) The Irish Compliance Bureau.
2. What legal Act are Insurance Companies and Brokers obliged to operate in accordance with?
3. What is 'Underwriting a Risk'?
4. (a) What is a Premium and what factors will dictate how high or low it is?
   (b) What businesses have to pay higher insurance premiums and why?
5. What are the most common types of insurance policies?
6. With regard to Motor Insurance differentiate between third party, third party fire and theft, and fully comprehensive insurance.
7. What is a No Claims Bonus?
8. What is Public Liability Insurance and who avails of it?
9. Who are the VHI and do they still maintain a monopoly in Ireland?
10. (a) Who provides travel insurance?
    (b) What are the EMU implications for Travel Insurance?
11. (a) What is the difference between Insurance and Assurance?
    (b) What is Life Assurance and why is it so important?
12. What is Fidelity Guarantee?
13. List the Principles of Insurance and explain them briefly but with clarity.

Sample Assignment Briefs

QUESTION 1.

Choose a Bank or Financial Institution and examine the following aspects of the Institution:

1. The types of loans offered categorised as Short, Medium or Long term.
2. The Procedure for getting a loan.
3. The most common services offered and charges incurred relating to personal customers.
4. The most common services offered and charges incurred relating to business customers.

QUESTION 2.

Choose an Insurance Company or Broker and do an analysis of the business and examine a range of the following aspects of the organisation:

1. Brief history and organisational structure
2. The types of insurance policies and cover offered and charges categorised with reference to the section on insurance in Chapter 3.
3. How the Principles of Insurance tie in with the policies offered.
4. How a claim is handled by the business – process of claim from point of receipt to point of payment.
- Include in your assignment
   (a) An Insurance Claim form
   (b) An Insurance Proposal form.

4. Human Resources

Human Resource Management or Personnel Management is concerned with recruiting employees, looking after existing staff needs, dealing with employee grievances and disciplining or dismissing employees if the need arises. This management is also obliged to inform employees of their statutory rights regarding their employment in the organisation and is responsible for drawing up and maintaining documents (attendance records, personnel files and contracts of employment) in the Human Resources Department.

Manpower/Workforce Planning

This involves the forecasting of future labour requirements and is based on the estimated 'Manpower Gap' expected to occur. A manpower gap is the difference between current employee numbers and future requirements. Manpower planning is also referred to as 'Human Resource Planning'. The likely availability of a suitable Labour Supply will dictate whether the manpower gap is bridged.

SHORT-TERM MANPOWER GAP (UNDER ONE YEAR)

If a female employee has informed her superior that she will be taking maternity leave from a certain date, immediate manpower planning is required. This future temporary worker requirement must be matched by a 'suitable substitute'. This will be based on a suitable future supply of appropriately skilled labour to fill the temporary vacancy. Employee sickness requires short-term manpower planning also. This type of manpower gap can be difficult to bridge because of short notice.

MEDIUM-TERM MANPOWER GAP (ONE TO FIVE YEARS)

If an employee decides to take a career break (his/her position can be held for a maximum of five years in many state employments), the position must be filled in a temporary capacity. If a company undertakes an assignment or project, it will interview interested and suitably qualified candidates and appoint them for the period of the contract.

LONG-TERM MANPOWER GAP (OVER 5 YEARS)

The interviewers would carefully assess any position that would be foreseen as long term. Senior management positions are often (not always) long-term appointments. The suitability of the successful candidate is paramount in the mind of the interviewers. Permanent state jobs tend to fall into this category. Another example would be secondments (explained later in this chapter under the heading 'Internal Sources of Labour').

How to Assess the Manpower Gap

Management normally carries out an 'Employee Assessment or Audit'. This involves analysing the current workforce, taking into account the total number of employees and how they are categorised in terms of their posts of responsibility and their seniority. The diverse skills of each employee should be listed, as well as their qualifications. The future requirements should then be weighed up. Natural wastage (retirement, redundancy and unexpected disability) must be taken into account and the cost of training (if applicable) must be estimated. Some businesses must look carefully at the cost of overtime and the willingness of employees to work overtime. If employee turnover or absenteeism is high, a panel of part-time employees should be available to management to cover requirements.

The Importance of Good Manpower Planning:

It is important that managers have the appropriate back-up facilities to cover short-term labour shortfalls. Otherwise the business profile might be damaged and it could affect customer loyalty and/or sales. All manpower planning is difficult and is based on the following factors:

1. Social Factors – people matters – considerations like, will people's home situations reduce work effort and contribute to absenteeism.
2. Technological Factors – skills, the need for retraining and the question of whether more labour or less labour is needed based on more modern high tech equipment being used in the business.
3. Demographic Factors – considerations like the need to relocate in order to take up the job and the expenses connected with this decision.
4. Political Factors – qualifications and job specification to match with job description as advertised; the recruitment option – open competition and equal opportunity legislation considerations (discussed in the next section).

Recruitment Options

The methods used to hire labour and to make appointments. Both Internal (recruiting from within the organisation) and External (recruiting from outside the organisation) sources of labour are discussed below.

External Sources of Labour

OPEN COMPETITION

Advertising in newspapers is the common method that is used by companies in order to be seen to comply with 'Open Competition' requirements for hiring staff. The advertisement will generally consist of:

1. *THE JOB DESCRIPTION:* This consists of the job title, location, duties attached to the post and any other special features connected with the post.

2. *THE JOB SPECIFICATION:* This refers to the special qualities, qualifications and skills that are sought by the company.

> The companies in question will usually refer to their 'policy of equal opportunity' and a closing date for receipt of applications. They will also refer to competitive interviews assessed by interview boards based on appropriate qualifications and applicable work experience. They will state that applications will be treated in strict confidence (complying with the Freedom of Information Act and the Data Protection Act 1988) and in some cases will draw up a set of criteria to shortlist candidates. A usual statement 'Canvassing will disqualify' is most likely to appear also. This type of selection procedure is seen to be fair and non-discriminatory.

STAGES TO BE FOLLOWED IN RECRUITING THROUGH OPEN COMPETITION:

Stage 1: Design of application form for job vacancy.

Stage 2: Evaluation of selection procedure by selection board and management.

Stage 3: Paper advertisement (samples below).

Stage 4: Application forms are sent to interested parties.

Stage 5: Candidates are shortlisted on the basis of their application, qualifications, suitability and the number of vacancies. References are verified at this stage.

Stage 6: Selected candidates are invited to attend a preliminary interview and/or other qualifying tests (psychometric tests). The aim is to assess the merits of each candidate. (This does not always apply.)

Stage 7: Subsequent final interviews might be arranged.

Stage 8: Job offers and contracts of employment (which include regulations and conditions of service) are sent to successful candidates. They must return the documents signed, by a set date, if they decide to accept the job offer. The offer is normally subject to the candidate's successful medical examination.

Stage 9: In the case of state jobs the appointments must be sanctioned by the particular government department that the position is connected with.

MANPOWER/MANAGEMENT CONSULTANTS

Executive search agencies are often employed by companies to search for and locate suitably qualified candidates for different positions where vacancies arise. It is usually when businesses are head hunting or searching for top-class management candidates that they employ consultants to do the groundwork for them. Head hunting usually involves a business offering the person a more attractive remuneration (wage) than he/she is currently earning. The cost of employing search agencies is usually very high. The recruitment company Marlborough is an example of a company that offers indigenous (within the economy) and multinational clients a range of personnel for their requirements.

EMPLOYMENT AGENCIES
1. Private agencies: are usually relatively expensive to employ but many companies utilise their services.
2. State or semi-state agencies: Foras Áiseanna Saothair (FÁS) is the main government agency providing training and employment services in the country. One of its functions is the provision of a placement service. There is no cost for the service. FÁS grants are often given to businesses if they undertake to recruit FÁS employees for periods of at least thirty-nine weeks.

Internal Sources of Labour

INTERNAL PROMOTIONS

These types of openings are usually advertised on notice boards within the particular establishment where the promotion is due. The criteria to award the promotion are usually based on suitability and merit (the ability and qualifications to do the job), as well as seniority and length of service in the particular area of promotion.

INTERNAL DEMOTIONS

When a person gives up or loses a post of responsibility, the vacancy remaining creates the need for more labour. Usually positions like these are filled from the internal source of labour on the existing staff.

CAREER BREAKS AND SECONDMENTS

When employees take a career break (maximum five years) or if they are granted a secondment away from their usual line of work, these decisions create temporary vacancies. These vacancies would be, if possible, filled in a temporary capacity by existing part-time staff.

An employee may look for a secondment if they are full-time and permanent employees in state jobs and their aim is to work for another government-run body or for the same government body in a different section. The work must be connected with their main employment and the work experience that is gained from it must be seen to directly contribute to their main employment.

REDEPLOYMENT OR TRANSFERS

Redeployment is the unavoidable transfer of staff to a different location or branch due to closure.

Voluntary Transfer happens when an employee requests a transfer to a different branch. The managers in the section that they wish to work in usually request the transfer. Their main employment position is held open (a temporary substitute is recruited) for them while they are on secondment.

Recruiting Options (Informal Methods)

These methods can range from existing staff recommending their friends or relatives as suitable candidates for positions, to sending unrequested CVs, career guidance officer recommendations and media or paper/magazine advertisements to prospective employers.

PRACTICE QUESTIONS

1. Define 'Human Resource Planning'.
2. How does the term 'Human Resource Planning' differ from the term 'Manpower Gap'?
3. Give *one* example each of a short-term, a medium-term, and a long-term Manpower Gap.
4. Define the following terms:
   (a) Employee Audit.
   (b) Natural Wastage.
   (c) Employee Turnover.
5. Why is Manpower Planning so important to managers?
6. How does the term 'External Source of Labour' differ from the term 'Internal Source of Labour'?
7. Make a clear distinction between 'Job Description' and 'Job Specification'. Give *one* example.
8. What do the following terms mean?
   (a) Head Hunting
   (b) Remuneration
   (c) Promotion and Demotion
   (d) Career Break
   (e) Secondment
   (f) Redeployment
   (g) Voluntary Transfer.
9. List the Formal and Informal methods used to recruit staff.

Functions of the Human Resources Department

The term 'Personnel Management' is now generally referred to as Human Resource Management. It can be defined as 'all those who have responsibilities for people matters'. Its purpose is to ensure that the employee has good working conditions. This in the long run helps towards job satisfaction and a pleasant working environment. Human resource management represents the formal recognition of the need for specialist individuals to deal with people management issues.

The Role of the Human Resources Department

The Human Resource Manager or the Personnel Manager's responsibilities include:

1. STAFF WELFARE:

The human resource department provides the employee with information on statutory and voluntary employee benefits.

Statutory benefits: employee benefits underpinned by law. Entitlements and obligatory contributions:

Maternity leave
Holidays and holiday pay
Employment pension schemes
Sick pay
Company cars (if applicable).

Voluntary benefits:

Sports and recreation facilities connected with employment
Child care facilities
Health insurance
Career breaks and secondments
Option of extra pension subscriptions.

2. STAFF DEVELOPMENT

The 'human factor' determines levels of productivity (efficiency and speed of work). The impact of work conditions on performance has encouraged companies to set up staff seminars and staff development groups made up of a varied staff group to investigate the levels of satisfaction or dissatisfaction with the work environment. This development is an important mechanism that is encouraged by the Human Resource Department in order to keep staff happy. It also gives staff the opportunity to suggest improvements to existing working conditions.

3. STAFF MOTIVATION

Motivation means a stimulus to work hard to achieve objectives and targets. In 1943 Maslow, a clinical psychologist, analysed human needs in an effort to understand human drives and enthusiasm. His studies became the building blocks of subsequent research on staff motivation, career counselling and the understanding of the human condition. Maslow's Pyramid of Hierarchy of Needs describes how all behaviour is driven by needs. The basic physiological needs are food, shelter and security. Humans must experience security on the lower steps of the ladder to progress to the next step. The need for love, acceptance and recognition is experienced at this stage. The top two steps of the ladder, self-esteem and self-actualisation, are experienced as a result of a positive response, i.e. acceptance, respect, recognition, appreciation and praise.

MASLOW'S PYRAMID OF HIERARCHY OF NEEDS

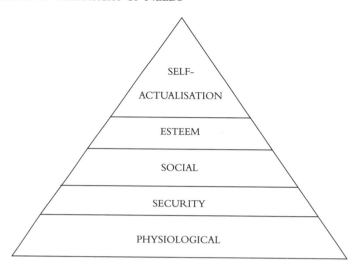

The understanding of human needs is directly applicable to the analysis of employee behaviour. Appropriate understanding of people and their behaviour within their work environment leads to good worker-manager relations and therefore avoids industrial relations problems, strikes and work to rule (deliberate slowdowns in the workplace).

The key terms in describing Maslow's hierarchy with regard to employees might be:

1. Recognition for work done.
2. Appreciation for work done.
3. Respect for employees.
4. Praise.

I have attempted here to interpret each step of the hierarchy in a 'staff needs' context as follows:

1. Physiological needs: Maslow's pyramid shows how staff members have material and personal needs.
   • Material needs are those physical things like equipment and room space which employees feel they have a right to or ownership of.
   • Personal needs, like the manager or superior creating a sense of well-being in the employee – a feeling that needs are being met, their efforts are valued, and that they matter to the organisation.
2. Security: When the manager or superior is meeting material and personal needs, it gives the employee a sense of security and well-being.
3. Social: This refers to the effective communication flow between the manager and the employee (superior and subordinate).

4. Esteem: When employees experience esteem, they realise they are appreciated and respected by their superior, resulting from effective communication flow and praise.
5. Self-actualisation: The employee will respond eagerly to positive signs and, in turn, will respond to the manager or superior's needs. Their self worth will be fully realised, creating greater work effort and stimulating motivation.

Ultimately, the recognition of employees as people, not just as 'work machinery', is the key to good employer-employee relationships.

HERZBERG'S OBSERVATIONS

Frederick Herzberg (1966) observed that:
(a) Highly motivated workers characteristically
  (i) enjoyed the challenge of the work
  (ii) were involved in the decision-making process
  (iii) gained recognition and were given the opportunity to advance their careers or gain promotion.
(b) Workers with low motivation characteristically
  (i) were governed by too many rules – oversupervised
  (ii) had a bad relationship with senior staff and superiors
  (iii) were frustrated by workplace attitudes or bullying
  (iv) had a bad relationship with colleagues, leading to low self-esteem
  (v) had a cynical or divisive outlook
  (vi) had poor working conditions.

4. CAREER COUNSELLING

In most organisations induction seminars, in-service courses and training are provided to guide and advise employees how they should approach their jobs. These sessions are organised by the Human Resources Department, which will also readily provide information regarding promotional posts, secondments (already defined) and any other paths that might lead to career advancements if so requested by employees.

5. DISCIPLINARY PROCEDURES AND DISMISSAL

Employees have to adhere to the organisation's rules and regulations regarding behaviour, absenteeism, punctuality etc. If they do not, then the disciplinary procedures laid down will involve:

1. A verbal warning from the employee's immediate superior for an occasional lapse in behaviour or work standards, e.g. being frequently late or swearing at a superior.
2. A formal written warning from the manager following an investigation into the case, if the employee re-offends in the same way, having taken no notice of the verbal warning and where more serious offences have taken place. Usually a copy of this written warning will be sent to the Human Resources Department.

3. A further written warning that dismissal is the next step. This subsequent disciplinary action is based on the unwillingness of the employee to adhere to previous warnings.
4. Management investigating and hearing the employee's case, followed by final warning.
5. Suspension or dismissal.

When employees are hired, they are given a copy of their conditions of employment and this would include a Code of Conduct they are expected to adhere to.

PRACTICE QUESTIONS

1. What is the meaning of the term 'Human Resource Management'?
2. Name the functions of the 'Human Resources Department'.
3. What are the differences between Statutory and Voluntary Benefits with regard to Staff Welfare?
4. What is Productivity and why is it so important?
5. What is the meaning of the term 'Motivation'?
6. Explain how Maslow's Pyramid of Hierarchy of Needs is applied to staff.
7. What steps are taken by the Human Resources Department regarding the following issues?
   (a) Career Counselling in employment
   (b) Disciplinary Procedures in employment.

Purpose of Maintaining Documents in the Human Resources Department

The basic functions of the Human Resources Department that have already been discussed include: the selection, recruitment, training and deployment of suitable types and numbers of employees, as well as staff welfare, staff development, staff motivation, career counselling, staff discipline, staff dismissal and interacting with union representatives to discuss and hopefully solve disputes.

Documents such as employee statistics and personnel files, attendance records (including sick leave taken – both self-certified and medically certified), wage records and job specifications must be kept on record in the Human Resources Department for future reference. Safety and welfare procedures, codes of conduct and disciplinary procedures are also recorded in the department.

1. An employee may leave the employment and require a job reference and a P45 termination of employment form containing details of pay to refer on to the next employer.

2. Employee pension rights and payments may need to be reviewed or estimated.

3. Appointment (converting an employee's status from part time to full time) or promotional suitability (an employee's future potential) might need to be reviewed based on qualifications that are kept on record in the department. The manager can assess previous work done by employees and by choosing a suitable candidate can achieve and sustain high job performance to ensure the survival and success of the business (performance appraisal).

   A manager can assess an employee's potential to take on wider responsibilities by referring to their employment records held in the Human Resources Department.

4. An employee's attendance is monitored (with the help of attendance records and time sheets) and the level of absenteeism is noted. It could be a deciding factor with regard to future promotional prospects.

DATE	DAY	TIME	
13/07	Monday	9.00	IN
		13.00	OUT
13/07	Monday	14.00	IN
		17.00	OUT
14/07	Tuesday	–	IN
		–	OUT
14/07	Tuesday	14.00	IN
		17.00	OUT
15/07	Wednesday	9.00	IN
		13.00	OUT
15/07	Wednesday	14.00	IN
		17.00	OUT
15/07	Wednesday	17.45	IN
		19.45	OUT
16/07	Thursday	–	IN
		–	OUT
16/07	Thursday	–	IN
		–	OUT
17/07	Friday	9.00	IN
		13.00	OUT
17/07	Friday	14.00	IN
		17.00	OUT
17/07	Friday	17.30	IN
		21.00	OUT

CLOCK CARD/TIME SHEET

TOTAL BASIC HOURS

BASIC PAY

TOTAL OVERTIME

O/T PAY

TOTAL HOURS

TOTAL GROSS PAY

Managing vital resources

Organisations are increasingly looking
for better ways to manage their
human resources.

Barry McCall

Walk into almost any organisation's premises and you will find massive investments in IT geared towards managing productivity, costs, assets and so on. A manufacturing concern will be able to tell you to the nearest gram its output on any given day; you will also be able to find out exactly how much stationery it consumes in a month, how much coffee was drunk last year, and the age and value of every car in the company fleet. All at the touch of a few buttons on a PC.

The efficiency gains of organisations – both commercial and otherwise – during the 1990s was largely attributed to the IT revolution. Companies installed hugely sophisticated enterprise resource planning (ERP) systems which could track almost every aspect of the organisation's activities and ensure that tight controls were kept on costs while productivity was maximised through sophisticated JIT purchasing and manufacturing techniques.

However, against this background of heavy investment in business automation one area remained almost untouched, and that area was usually responsible for the heaviest cost burden – human resources. Human resource departments were still manually recording all employee details from hours worked through holiday entitlements to pension arrangements. Massive amounts of data were created and stored although little of it was turned into actual information.

For example, to make a simply query such as the amount of employees that took two weeks holidays during the

month of August would usually require either a manual search of holiday records or, at the very least, the writing of a macro to run on the holiday date spreadsheet.

And all the while the amount of data required to be kept was growing. For example, the EU Working Time Directive means that employers have to keep accurate records of the hours worked by its employees to ensure that they are in compliance with the law. Health & Safety Regulations mean that manufacturing companies have to keep huge volumes of data on file relating to safety training, the times of rest breaks, and so on. Furthermore, with employment legislation becoming increasingly complex detailed records of an employee's work performance and disciplinary record must be kept.

And this is just the straightforward stuff. Organisations which offer employees flexitime or other flexible working arrangements need to keep track of a whole variety of different data while other companies which have flexible reward packages which allow the trade off of holidays for pay, pension, insurance or other entitlements again have to have the means of recording all of these items for hundreds of employees.

There is also the relatively simple matter of pay. When a person gets promoted their pay and other conditions have to be improved. In many organisations this still requires a veritable flurry of paperwork with one department telling the HR department of the changes in the person's role, the

HR department telling the accounts department and so on and so on.

For this reason many companies began to view their HR departments as pen pushing operations rather than strategic resources – simply because they were overwhelmed by the amount of data required to be recorded and processed. They were unable to make a strategic input into the management of the organisation because they were too deeply involved in the day to day management of data.

With the increased focus on human resources over the past few years, largely prompted by skills shortages in some key areas, has come a realisation that the HR function needs to be automated and integrated into the rest of the business in much the same way as the accounts or purchasing operations are. Automated HR systems are no longer seen as a 'like to have' by many organisations, they have become a 'must have'.

This has seen a relative upsurge in the uptake of such systems over the past two years. 'As people did the whole ERP thing a few years ago HR wasn't seen as that important,' says John Caulfield, pre sales manager with Oracle Ireland whose customers in the HR area include Aer Rianta, Bord na Mona and Dublin City Council. 'They got away with doing it manually up to a point. But HR departments were doing too much paper pushing and not making the strategic input which they were capable of. Take employee appraisals for example. To ensure that they are fair and reasonable a lot of details about an employee's history has to be kept on file. Then there are the basic things like attendance details, holidays and so on.

And on top of that you can have organisations which operate what is known as total compensation management where employees can choose to have shorter holidays in favour of better pensions, or better life assurance and not such a high level of health insurance and so on. This not only means that every employee is potentially on a different package but that the company has to ensure that it has the right life assurance package to cope with this or that it is getting the best possible deal from the health insurer.

Due to these factors Oracle has seen a major increase in the sales of HR systems over the past two years. We have been seeing a huge increase over the past two years,' says Caulfield. 'Up until then we would have sold a lot of ERP systems but since then we have been selling lots of ERP systems with HR systems built in or indeed HR systems on their own.'

He also points out that the systems are more than simply about managing data efficiently. 'It's about the smooth running of the organisation,' he says. 'Take the issue of expenses claims. Everyone operates in some sort of approvals hierarchy for expenses. I need someone to approve mine before they will be paid. They are then apportioned to one budget or another and set off as a cost against a particular part of the business. But what happens if I move department or division? I will not only require a different person to approve my expenses but the cost centre to which they are attributed might well change as well. With a good HR system these changes can be implemented quickly and in a matter of seconds – but with the old manual systems it could take days or weeks of memo writing to sort out.'

Competence management is another important area.

'In large companies you need to be able to analyse your requirements for skills and competencies and measure that against what you have,' says Caulfield. 'After that you can make decisions on training or recruitment or whatever. And you need to stay constantly up-to-date with the skills and competencies of staff to ensure that they are utilised to the best advantage. This would be almost impossible without a good HR system in place.'

'HR departments are now using the internet and corporate intranets to deliver information and services to employees more efficiently and effectively than ever before,' says Dianne Flood, HR analyst with Softworks Computing. 'After initial fears that web applications would take the 'human' out of human resources, HR departments have embraced the web to re-engineer their processes. An idea that was initially spawned in the US, the implementation of web self-service applications for checking benefits, updating employee information and posting job requisitions has now expanded to include employee time and attendance information.'

Established in 1990, Bray-based Softworks Computing,is Ireland's largest supplier and developer of client server and web-based time and attendance /flexitime solutions and has been recognised as the fastest growing Technology Company in its field in Europe in the recent Deloitte Touch Tohmatsu European Fast 50 awards. 'We have concentrated on time management and the management of labour resources since our foundation,' says Dianne Flood. 'We have proven our ability to increase productivity and decrease costs, through improved management of human resources in our many customer sites. Our qualified and experienced staff are committed to meeting any unique requirements a customer may have through our project management,

customisation, implementation, training and support services.'

The company's 'Wise' software suite can be used for all aspects of time management, from the basic recording of hours/flexitime, overtime, and absenteeism, to extremely advanced but user-friendly management reporting capabilities. The integral report writer can produce any number of user-definable reports, providing information on absenteeism, lateness, overtime etc. by frequency, reason, percentage and cost to the company. It enables an organisation to identify any potential problems before they become serious, and thus manage and control them accordingly.

'Our customers, including companies such as Mercer, Coyle Hamilton, EMC, and Ordnance survey Ireland, as well as various Government departments, have realised that leveraging the power of the internet is critical to streamlining performance and enhancing employee job satisfaction and productivity,' says Flood. 'By embracing a web-enabled employee self-service portal, these companies have given their employees 'the keys to the car', when it comes to getting information about their holiday balances, entering absences and checking hours or flexitime earned. Tasks that once required layers of approvals and piles of paperwork are being automated, if not eliminated. Not only can employees book their holidays on line but an email notification is automatically routed to the relevant manager, who then decides whether to approve it or not. At the click of a button, management can approve or deny requests or applications.'

With a range of software and systems available to suit any company, regardless of size, and the growing use of the self-service option it looks as if HR departments will at last be freed from the relative drudgery of masses of paperwork and allowed to make real ...
(Sunday Tribune, August 2002)

Basic Rights of Employees as Protected under Current Legislation (refer to www.irlgov.ie)

The following employee rights were referred to under 'Staff Welfare': maternity leave, holidays and holiday pay, employment pension schemes, sick pay and company cars (if agreed as part of the job package). Other rights consist of entitlements to view the organisation's current 'Safety Statement' and to highlight inconsistencies with regard to health and safety in the workplace.

- Maternity Protection Act 1994
  - entitles a full time female employee to maternity leave of 18 consecutive weeks plus the option of a further 8 weeks unpaid leave.
- Holiday Act 1973 and the Worker Protection (Regular Part-time Employees) Act 1991
  - entitles employees to annual leave depending on hours worked.
- Payment of Wages Act 1991
  - entitles employees to a statement of wages and mode of payment and protection against unlawful deduction out of the paypacket.
- Minimum Notice and Terms of Employment Acts 1973–94
  - entitles employees to information about their terms of employment in writing and the period of notice indicated.
- Protection of Young Persons (Employment) Act 1977
  - outlines restrictions regarding the employment of workers under the age of 18 years
- Safety, Health and Welfare at Work Act 1989
  - entitles workers to a safe and healthy work environment, free from undue risk to the person. This includes employer obligations regarding protection clothing etc. as well as the preparation of a written 'Safety Statement' to outline potential hazards.
- Anti-Discrimination (Pay) Act 1974
  - entitles men and women to equal treatment in employment.
- Employment Equality Act 1977
  - makes it illegal to discriminate against a person on the basis of sex or marital status, with some exceptions like 'acting', where employment of a specific sex might be required.
- Unfair Dismissals Acts 1977–93
  - protects employees from being dismissed unfairly, i.e. where the dismissal is unjustified (some employees are excluded from this Act, particularly those in training).
- Redundancy Payment Acts 1967–91
  - protects employees made redundant and places an obligation on the employer to pay lump sum payments to those workers that are to be made redundant

based on age, years of continuous service and gross weekly wages. It does not apply to employees that leave voluntarily or where their contract expires.

If the employer becomes insolvent, the state will finance any outstanding sums to be paid to employees.

Parental Leave

The Parental Leave Act 1998 became law on 3 December 1998, with an amendment on 19 July 2000. The act states that employees with one year's continuous service who have a child born after 3 June 1996 are entitled to 14 weeks **unpaid** leave (per year) to take care of their child up to the age of five. Both parents are entitled to Parental Leave in respect of each child, and it can be taken in one block, in weekly blocks, in days or even hours. It is calculated on a *pro rata* basis in the case of part-time workers. The employee must inform his/her employer six weeks in advance, in writing, that they wish to take the leave. A 'confirmation document' is drawn up by the employer on receipt of the birth certificate of the child and at least four weeks in advance of the date of departure. The document is signed by both parties and kept by them. Parental leave does not affect any other holiday entitlements, maternity leave, sick leave or public holidays. An employer cannot refuse the leave but can defer it for a maximum of six months if it is thought to have a 'substantial adverse effect' on the operation of the business.

'FORCE MAJEURE LEAVE'

The Parental Leave Act also provides for 'Force Majeure Leave'. This is where a maximum of three days in one year or five days over three years can be taken. This can be taken in case of sudden illness or injury to an immediate family member, i.e. spouse/partner, parent, child, sibling or grandparent. This leave is paid leave.

Freedom of Information Act 1997

This act obliges government departments, health boards, local authorities and a range of other statutory agencies to publish information on their activities and to make personal information available to citizens. In addition, the Act establishes three new statutory rights:

1. The legal right for each person to access information held by public bodies.
2. A legal right for each person to have official information relating to himself/herself amended where it is incomplete, incorrect or misleading.
3. A legal right to obtain reasons for decision affecting himself/herself.

The C and A Machinery

This refers to the processes of Conciliation and Arbitration.

Conciliation is the attempt by a third party to help in the settlement of an industrial dispute by hearing all sides of the dispute and suggesting terms for settlement. The Labour Relations Commission provides a conciliation service.

Arbitration is a way of settling a dispute when both parties to the dispute request a third party to make a decision that they both agree to accept. This would come under the auspices of the Labour Court. Most disputes are settled by conciliation and there is a general unwillingness to refer disputes to arbitration.

The state provides the following specific institutions (all of which have various responsibilities for matters concerning employee relations) that are underpinned by current legislation. Employees can seek help with the appropriate institution to resolve problems that occur in connection with their workplace and/or in connection with alleged discrimination by management against employees in their workplace.

1. The Labour Relations Commission:

The commission's functions are derived from the Industrial Relations Act 1990 (sections 24 and 25). Its aim is to promote good industrial relations by embodying employer, trade union (employee representation) and independent representation. The services it provides aim to prevent disputes and if this is not possible to resolve existing disputes.

SERVICES

(a) Advisory body: It is an industrial relations advisory body. It helps and advises Labour Committees and Industrial Councils to carry out their functions.

(b) Resolution of disputes: The commission provides a conciliation service (involving negotiation and dialogue), taking steps to resolve employee industrial relations disputes before they require full Labour Court investigation. It reviews and monitors these developments. The success rate has to date been high. Basic pay claims, special pay increases and conditions of employment are the usual issues dealt with as part of this service.

(c) Prevention of disputes: The commission provides an advisory service to help identify and prevent situations that might eventually cause industrial relations problems (employee relations difficulties). It strives to provide this service by encouraging good industrial relations policies. It advises on and develops acceptable codes of practice for organisations and it analyses and researches problematic areas involving union/management agreements for both the private sector (firms and companies privately owned and operated) and the public sector (government and semi-state organisations). It helps government, employers and trade unions to co-operate and work together to everybody's satisfaction.

(d) Equality: It is responsible for ensuring that an equality service is provided in organisations and it is also responsible for the appointment of Equality Officers. The selection and nomination of persons for appointment as Rights Commissioners is also within its brief.

The Rights Commissioner

The Minister for Labour (underpinned by the Industrial ⌐
the Rights Commissioner after suitable persons for the job ha
the Labour Relations Commission. Rights Commissioners wou
Relations Commission and investigate disputes relating to indiviᴄ
cerning industrial relations matters, unfair dismissals (1977 Act), ma
(1981 Act) and the Payment of Wages Act 1991. They only investigate
Labour Court is not already handling it, only if it concerns an individual,   up,
and if there is no valid objection by any party in writing. Objections tᴄ ⸝ending
investigations into disputes and to recommendations by the Rights Commissioner
following an investigation must be made within three and six weeks respectively.

Equality Officers

Equality Officers work as part of the Labour Relations Commission but perform
their duties independently. They investigate and make recommendations on issues in
relation to claims for equal basic rates of pay (alleged sex discrimination), or marital
status (allowances and maintenance), redundancy payments, overtime entitlements
that are covered under the Anti-Discrimination Pay Act 1974 and alleged discrimination in relation to access to employment, conditions of employment and working
hours, alleged sexual harassment, and promotion, that are covered under the
Employment Equality Act 1977.

If the parties involved are not happy with the recommendations made by the
Equality Officer, they are allowed to make an application to the Labour Court within
forty-two days of the recommendation. The Labour Court's judgment on the case
will then be legally binding.

Refer to **www.lrc.ie** for further information.

2. The Labour Court

The functions of the Labour Court are also derived from the Industrial Relations Act
1990. It is also underpinned by section 20 of the Industrial Relations Act 1969. If the
Labour Relations Commission fails to resolve a dispute, the parties involved can ask
the Labour Court to hear their case.

The dispute must be referred to the Labour Court by:

(a) The Labour Relations Commission (via written and oral reports through the
    chairperson of the Commission, a Rights Commissioner or an Equality Officer).
(b) The Minister for Enterprise, Trade and Employment.

The hearing usually involves a trade union representative, an employer, and an
independent chairperson where the representatives are cross-examined and written
and oral submissions are presented.

The Labour Court, on hearing the case, will issue a recommendation that is not legally binding but that employers and trade unions are encouraged to put in place.

3. The Employment Appeals Tribunal

The Tribunal operates under the Unfair Dismissals Act 1977. The decisions it makes are decided by reference to this Act as well as the Unfair Dismissals (Amendment) Act 1993, the Maternity (Protection of Employees) Act 1981, the Terms of Employment Act 1994 (covering minimum notice etc.) and the Redundancy Payments Acts 1967–89.

As suggested by the Acts above, the Tribunal hears cases that concern unfair dismissals, maternity protection of employees, the protection of employees following employer closure and liquidation, and regular part-time worker protection, minimum notice and terms of employment, and redundancy payments.

PRACTICE QUESTIONS

1. Name and briefly explain the main legal Acts that protect employee rights under current legislation.
2. Name the *three* institutional frameworks from which employees can seek help when problems occur in connection with their workplace.
3. What are the functions of the Labour Relations Commission?
4. What are the functions of the Rights Commissioner?
5. How is the right to equality protected under current legislation?
6. What are the functions of the Labour Court?
7. What are the functions of the Employment Appeals Tribunal?

A Brief History of the Trade Union Movement

The concept of trade unionism established itself in the mid-nineteenth century. In Ireland James Larkin founded the ITGWU (Irish Transport and General Workers' Union) in 1909. Employees were poor and dissatisfied with their wages and conditions of employment. Larkin called for a strike in the Dublin Tramways Company in August 1913. Employers locked all ITGWU members out of their places of work. By September 1913, 25,000 people were locked out in Dublin, aptly named the '1913 Lock-out'. This incident marked the beginning of the trade union movement in Ireland.

The Role of a Trade Union within the Workplace at Branch and National Level

A trade union is defined as 'a continuous association of wage earners with the objective of improving or maintaining conditions of employment'. Trade unions fall into three broad groups, employee associations (like SIPTU), employer associations (like IBEC) and trade associations (like the Irish Nurses Organisation, INO).

Employee trade unions are further categorised into three main types in Ireland: Craft unions, General unions, and White Collar unions.

CRAFT UNIONS: are trade unions that protect workers that are in the 'skilled' category. Workers must have a period of apprenticeship appropriate to their work before they will be accepted into the union. Examples of Craft unions are the Electrical Trade Union and the Irish Print Union.

GENERAL UNIONS: are trade unions that cater for semi-skilled and unskilled workers and attract members from different industries. The main general union is the Services, Industrial, Professional and Technical Union (SIPTU) explained later.

WHITE COLLAR UNIONS: are trade unions catering for professional, office and service occupations. Examples of these unions are the Teachers' Union of Ireland (TUI), Association of Secondary Teachers of Ireland (ASTI), Irish National Teachers' Organisation (INTO) and the National Union of Journalists (NUJ).

The main objectives of trade unions are:

1. To unite employees who have common interests.
2. To secure improvements in members' conditions of employment and rates of pay through negotiation with employers and the government. (Refer to 'Social Partners' and 'Collective Bargaining' discussed later.)
3. To maintain agreed conditions of employment, which include making sure that promises of any pay increases are honoured.
4. To negotiate on behalf of members when disputes arise.
5. To protect their members and strive to ensure security of their jobs.
6. To provide a mechanism allowing members to express any job dissatisfaction and to highlight any developments at local level that might conflict with their job specification and job description (defined earlier).
7. To minimise exploitation of workers.
8. To control activities of members and discipline them if necessary.
9. To provide members with other services like information services regarding pension rights, car insurance schemes and advice regarding any areas of doubt concerning union directives.
10. Training courses for union representatives.

Social Partners and Collective Bargaining

The Social Partners, that is, the unions (on behalf of employees), employers and government representatives collectively discuss and negotiate issues concerning the conditions of employment and pay revisions. This is referred to as Collective Bargaining. It replaces individual bargaining that, generally, is not very effective and would fail to secure agreement with management on many issues. The conflicts of interest that usually exist between management and workers are best ironed out using the collective bargaining mechanism.

There is no constitutional provision for trade union recognition. This means that employers that are not part of any union themselves are not obliged to recognise employee grievances that are highlighted via the employee trade union.

Why should employers recognise trade unions?

The employee's right to be represented by the union will:

1. Be beneficial for the employee, providing a good degree of security that will lead to better work effort and job satisfaction.
2. Be beneficial for the employee, as it is possible to have proper negotiations over pay and working conditions.
3. Be beneficial for the employer, placing management into a good position to influence union attitudes. There is the possibility for management to create a good atmosphere in the firm by being seen to be fair with regard to decision-making.
4. Be good for the business itself, as a framework exists that can be used to sort out disputes.
5. Minimise the risk of strikes and the occurrences of work-to-rule situations.
6. Be good for all parties, as it imposes certain defined conditions on the conduct of business activities.

Different Employee, Employer Organisations and those Representing the Unemployed

IRISH BUSINESS AND EMPLOYERS' FEDERATION (IBEC)

The Federation of Irish Employers (FIE) and the Confederation of Irish Industry decided to amalgamate in 1993 to form IBEC, the largest employer association in Ireland.

Functions:
1. It represents employers when the Social Partners (unions, employers and government) meet to discuss economic issues and employee/employer disagreements and disputes.
2. IBEC representatives attend important conferences which deal with issues that directly affect employers, and relate back to their members that number over 4,000.

3. Economic and Social Policy (involving grant-aid for investment) is a main area of interest and IBEC represents Ireland when representatives take part in meetings of the Union of Industry and Employer Confederations in Europe (UNICE) and at meetings of the European Trade Union Confederation (ETUC) on behalf of its members.

4. It carries out research on behalf of employers.

5. It provides a consultancy service and advises employers on issues like health and safety.

6. It produces publications and provides training for employers.

IRISH SMALL AND MEDIUM ENTERPRISES ASSOCIATION (ISME)

ISME is the main small business lobby group (privately funded) in Ireland that has an input into Social Partner discussions (e.g. National Wage Agreements, Partnership 2000). It discusses economic issues and other issues that might affect small and medium-sized businesses with the managers of those businesses and with the other Social Partners. It keeps its members up to date with newsletters.

ISME works in close co-operation with the Minister and with 'Enterprise Ireland' the body set up by the Minister, which aims to further promote small and medium-sized indigenous (home) industry.

SMALL FIRMS ASSOCIATION (SFA)

The Small Firms Association represents and provides economic, commercial, employee relations and social affairs advice and assistance to small and medium enterprises (SMEs). There are 7,000 member companies. Information packs on health and safety requirements in the workplace, management training and development, discount schemes, IT management, business and economic trends and employee relations are available to meet the needs of small and medium companies.

Employees are also entitled to be members of an affiliated trade union that represents the employees of that organisation. Employees can make their grievances known through their trade union representatives and can pursue matters until satisfactory resolutions are found.

SERVICES, INDUSTRIAL, PROFESSIONAL AND TECHNICAL UNION (SIPTU)

The beginning of the 1990s saw the birth of a new union, SIPTU, when on 1 January 1990 the amalgamation of the ITGWU and FWUI took place. SIPTU is by far the largest trade union in Ireland. Members of the Irish Transport and General Workers' Union (ITGWU) and the Federated Workers' Union of Ireland (FWUI) were balloted in November 1989 and the amalgamation was the result of the ballot. Other membership groups have been accommodated within the SIPTU structure without difficulty, retaining their distinctive characters, while at the same time benefiting from the additional resources, services and protection that the SIPTU umbrella provides. Groups accommodated in this way were:

- Federation of Rural Workers
- Irish Advertising and Design Associates
- Irish Agricultural Advisory Organisation
- Irish National Painters' and Decorators' Trade Union
- Local Authority Professional Officers
- Medical Laboratory Technologists' Association
- National Association of Transport Employees
- Racing Board Tote Staff Association.

Many other groups of employees are affiliated to and represented by the trade union:

- Association of Artists Ireland
- Association of Irish Composers
- Irish Actors Equity
- Society of Irish Playwrights
- Employees in banking, clerical, administrative, supervisory, sales, hotel/catering and many other occupations.

IRISH NATIONAL ORGANISATION FOR THE UNEMPLOYED (INOU)

This is the lobby group that represents the interests of both the short-term and the long-term unemployed in Ireland. It has significant input into Social Partner discussions and national wage agreements like Partnership 2000. Changing economic circumstances like decisions taken by both the private sector (firms and businesses) and the public sector (government) are the concern of the INOU if they are seen to be a future cause of unemployment. The privatisation of companies (decisions to sell government-owned companies to private firms) can be a major cause of unemployment, as can the proposed withdrawal of foreign companies (e.g. Digital) from the country. In recent years the INOU has had a greater input into decisions that have been made, in particular in relation to Partnership agreements.

Note: **Refer to the section on Trade Union Operations at National Level under 'The Features of Grievance Procedures' in the next section of this chapter for information on Partnership Agreements.**

The Irish Congress of Trade Unions (ICTU)

This is the co-ordinating umbrella body to which many individual trade unions are affiliated. The congress itself is not a trade union, so therefore it has no legal status.

Functions:
1. It provides a framework to co-ordinate the activities of trade unions in Ireland.
2. It consults with government on matters affecting industrial relations – wage agreements etc.
3. It represents collectively the trade union movement with regard to industrial relations, and legislative and administrative matters.
4. On the request of affiliated unions, it may negotiate at national level with employers' organisations on policy and principles relating to pay and conditions of employment.
5. It promotes unity within the trade union movement as a whole.
6. It aims to reconcile views and relationships of unions that have similar classes of workers in their membership.
7. It aims to encourage (in some situations) amalgamation of similar unions to help strengthen their structures.
8. It provides affiliated trade unions with advice and information like legal advice and educational information and facilities.

Note: **Some trade unions are registered with the Registrar of Friendly Societies. Some trade unions are registered with both the ICTU and the Registrar.**

SAMPLE LIST

Trade Unions affiliated with the ICTU **(Source: The Irish Congress of Unions)**	Trade Unions Registered with the Registrar of Friendly Societies **(Source: The report on the Registry of Friendly Societies, Government Publications Office)**
Amalgamated Engineering and Electrical Union	
Prison Officers' Association	The Association of Electrical Contractors (Ire)
Association of Secondary Teachers Ireland (ASTI)	Irish Hairdressers' Federation
Bakery and Food Workers' Amalgamated Union	Irish Airline Pilots' Association
	Irish Bank Officials' Association
Irish National Teachers' Association (INTO)	Irish Postmasters' Union
Mandate (The Union of Retail, Bar & Admin. Workers)	Irish Printing Federation
	Irish Taxi and Hackney Owners' Association
Irish Nurses' Organisation	
National Union of Journalists	Irish Veterinary Union
Teachers' Union of Ireland (TUI)	Licensed Vintners' Association
SIPTU	National Bus and Rail Union
National League of the Blind of Ireland	Retail Jewellers of Ireland

- Many more organisations are listed in the source documents mentioned above.

Features of Grievance Procedures

Some trade unions operate at three different levels – workplace level, branch level and national level.

If an employee feels that he/she has been badly treated by colleagues, superiors or 'the system', he/she would:

(a) Bring the grievance to the attention of the workplace union representative/s.

(b) Arrange a meeting with the workplace manager/s.

(c) If a satisfactory resolution is not achieved at this stage the workplace representatives would bring the matter to the attention of the branch union representatives who would request a meeting with the manager/s.

(d) If a satisfactory agreement is not reached at this stage and if a head office governs the workplace, the branch-union representatives would request a meeting with the chief executive or executives based in the head office. (Note: Sometimes this stage structure does not apply depending on the type of organisational structure that exists.)

(e) Having found no resolution the branch representatives would then either
   1. put a strike action motion to the union branch committee that must be voted on; or
   2. recommend that the employee refer the matter on to the Labour Relations Commission which might refer it on to the Labour Court.

TRADE UNION OPERATIONS AT WORKPLACE LEVEL

Workplace union representatives are usually called Shop Stewards. They are elected by fellow staff union members. Their representation involves:

1. Posting union business and information received in the mail on to the union bulletin board to keep members informed on current events within the union.
2. Providing staff that wish to join the union with application forms and information regarding subscriptions and collecting subscriptions when applicable. (Many union subs are collected using the DAS method which means Deduction at Source. The subscriptions are taken directly from their wages with their approval.)
3. Attending branch meetings approximately once a month and whenever other emergency or special meetings occur. Shop stewards are not paid to attend these meetings on behalf of members.
4. Liaising with union head office.
5. Negotiating with management and representing fellow members when disciplinary and grievance issues arise.

TRADE UNION OPERATIONS AT BRANCH LEVEL

Branch representatives are usually part of the Branch Committee which includes the Branch Secretary, the Branch Treasurer, and the Equality Officer. These members are elected at the union's AGM (Annual General Meeting). They are made up of employees from different organisations that are employed by the same body located within the one geographical area.

The business of the branch is:

1. To negotiate better terms and conditions for all branch members (all branches). This involves formally meeting with managers of different branches of the organisation to help negotiate fair and better conditions and to help resolve disputes that arise between individual members and management.
2. To manage the internal affairs of the union.
3. To make representations (put forward motions to improve members' pay and conditions) at the Annual Congress held once a year. Delegates that are to attend the Congress are elected at the AGM.

TRADE UNION OPERATIONS AT NATIONAL LEVEL:

Union officers are elected at the Annual Conference. The conference itself is the national forum where motions are put forward, resolutions are passed and union policy is determined. The union's National Executive is the body that is responsible for ensuring that decisions made at the conference each year are implemented. The people that head the union are full-time employees of the union – called General Officers. They are the President of the union, the Vice-President, the General Secretary, and the Union Treasurer.

The National Union Meeting:

This is a meeting of all the members of the union in the country and is referred to as a Congress or an Annual Conference. A specific number of delegates are put forward and elected from individual branches to attend the Congress and speak on (debate) motions in a public arena before a vote is taken to pass or reject these motions. The motions passed then become resolutions that are later discussed with the other Social Partners, i.e. employer representatives (IBEC Irish Business and Employers' Confederation), and government representatives. Wage agreements like the Programme for National Recovery 1987, the Programme for Economic and Social Progress (PESP) 1991, and the Programme for Competitiveness and Work (PCW) 1994, were negotiated based on resolutions that were reached at Congress and the Annual Conferences.

Essential Ingredients of a Contract of Employment

A Contract of Employment is an offer in writing of:

(a) Temporary Employment – usually a fixed-term employment contract – usually a maximum commitment of three years or less; or
(b) Permanent Employment.

A temporary contract will contain a statement of the terms and conditions of employment broken down into:

(a) Nature of post of employment – temporary
(b) Duration of employment – annual fixed-term employment (or otherwise)
(c) Duties and extra duties required from time to time
(d) Working hours
(e) Salary
(f) Travel and subsistence allowances (if applicable)

(g) Holiday entitlements – also referred to as annual leave

(h) Special leave – e.g. compassionate leave or exceptional circumstances

(i) Sick leave entitlements

(j) Notice of termination of employment

(k) Maternity procedures and entitlements

(l) Grievance and disciplinary procedures

(m) Medical examinations (if applicable)

(n) Declaration and signatures – employee and employer (counter signature)

A Permanent Contract will contain a statement including most of the terms and conditions mentioned above, but will usually also include Probation requirements.

(A Sample Contract of Employment is located on the next page.)

A Sample Contract of Employment

Dear

We have a temporary vacancy in . . . . and I have pleasure in offering you temporary employment in this post.

A statement of your Terms and Conditions of Employment is enclosed. I should be grateful if you would signify your acceptance of the offer by signing the attached copy of this letter and <u>returning it to</u> . . . .

Your employment is temporary, commencing on Monday 19 June 2XXX and terminating on Friday 28 July 2XXX. The Unfair Dismissals Act 1977–1991 shall not apply to a termination consisting only of the expiry of this term without its being renewed.

Please report for work to . . . . at 9.00 a.m. on . . . . You should bring with you your Income Tax Form P45. As you will see from the attached Terms and Conditions, your salary will be paid monthly, one month in arrears. This payment will be made on the second Friday of each month for any employment with us during the previous month – therefore, you may be with us 6/7 weeks before you receive any payment. If this is likely to cause you any difficulty you should approach your Assistant Manager concerning the arrangement of advance payment of some of your salary.

If you are unable to start on that date, please contact me without delay. If you require further information or clarification on any aspect of this correspondence, please get in touch with myself at ext. . . . .

I would like to take this opportunity to wish you every success and happiness during your period of temporary employment with us.

Yours sincerely,

I accept the temporary position as offered. I acknowledge receipt of a statement of the general terms and conditions of my employment and Staff Rules. I have read these and I accept them as the terms and conditions of my contract of employment with . . . . . . I shall report for duty as requested.

SIGNED: _____   DATE _____

STATEMENT OF TERMS AND CONDITIONS OF EMPLOYMENT – REPUBLIC

1. NATURE OF EMPLOYMENT

You will be employed on a temporary basis.

2. SECRECY

You are required to treat all information gained as a result of your employment with . . . . . as strictly confidential, both during and after your employment with . . . . For this purpose you will be required to sign a Declaration of Secrecy Form.

3. WORKING HOURS

The normal working week is from Monday to Friday inclusive.

The normal working day may vary, but overtime is calculated on a daily basis in respect of each completed quarter-hour worked in excess of 7.25 hours (exclusive of one hour's lunch-break).

Your normal starting and finishing times will be advised to you by your Manager/Head of Department.

Payment for overtime work will be at such rates as are in force from time to time, and is based on completed quarter hours worked in excess of the normal day.

(Details of eligibility and current overtime rates are available from Managers/Heads of Departments).

4. SALARY

Your salary will be at the rate of . . . . . . per week payable monthly. In addition, overtime is payable at the current agreed rates, at present . . . . . per hour.

5. HOLIDAYS

Provided you have worked at least 120 hours in a calendar month, you will be entitled to holidays at the rate of one and three quarters working days per month worked, this leave to be taken by agreement with your Manager/Head of Department but before six months continuous employment has elapsed.

If you have worked less than 120 hours in a calendar month you will be entitled to 6 hours paid leave for every 100 hours worked and to proportionately less for periods of less than 100 hours worked provided:

- you are normally expected to work at least 8 hours per day.
- you have at least 13 weeks continuous service. These 13 weeks are not included when calculating annual leave entitlements.

Holiday pay and payment in lieu of accrued holidays on termination of employment will be paid at the rate of . . . . . per day.

You will be entitled to the same Bank/Public Holidays as permanent Officials, details of which are available from your Manager/Head of Department (if you have worked 120 hours in the 5 weeks preceding the holiday or have 13 weeks continuous employment and are normally expected to work more than 8 hours a week).

You will be entitled to the same Bank/Public Holidays as permanent Officials, details of which are available from your Manager/Head of Department (if you have worked 120 hours in the 5 weeks preceding the holiday or have 13 weeks continuous employment and are normally expected to work more than 8 hours a week).

6. **BENEFITS NOT APPLYING TO THIS EMPLOYMENT**
You will not have entitlement to benefits applicable to permanent employees,

  e.g.   – club subscriptions
         – pension benefits
         – staff loan facilities, etc.

7. **SICK LEAVE**
If you are unable to attend work because of illness, your Manager/Head of Department should be notified as early as possible on the first day.

Where you have cumulative service of one year or more you become entitled to paid certified sick leave up to a maximum of four weeks in any one year. However there will be no pay for absence due to sick leave during the first year of employment. You may be required to see the company doctors or a doctor nominated by the Bank at any stage during your employment. You will be entitled to see any medical report made at the request of the Bank and said report shall not be used by . . . . except for lawful purposes.

8. **NOTICE OF TERMINATION OF EMPLOYMENT**
The Minimum Notice and Terms of Employment Act 1973 will apply to notice of termination by . . . . or by you of your employment. The statutory minimum notice which must be given is one week.   . . . . . . reserves the right to give payment in lieu of notice.

9. **MATERNITY**
The Maternity Protection of Employees Act 1981 shall apply to female temporary staff regarding maternity leave and the right to return to work. The requirements in each of sub sections (1) and (2) of Section 22 of the Act are mandatory. (Details available from Personnel Manager).

10. **PARENTAL LEAVE**
The Parental Leave Act 1998 shall apply to temporary staff and will be calculated on a *pro-rata* basis (details available from personnel manager).

11. **GRIEVANCE AND DISCIPLINARY PROCEDURES**
A listing of the principal staff rules is attached. Detailed Grievance and Disciplinary Procedures have been devised to ensure that fair and prompt arrangements exist for dealing with grievance or disciplinary matters. Grievance and Disciplinary Procedures will be provided on request.

12. **ALTERATIONS IN TERMS AND CONDITIONS**
Alterations in your Terms and Conditions of Employment will be advised, normally by general Circular or Memorandum to Branches/Departments, as they occur from time to time.

13. **GENERAL**
It is understood that you will perform, to the best of your ability, all duties assigned to you and will at all times obey all reasonable instructions given to you.

Data Protection Act 1988

The following individuals, firms and other bodies who keep personal information on computer are required to register:

- Public authorities and other public sector bodies
- Financial institutions, insurance companies and individuals or firms whose business consists wholly or mainly in direct marketing or direct mailing, providing credit references or collecting debts
- Any others who keep personal information on computer relating to racial origin, political opinions, religious or other beliefs, sexual life, criminal convictions or health (other than health information on employees kept in the ordinary course of personnel administration and not used or disclosed for any other purpose)
- Those whose business consists wholly or partly in processing personal data on behalf of others.

It is an offence for anyone who is required to register but has not done so to keep personal information on computer.

Note: All those who keep personal information on computer, whether or not they are required to register, must comply with the data protection provisions of the Act from that date.

Application forms for registration, notes on how to register and a Guide to the Act may be obtained from the Office of the Data Protection Commissioner, 74 St Stephen's Green, Dublin 2

TERRITORIAL APPLICATION OF THE DATA PROTECTION ACT

1. If a data controller is **based outside of Ireland** and does not use any equipment for data processing (the processing of personal data) in Ireland and does not have any branches or agencies acting on its behalf in Ireland, the data controller is not subject to the act.

2. If a data controller is **based in Ireland**, then the act applies.

3. In unclear cases where headquarters are not in Ireland or are in Ireland but carry on all of their activities in other countries, the new European Communities (Data Protection) Regulations, 2001 allows for the replacement of section 23 of the Data Protection Act. In general the regulations apply only to data controllers established 'in the state' – where equipment is used in Ireland. This does not include Northern Ireland.

4. In general, data controllers in EEA (European Economic Area) countries are subject to data protection laws in the EEA country in which they use equipment to process personal data and in which they are based.

The Services of the Irish Ombudsman

The Ombudsman deals with complaints against government departments, local authorities, health boards and An Post. The first Ombudsman was appointed in 1984. Ombudsman is a Swedish name meaning 'representative of the people'.

The basis for the services provided by the Ombudsman is the Ombudsman Act, 1980. Important features of the act are as follows:

1. The appointment is made by the President, where the office is held for six years.
2. The Ombudsman can be removed from office by the President due to misbehaviour, incapacity or bankruptcy and must vacate the office on reaching the age of 67 years.
3. The Ombudsman is empowered to make recommendations only – his or her findings are not binding and these recommendations are dealt with in private in the first instance to allow the body concerned to make their own representations.
4. He must report on the response of the body complained against and if a response to one of his recommendations is not satisfactory he may make a special report to the Oireachtas.
5. Excluded from investigation are:
   (a) Cases where the matter is before the courts or where a court decision is being appealed against.
   (b) Cases relating to recruitment or terms and conditions of employment (dealt with by LRC – Labour Relations Commission).
   (c) Cases relating to aliens or naturalisation (emigration).
   (d) Cases relating to prison pardons or sentences or court penalties.
   (e) Cases relating to the administration of prisons.
6. A Minister of the government can request that a particular case not be investigated. The Ombudsman must cease his investigation immediately.

The European Ombudsman

The institution of the European Ombudsman was created by the Maastricht Treaty in 1992. The European Parliament elected the first European Ombudsman, Mr Jacob Soderman from Finland in 1995.

The European Ombudsman investigates and reports on maladministration in the institutions and bodies of the European Community, such as the European Commission, the Council of the European Union and European Parliament based only on complaints made. Only the Court of Justice and the Court of First Instance do not fall within his jurisdiction. Any citizen of the European Union or resident in

Super Ombudsman with no super powers

Ed Micheau applauds the creation of Ireland's new 'Super' Ombudsman, but has a couple of questions about the Office

The timetable for the creation of a statutory Ombudsman for the financial services sector has been stepped up, with a Bill for its creation now scheduled to be brought before the Oireachtas in the autumn. The Ombudsman could be in place by early 2003.

The 'Super' Ombudsman will field complaints currently heard by voluntary Ombudsmen in the areas of insurance and credit provision. The remit of the Ombudsman is not yet clear, but the precise details of its rules of engagement will be of interest to the consumer, the suppliers and the voluntary Ombudsmen alike.

For example, will the Ombudsman replicate the powers and actions of the Financial Ombudsman in the UK, which came into being on December 1, 2001?

The Financial Ombudsman has been in the news of late, after a series of rulings made against a number of mortgage providers, including Abbey National and Halifax. The latter two have had their knuckles rapped by the Ombudsman following complaints by consumers that the mortgage providers had discriminated against them by offering two different variable rates – one for new customers and another for existing customers. The complaints were received from existing customers who were peeved at not being offered the same, or lower, rate that were being offered to entice new customers.

The Ombudsman in the UK does not have the power to force the mortgage providers to drop dual pricing, but it did force them to at least offer the lower rate to the aggrieved existing customers.

Under existing rules in Ireland, mortgage customers would not enjoy the support of the Ombudsman for Credit Institutions. The Ombudsman is opposed to forcing the hand of mortgage providers as it would breach the contract freely entered into by the consumer.

The Ombudsman says the issue is further complicated in the UK, as the banks and building societies – unlike the system in Ireland where a decision is binding – can appeal a decision to the courts. It opens up the vista of consumers finding themselves fighting their mortgage provider in the High Court.

But then you could argue that the Ombudsman would say that – do turkeys vote for Christmas? With the arrival of the 'Super' Ombudsman, will there still be a role for the two existing watchdogs? Will they become redundant, or will a parallel system of scrutiny be plausible?

Alternatively, the 'Super' Ombudsman could opt for a third way, similar to that in place in Australia. There, the Securities and Investment Commission (SIC) does not review individual cases but supervises the Ombudsman's office.

Just what course of action is adopted will soon be revealed. Whatever the details, the Irish Financial Services Regulatory Authority (IFRSA) will want the Ombudsman's office to have real teeth.

In the present climate of fear and loathing concerning company accounts and corporate governance, the mandarins at the Department of Finance will be anxious to ensure that the consumer is king under the new regime.

a member state can lodge a complaint. If an attempt at conciliation fails, the Ombudsman can make recommendations to solve the case. If a problem arises he can make a special report to the European Parliament.

Many complaints made to the European Ombudsman concern:

- Administrative delay, lack of transparency or refusal of access to information.
- Work relations between the institutions and their agents, recruitment of staff and the running of competitions.
- Contractual relations between the institutions and private firms, for example in case of abrupt termination of contract.

The European Ombudsman produces an Annual Report to the European Parliament and this is translated into all the official languages of the European Union. He also visits all member states.

PRACTICE QUESTIONS

1. Define the term 'Trade Union'.
2. There are *three* different types of employee unions. What are they?
3. What is the purpose of an employer association?
4. List *five* main objectives of trade unions.
5. Who are the Social Partners and how are they connected with Collective Bargaining?
6. List *three* benefits to employers of recognising trade unions.
7. What is ICTU and list *four* of its functions.
8. Explain the basic differences between the *three* levels at which Trade Unions operate.
9. Write notes on:
   (a) Shop Steward
   (b) DAS.
10. The Trade Union Annual Conference displays how it operates formally at National Level. Why is this meeting so important?
11. Give *five* reasons why documents are kept on file in the Human Resources Department.
12. What are the essential ingredients of a Contract of Employment?
13. What is the substance of the Data Protection Act 1998?
14. Write notes on
   (a) The Ombudsman
   (b) The Director of Consumer Affairs.

A Sample Student Trade Union Assignment

The Association of Secondary Teachers Ireland (ASTI)
Compiled by Shane Creedon, Computer Applications and Business student in
Crumlin College 1995–1996

History of Trade Unionism and ASTI

In 1889, the first effort to organise unskilled workers into unions began. Craft unions had been in place for 150 years before. By 1890, only 7,500 people had been members of a union. It was slow to grow as owners were opposed to trade unions. In Ireland, the Irish were concerned with the Land Question, so the rights of individuals in towns and cities were ignored. People were slow to join, for fear of being fired. In 1900, the union had more than 60,000 members who were involved in strikes in Dublin, Cork, Belfast and Wexford.

In the twentieth century, wages were low and there was a lot of unemployment. People knew that strikes could bring about change. The ITGWU was growing in size and strikes brought about wage increases. The most notable strike was the 1913 Lock-out.

Trade unions were eventually accepted in the workplace. The membership was growing, and a number of new, individual unions were being formed in the workplace in the 1930s. This caused problems both for the workforce and employers. Different unions wanted to strike for different reasons. There was great rivalry between unions. A new body of trade unions was set up, the ICTU. This was because, at a meeting of trade unions in London the ITGWU did not want to breach Ireland's neutrality. So the ICTU was set up in 1959.

In the 1960s, there was economic growth, and white-collar unions were beginning to grow. New companies were coming to Ireland and trade unions were eventually accepted.

In the 1970s, all-out strikes were used to pursue demands. Also, national pay agreements were introduced. This meant that unions could negotiate with employers.

The ASTI was founded in 1909. It was set up to achieve a system of registration, an adequate salary scale, reasonable security of tenure and good service pensions. To meet their demands, they launched a sophisticated lobbying campaign. In 1912, parliament gave a grant for lay secondary school teachers' salaries of £40,000. Registration and security provisions were made.

The Molony Committee recommended changes in administration financing. They wanted wages increased from £180 to £450 per annum. The final offer was a £40 increase for men and a £30 increase for women. In 1920 the ASTI had their first strike In 1923 the first annual delegation took place. In 1924 the Department of Education was set up, and in 1929 the secondary school superannuation scheme was set up. The union eventually succeeded in getting a registration of teachers, and an eight to twelve per cent salary increase. Membership has grown to 14,236 in 1994 and there is now job security for teachers.

ASTI Union Structure

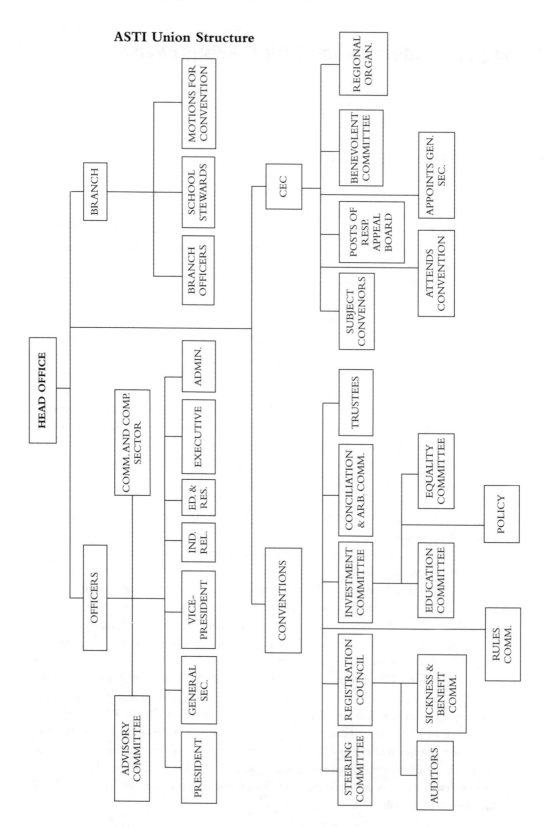

Election Procedures for ASTI

The ASTI is organised in branches of schools in geographical regions. Each school is affiliated to a branch. Members of branches elect a number of their members to the Central Executive Council. Each branch also elects members as delegates to the Annual Convention.

A standing committee of twenty-three members manages the business of the association. A president is elected at the Annual Convention. The term of office runs from 1 August to 31 July. (He/she is the president-elect for the period running from the Annual Convention to 31 July.)

The Honorary National Organiser and regional organisers are elected by the CEC. A school steward is elected to liaise with the local branch, CEC members and Head Office.

Election of School Stewards

The election of school stewards should take place annually. Each branch arranges that a school steward is elected by the ASTI members of the staff of every school within its area which has more than once teacher who is a member of the association. This election takes place on 1 May of each year. The newly elected school steward, as soon as possible, notifies Head Office using the appropriate form, the Regional Organiser, the Honourable Secretary of his/her branch, and the Hon. secretaries of the branches concerned, of his/her election. The General Secretary informs each school manager of his/her branch, concerning the school steward they elected after 15 May.

Membership of ASTI

There are four classes of membership in the ASTI
- Full membership (for serving lay teachers with the relevant qualifications)
- Associate membership (for lay Higher Diploma or final year college students)
- Emeritus membership (for members who retire on reaching retirement age)
- Honorary life membership (conferred only in recognition of outstanding service to the association).

ELIGIBILITY FOR FULL MEMBERSHIP
- All lay serving assistant teachers who hold qualifications for registration as a secondary teacher
- If they hold a primary university degree
- If they are entitled to become a member.

ELIGIBILITY FOR ASSOCIATE MEMBERSHIP
- H.Dip. in Ed. lay students in their final year or when they have qualified are eligible for associate membership.

ELIGIBILITY FOR EMERITUS MEMBERSHIP

All serving teachers who have retired on reaching the required age, or due to medical grounds, can become an Emeritus member.

APPLICATION FOR MEMBERSHIP

- Fill in the correct application form agreeing to the rules.
- Agree deductions from salary.
- Be proposed and seconded by branch members.
- Pay one-quarter annual subscription for full membership, if not deducted from salary.

INELIGIBLE FOR MEMBERSHIP

- A branch may refuse membership where there is a valid objection by standing committee or CEC.
- Principal teachers with sole power to appoint or dismiss teaching staff are not eligible for membership.
- The decision of the Central Executive Council to accept or reject is final.

Roles and Services of the ASTI

The role of the ASTI is to promote increases in funding for education, and improvements in facilities. It is directly involved in curriculum content and reform. It has direct representation on the National Council for Curriculum and Assessment, Syllabus Committees, the Registration Council, on the Public Services Committee of the ICTU and Posts of Responsibility Appeals Board.

It also represents its members at meetings with the Department of Education, the government and the political parties. Through press releases, conferences and the media, it seeks to improve the teachers' working environment.

At local level, it gives advice on rationalisation, contracts, adequate staffing levels, redeployment and leave entitlements. School stewards, CEC, branch officers and Head Office give advice and information on trade union and professional matters.

ASTI Services:

1. It is represented on
   - School authorities and boards
   - Managerial bodies
   - Government departments
   - Media and general public.
2. It negotiates to
   - Increase salaries and hourly pay
   - Improve and protect working conditions
   - Secure jobs
   - Develop curriculum

3. It advises on
   - Career and professional matters
   - Access to information
   - School stewards availability in schools
   - Branch representatives
4. It gives legal assistance on
   - Urgent legal counselling
   - Legal expenses
5. It gives benevolent funds to
   - Members retiring through illness
   - Dependants of deceased members
6. It gives sickness benefit
   - Illness-related expenses
   - Optical and dental benefits
   - Prescribed hearing aid benefits
7. It gives seminars and training on
   - Equal opportunities
   - Child abuse
   - Adult education/training
   - Annual Education Conference
   - European Social Fund for schools
   - Training for school stewards and branch officers
   - Health and safety
   - School libraries
8. It has a contingency fund
   - For financial benefits for members during disputes
9. It has a salary protection scheme
10. It has car a insurance scheme for
    - Reduced car insurance costs
    - Open to spouses of members
11. It has publications
    - *ASTI* monthly journal
    - *Secondary School*, a quarterly educational journal
    - *Nuacht*, current affairs journal
    - *School Year Diary*
    - Regular publications and leaflets on education matters
12. It has library/information centre for
    - All members
    - Books and magazines on education
    - Computerised documents
    - Access to educational databases

- Comprehensive media file
- Education and research officer

13. It has other benefits

- Rail vouchers
- VHI group scheme
- ASTI credit union.

The ASTI's main aim in 1909 when it started was to:

- Have a registry of teachers
- Adequate salaries
- Employment security
- A good pension scheme.

The ASTI has achieved for secondary school teachers the following.

1. A growth in membership.
2. Salary increases.
3. Job security (protecting employment and redeployment protection for teachers)
4. Pupil teacher ratio improved
5. Provisions for disadvantaged students (guidance teachers)
6. Curriculum development (introduction of the Junior and Senior Certificates).
7. Career options (career breaks, job-sharing).

It has done this through successful lobbying, campaigns, public meetings and demonstrations and media publicity to bring about these changes.

Bibliography

ASTI, Members' Handbook.
ASTI, Membership Information.
ICTU, *Understanding Trade Unions: Past & Present.*

Sample Assignment Briefs – Human Resources/Trades Unions

1. Carry out a brief profile of an Irish Trade Union using the following headings as a guide:
   (a) History, size and membership and general purpose of the union.
   (b) Mission Statement.
   (c) Organisational Chart of some aspect of the Trade Union (can be the complete chart, a breakdown of head-office staff or a branch profile or equivalent e.g. general secretary, vice president of the union etc.)
   (d) Functions of members mentioned on Organisational Chart(s) explained.
   (e) Union Meetings.
   (f) Grievance Procedures.

2. Analyse the workings of any Human Resources Department using the following headings as a guide:
   (a) History, size and ownership of the business.
   (b) Size and layout of the H.R. Department (with visuals, staff numbers etc.)
   (c) Organisational Chart of the H.R. Department and H.R. staff functions explained.
   (d) Filing methods and general H.R. Department day-to-day functions/duties.
   (e) Recruitment Procedures.
   (f) Disciplinary Procedures.

3. The student brief is as follows:
Select and cut out *four* advertisements for various types of jobs from the newspaper. For each advertisement:
(a) Identify what type of Company or Organisation is advertising.
(b) Identify at what level in the organisation the person will work.
(c) Identify what type of Recruitment Option is being used.
(d) Identify who the applicant will be responsible to and what is the extent of his/her job specification (some imagination and knowledge of the world of work should be evident).
(e) Identify what type of person (qualifications, attributes, skills, experience etc.) is required.
(f) Outline any available information about remuneration with reference to 'flat rate', bonuses, overtime, or other incentives.

Note: The Examiner marking the assignment will take variety of advertisements, clarity of analysis, extent of knowledge, imagination in interpretation and neatness of presentation into consideration.

Sample Questions for Student Research on 'A Trade Union'

1. Could you give me some information on the history of the Trade Union?
2. What is its Mission Statement?
3. Where are the Trade Union offices located i.e. head-office, branches?
4. Is the Trade Union affiliated to the ICTU (Irish Congress of Trade Unions)?
5. How many and what categories of members has the Union got?
6. Could you provide me with an Organisational Chart of the Trade Union? (E.g. President, General Secretary, Assistant General Secretary etc.)
7. What are their functions?
8. What is the structure in place with regard to union meetings?
9. What grievance procedures can members avail of?

Sample Questions for Student Research on 'The H.R. Department'

1. When did the business become established? Did it relocate?
2. How many branches/departments are there?
3. What products or services does it offer?
4. What type of ownership is there (e.g. sole trader, partnership, private, public company etc.)?
5. Who owns the business (shareholding)?
6. Could you provide me with an Organisational Chart of staff in the H.R. Department? If not, can you help me to compile one?
7. Can you explain the basic functions of the staff in the H.R. Department?
8. What filing systems are used in the H.R. Department, e.g. alphabetical, numerical, historical, mixture?
9. What are the recruitment procedures of the business, e.g. open competition, agencies used, word of mouth etc.?
10. Could you provide me with a copy of a sample newspaper advert, letters of reply or contracts of employment to include in my project?
11. How do you discipline staff, e.g. reminders (memos), verbal, written warnings, suspensions, dismissals?
12. Do you hold staff development days? If yes, do you think they help to motivate staff and increase work effort?
13. How are the staff motivated – by career advancement/promotions etc.?

5. Preparing for Meetings

A 'meeting' is a forum that allows for communication within a group of people.

Role of a Meeting within the Organisation

Meetings are designed to:

1. Allow immediate face-to-face verbal exchange, feedback and presentation within a controlled framework, where a chairperson's job is to provide this control and regulation of activities.
2. Help to enhance understanding and act as a forum for persuasion.
3. Humanise the context of the organisation's communication channels by opening the parties to personal contact and each other's direct scrutiny and by exposing the characteristics of individual personalities. Open and spontaneous communication is usually encouraged with constructive criticism being paramount to improvements and more satisfactory work arrangements.
4. Spread information quickly and efficiently with full advice on and explanations of business given to participants, to avoid misunderstandings.
5. Create possible decision-making forums usually with detailed discussion before decisions are arrived at, and where previous unfulfilled commitments can be discussed further and sometimes enforced.
6. Iron out difficulties (problem-solving) and to promote better 'people relationships' and co-operation.

Different Types of Meetings

Meetings are generally set up by posting a *Notice* informing people where and when the meeting is to be held, together with an *Agenda* briefly detailing what the meeting is about.

1. Informal meetings usually have a chairperson who regulates activities by keeping order and by encouraging contributions to the discussion when necessary. He/she informally guides the discussion along the lines set by the agenda.
2. Formal meetings differ from Informal meetings because as well as the requirements for a Notice to be posted or sent and an Agenda to be drawn up:
   (a) The participants are governed by legal requirements, where they have the right to have an item included on the agenda provided that they give due notice of it to the chairperson.

(b) A sufficient number of participants must be present at the meeting in order to form a *Quorum* (a required number of participants to vote).

(c) The participants usually sign an attendance book to prove that they were present at the meeting.

(d) The participants presiding over the meeting have formal titles like *chairperson* and *secretary*. When these people are not available 'Acting' participants take their places temporarily.

(e) Formal *Minutes* of the meeting (an accurate summary of proceedings) are taken usually by the secretary.

(f) A formal *Report* of the meeting is usually compiled by the secretary and sent to participants.

(g) The *room layout* of the meeting and the seating arrangements of the participants are sometimes sketched to provide further evidence of attendance and formal procedures being adhered to.

(The terms written in italics will be discussed later.)

EXAMPLES OF DIFFERENT TYPES OF MEETINGS:

Types of meetings run from the Most Formal to Less Formal to Informal.

The Most Formal meetings are usually Annual General Meetings (AGMs), Annual General Conferences, Board Meetings, Extraordinary General Meetings (EGMs), Department Meetings, Union Meetings, Public Inquiries and Council Meetings.

Less Formal Meetings might be Staff meetings, Club committee meetings, Sub-committee meetings, Task groups and Quality Circle meetings.

Informal meetings might be staff development meetings, authors informally meeting with editors, inter-departmental meetings.

- Formal procedures involve thorough preparation by presiding participants with full written records, official rules of procedure, participant behaviour and rules of law governing the meeting being strictly adhered to.
- Informal arrangements involve informal notes (if any) being taken for reference, with no formal rules for participants and an unstructured procedure being apparent. MBWA 'Management by walk around' is an informal technique that managers use whereby they regularly walk around about the workplace and have informal chats with subordinates. It is a deliberate means of stimulating motivation and can help to raise job satisfaction. On the other hand, employees can view it as an intimidating means of motivation.

Note: It is interesting to note that informal meetings can be the key to good organisation because many issues that are discussed informally gain universal agreement before the formal forum is set up. Also input from people who may not wish to voice their opinions or objections in a more public and formal setting can prove to be informative and useful to guide the final decision-making process. It ensures that everyone's needs are considered within the organisation. In short, everyone gets a look in. (Refer to Chapter 1 'The Organisation' where Formal and Informal Organisational Structure is discussed.)

The Functions of Specific Types of Meetings

1. THE AGM

The Annual General Meeting is held once a year by clubs, associations and companies that all shareholders or members are entitled to attend. An invitation is posted or sent to them. The Companies Act requires by law that companies hold an AGM. Officers (i.e. chairperson, vice-chairperson, secretary, treasurer and other typical posts like publicity officer, equality officer etc.) are elected or re-elected for the year ahead. Annual reports regarding issues and monies (the financial position of the business including profits/dividends) are dealt with and copies of these are made available to members or participants. Shareholders can question directors openly and satisfy themselves with regard to the current performance of and future plans for the business.

2. AN EGM

An Extraordinary General Meeting is held if a serious turn of events occurs like the possibility of the company going into liquidation. A good example where a meeting like this is required would be if a company merger was envisaged in the near future. This meeting that the board of directors or committee calls notifies all shareholders or members of an EGM to discuss the specific item of business.

3. BOARD MEETINGS

A Board Meeting or Committee Meeting is a meeting of a task force that heads the organisation. The members have delegated authority to make decisions, and can serve as people who can be consulted for the purpose of co-ordinating activities within the organisation. The board members have the authority to carry out the decisions arrived at by them at these meetings. This type of company meeting is underpinned by the Companies Act 1985.

An MPC is a Monetary Policy Committee meeting that a bank or financial institution might hold to review interest rates and the general financial policy of the institution. It is an example of a type of board meeting.

4. DEPARTMENT MEETINGS

Organisations divide up labour into departments. Usually each department has a 'head of department' and he/she calls internal department meetings that only apply to people directly connected with the department in question. These meetings take place approximately once a month. A review of the past month's activities with regard to that department only takes place. Participants make suggestions for change and engage in constructive discussion to allow for improvements within the department. Appropriate statistics and documentation is provided by the head of department to motivate and inform workers present at the meeting.

5. UNION MEETINGS

The different types of Union Representatives are discussed in detail in Chapter 4, 'Human Resources and Legal Aspects of Retailing', in the section 'The features of grievance procedures'. The corresponding meetings that are presided over by these representatives are:

WORKPLACE UNION MEETINGS

The staff union representative posts a notice and an agenda of the intended meeting on the union notice board. A satisfactory period of notice should be given to staff, usually a week. Sometimes it is necessary to call an emergency meeting where it is not possible to give this amount of notice to members.

The functions of these meeting are:

1. To keep members informed on current events within the union.
2. To discuss grievances that members wish to raise and to suggest ways that solutions may be found.
3. To decide by majority vote to strike or operate a work to rule in order to gain management's attention, which might result in better pay and conditions of employment.
4. To decide whether disputes at local level should be brought to the attention of the branch representatives.
5. To decide whether disputes might be resolved more quickly by taking the legal route (via the Labour Relations Commission and the Labour Court – discussed in Chapter 4).

BRANCH UNION MEETINGS

The union head office will send individual workplace union representatives notification of branch meetings which take place usually on a monthly basis. Notification is also given of special or emergency meetings from time to time. Usually the branch chairperson, the branch secretary, and from time to time other officers preside over the meeting. All the members of different branches are entitled to attend these meetings and to vote.

The functions of this type of meeting are:

1. To address and discuss grievances resulting in motions being put forward and agreed upon by 'the branch'. These motions must be sanctioned by the Union

Executive Body and by the General Officers if they are to be presented as motions that have the possibility of being converted into resolutions and of becoming union policy at national level (at the Annual Congress/Conference).

2. To address and discuss problems at local workplace level and decide on options to resolve these disputes to everyone's satisfaction.

3. To discuss issues regarding pay and conditions and discrimination and to put forward motions to deal with local problems in these areas.

4. Each branch has its individual Annual General Meeting once a year (the functions of an AGM have been discussed previously).

THE NATIONAL UNION MEETING:

This is a meeting of all the members of the union in the country and is referred to as a Congress or an Annual Conference. A specific number of delegates are put forward and elected from individual branches to attend the Congress and speak on (debate) motions in a public arena before a vote is taken to pass or reject these motions. The motions that are passed then become resolutions that are later discussed with the other social partners, i.e. employer representatives (IBEC, Irish Business and Employers' Confederation) and government representatives. Wage agreements like the Programme for National Recovery 1987, the Programme for Economic and Social Progress, PESP (1991) and the current Programme for Competitiveness and Work, PCW (1994) were negotiated based on resolutions that were reached at Congress and the Annual Conferences.

6. PUBLIC MEETINGS

Certain European directives and case-law precedents affect the holding and conduct of some meetings. This would apply to public inquires and tribunals which are types of public meetings. The legal Acts that underpin these types of meetings are the Public Meeting Act 1908, the Public Order Acts of 1936 and 1986, and the Representation of the People Act 1983.

Both the public sector (government, state and semi-state bodies) and the private sector (private companies and organisations) have meetings to regularise affairs within respective areas of authority. Together, the informal and formal organisational structure which also applies to meetings, is the driving force that leads to good communication networks that in turn leads to effectiveness and efficiency.

PRACTICE QUESTIONS

1. (a) Define the meaning of a 'Meeting'.
   (b) List *four* objectives of meetings.
2. What are the main differences between a Formal and an Informal Meeting?
3. Name *five* different types of meetings and explain how they differ.
4. What are the functions of a Workplace Union Meeting?

5. What are the functions of a Branch Union Meeting?
6. What are the functions of a National Union Meeting?
7. What legal Acts underpin public meetings like Tribunals of Inquiry?

Roles, Powers and Duties of Officers at a Meeting

THE CHAIRPERSON

A chairperson regulates activities at a meeting by keeping order and by encouraging contributions to the discussion when necessary. He/she guides the discussion along the lines set by the agenda (in the form of a sequence of business decided in advance). Anything that the chairperson has not been informed about in advance can be referred to under 'Any other Business' (AOB) if time permits.

In formal meetings, the chairperson has more complex responsibilities where set rules will be applied by him/her.

1. The chairperson will make out a chairperson's agenda that directly corresponds with the main agenda except personal notes that will appear under each item on the main agenda. (A sample is given later.) It provides a personal reference to guide the chairperson when he/she is chairing the meeting. The chairperson's agenda will allow him/her to implement the correct procedure (points of order) that must be observed in convening and constituting the meeting and in the conduct of the debate.
2. In the event of queries or complaints regarding procedure (points of order) the chairperson must give an immediate ruling.
3. He/she must deal firmly and exercise courtesy when participants engage in irrelevancies, long-windedness, interruptions, show a lack of courtesy or use improper language.
4. He/she must regulate proceedings when participants are voting upon issues in order to arrive at a clear-cut decision agreed by a majority.

A well-led meeting can be very productive and effective for the purposes of planning, consultation, problem-solving and decision-making, relaying decisions and instructions, downward and upward briefing (to subordinates and superiors), inter-departmental and cross-departmental liaison.

THE SECRETARY

A Secretary would normally
1. Have 'before-meeting duties' like fixing the date and the time of the meeting and preparing, posting and/or sending out the Notice and the Agenda to interested parties.

2. Be responsible for choosing and preparing the location of the meeting, ensuring appropriate size of venue, good accessibility, appropriate facilities (overhead projectors etc.) and suitable seating arrangements.

3. Have 'during the meeting duties' like making notes and assisting the chairperson regarding clarification of statements made etc.

4. Have 'post-meeting duties' like preparing the Minutes of the meeting based on the notes taken at the meeting, and might be required to communicate decisions taken based on the discussion at the meeting and/or act on these decisions (this does not always apply).

THE TREASURER

The functions of the Treasurer are:

1. To receive and record subscriptions from members of a club or union and to send the new member a receipt acknowledging receipt of the money.

2. To lodge the money into the appropriate club or union bank account.

3. To pay all club or union bills.

4. To keep the accounts (financial transactions) of the club or union correct and up to date.

5. To prepare a yearly Financial Report for the club or union's AGM and make the report available to members.

Terms Associated with Meetings
(including regulations governing meetings)

1. Clear Days: refers to the time required to convene a meeting outside of the day the notices are sent out and the day the meeting is held. (An organisation's rules may place a different definition on Clear Days depending on their requirements.)

2. In Camera: refers to a meeting that is held in private where the public or the press are not allowed to attend.

3. A Motion: is a proposal put to a meeting. For example, Motion No. 1 might be, 'I propose that Mary Smith be elected as Treasurer of this branch' (usually naming the branch of the organisation). There is usually a 'seconder' to back up the 'proposer'.

    Examples of Motions: I propose:
    'that the meeting postpone consideration of the subject';
    'that the debate be adjourned.'

Informational proposals can also be cast as motions, e.g. 'I propose to receive the report on the annual accounts given by the treasurer for the year ended . . .'

4. A Proposer: is a person who puts forward a motion at a meeting.

5. A Seconder: is a person who immediately supports the proposer's motion. A seconder usually signs the minutes of a meeting also.

6. A Resolution: If a motion is accepted, but has to be put to superiors or executives, it is referred to as being 'carried'. If, however, it is regarded as a decision, the motion then becomes a 'resolution'.

7. Standing Orders: are rules governing the conduct of meetings. A standing order might be invoked to move that a resolution be suspended. (This means that a decision is delayed pending certain conditions.)

8. An Amendment: is a proposal to change the wording of a motion, *before* it is put to a vote.

9. An Addendum: is the change that is made to the wording of a motion *after* a vote has taken place.

10. Substantive Motion or Resolution: When a motion is changed it becomes a substantive motion that must be voted on again. If carried, it becomes a decision, at which point it is a substantive resolution.

11. A Point of Order: To raise a point of order at a meeting might be to clarify a point that has already been raised or to disagree with it. The point of order should be dealt with immediately by a ruling from the chairperson. Points of Order are designed to ensure:

    (a) that regulations are being observed.

    (b) that the proceedings of the meeting are not later rendered invalid.

    (c) that voting procedures are being adhered to (e.g. making sure that someone who is not entitled to vote does not vote – they are not allowed to manipulate proceedings).

12. An 'Ad Hoc' Committee: is one formed for a special purpose.

13. A Quorum: is like a quota – the minimum number of people that must be present at the meeting before the meeting can begin discussions. (Most organisations have rules concerning a quorum for meetings.)

14. A Proxy: is a 'stand-in' or the person authorised to act and vote on behalf of a shareholder at an organisation's AGM, with the shareholder's approval. At some company meetings proxies have the right to be present but not to speak.

15. A Scrutineer: is one who checks the validity of votes on behalf of interested parties, e.g. at elections.

16. A Teller: is a person who counts votes.

17. A Debate: is a representation of participants' opinions on an item that appears on the Agenda. In a larger forum such as a Conference (Fianna Fáil or Fine Gael Ard Fheis, Teachers' Conferences etc.), motions are debated by different delegates which are then voted on and, if carried, become resolutions. The chairperson is usually the president, vice-president or a prominent leader of the organisation.

18. Through the Chair: It is the chairperson's task to guide the meeting through the sequence of short debates. One speaker is allowed to speak at a time. Speakers that wish to interrupt or to argue with others are urged to 'address the chair'. This is a way of controlling interruptions, heckling, and arguments among the participants at the meeting.

19. An Adjournment: is an interruption in the proceedings of a meeting before they have been completed. It can take the form of an interruption or a postponement to a later date.

    (a) If there is a problem regarding the holding of the meeting and the notice to convene has already been issued, the meeting cannot be postponed. The procedure is to hold the meeting, but to propose a motion for an adjournment before any business is done. The secretary may issue an advance notice to members that the adjournment will be proposed, so that they do not waste time coming to the meeting.

    (b) If the quorum is a minimum of two people (or higher) and someone leaves, the meeting must be temporarily adjourned because the quorum is lost.

    (c) If it is impossible to maintain order, the chairperson will decide to adjourn the meeting.

20. Casting Vote: When there is an equal number of votes 'for' and 'against', the chairperson has/may have a deciding vote.

21. Abstention: The free decision that all members have not to vote either for or against the motion.

22. 'Nem Con': This is a Latin phrase *nemine contradicente* meaning 'no one voted against the motion' but some members abstained.

23. Unanimously Carried: This means all members voted in favour of the motion.

24. *Sine Die*: This occurs when a meeting adjourns without fixing a date for the next meeting.

Procedures for Voting at Meetings

Voting is the mechanism used by members of an organisation, club or union to make decisions and to reach agreement regarding motions (proposals) and convey these decisions to members and to the chairperson.

It is often possible to reach agreement without voting at meetings. (Government mostly reach decisions without voting.) At many informal meetings it is not necessary to take a vote. However, when voting is necessary it is important that:

1. The motion (proposal) i.e. the matter for discussion and the point to be decided, be clearly explained and conveyed by the chairperson to the members voting. Voters should know exactly what is being proposed.

2. The regulations governing the meeting are strictly adhered to (discussed previously).

3. Those voting can confirm exactly what was decided.

HOW IS THE VOTE TAKEN?

1. By acquiescence: This is the approval of the motion by the members clapping.

2. By Voice (or acclamation): If all those in favour of the motion say 'Aye' and all those against the motion say 'Nay'. The decision has usually been temporarily agreed upon beforehand.

3. Show of Hands: The chairperson invites the members to raise a hand, 'All those in favour?' The teller or chairperson counts the votes. Then the chairperson invites 'All those against?' to raise a hand and the chairperson or teller counts these votes. Then the result of the count is declared. This system is based on 'one person, one vote' or if it is allowable the member's proxy will vote on his or her behalf.

4. By Proxy: The member nominates a person to vote on his or her behalf (or gives the nominee voting instructions) only if the organisation's rules permit.

5. By Poll: After the result of the show of hands, the chairperson must decide whether a poll is required, when members request it. It must either be taken immediately or a date set in the near future. If it is decided to vote by poll, the result of the show of hands must be withdrawn. Individual members then must sign a form (voting paper) indicating their preference 'for or against the motion'. Companies generally vote by poll and in these cases because of shareholdings the system might not necessarily be based on 'one person, one vote'.

6. By Ballot: This is the voting procedure for general and local government elections. Voters tick their preference on a voting paper and place it in a special ballot box. This method of voting represents a secret ballot.

7. By Division: Members voting walk into different rooms based on 'for' or 'against' preferences and tellers count the numbers and report back to the chairperson. Internal government voting is carried out in this way.

The chairperson declares the result and asks the secretary to include this detail in the minutes of the meeting. The item of business or the debate cannot be reopened for discussion during this meeting. It can, however, be agreed to reschedule it for another time.

Purpose of an Agenda

An Agenda (Latin for 'things to be done') is usually posted or sent out by the secretary, together with the notice, and is a brief description of what the meeting is about. It is usually drawn up in the form of a list of items to be discussed in order of importance.

It informs every participant about

1. The subject of items to be discussed. Speeches arguments and questions can be prepared in advance.
2. The order of items to be discussed. This will allow members to attend only when items of interest to them are being discussed.
3. The limited time schedule: the chairperson must make members aware that there is a time limit for debate.

A Sample Combined Notice and Agenda of a Business

The following is the Agenda for the AGM of Maryville Football Club.

Notice of the Annual General Meeting of Maryville Football Club

Notice is hereby given that the sixth Annual General Meeting of Maryville Football Club will be held.

MARYVILLE FOOTBALL CLUB

ANNUAL GENERAL MEETING

Friday 12 November xxxx at 8 p.m.
In Glenstall Hotel, Maryville

AGENDA

1. Apologies for absence.
2. Minutes of the previous AGM.
3. Matters arising from the minutes.
4. Chairperson's Report.
5. Treasurer's Report.
6. Election of Officers.
7. Any Other Business (AOB)
8. Date of next meeting.

Signed:

_____

Frank James
Secretary

MARYVILLE FOOTBALL CLUB

CHAIRPERSON'S AGENDA   **NOTES**

For the AGM to be held in the Glenstall Hotel
on Friday 12 November xxxx at 8 p.m.

1. *Apologies for absence*
   Mr J. Downey and Ms A. Malone are unable to attend.

2. *Minutes of the previous AGM.*

3. *Matters arising from the minutes*
   Subscriptions: Refer to updated report on estimated expected rise in
   subscriptions and consequent revision needed in facilities on the premises.

4. *Chairperson's Report* (attached).

5. *Treasurer's Report* (copy attached).

6. *Election of Officers*
   Proposals for Ms Kathleen Johnson as next year's Secretary replacing Mr
   Harry Black. And Mr Seamus O'Connor replacing Regina White as
   Treasurer.

7. *Any Other Business*
   Item 4: Mr John McCarthy has officially issued his resignation as Senior
   Grounds Supervisor and Mr Frank Fahy has been officially appointed to the
   position. Reminder to thank Mr John McCarthy for his years of service and
   to welcome Mr Frank Fahy to the position.
   Item 6: Ms Mary Fox has agreed to organise events and presentations at the
   Club's Annual Dance this year. Reminder to thank her.

8. *Date of next meeting*
   Friday 2 February xxxx at Maryville Clubhouse at 8 p.m.
   (subject to agreement).

The Notice sometimes appears in the page preceding the Agenda:

NOTICE

MARYVILLE FOOTBALL CLUB
ANNUAL GENERAL MEETING

Friday 12 November xxxx

At
8 p.m.
in
Glenstall Hotel, Maryville.

Signed:

_____

Frank James
Secretary

Purpose of the Minutes of a Meeting

The minutes of a meeting are a written record of the meeting taken by the secretary (or another nominated person). They are usually taken in the form of shorthand notes and later written up in a formal structure (example given later). The minutes represent a form of reported speech and insignificant outbursts (or personality clashes) are sometimes edited out of the minutes.

The benefits of writing up the minutes of a meeting are:
1. They propose to serve as a complete and concise record of business and as a source of reference regarding details of information, commitments, agreements and disagreements uttered orally by participants.
2. They provide some evidence and back-up and can be referred to regarding conflicts of facts about the meeting, where participants might deliberately forget or distort the account of speeches made at the meeting.

Types of Minutes

1. Resolution Minutes

Strictly only the decisions that were taken (excluding the debate or objections) will be detailed. These minutes might be used to disguise conflicts of opinion and objections raised. For example 'It was resolved that Maryville Football Club AGM should be held on Friday, 12 November xxxx, at 8 p.m. in Glenstall Hotel, Maryville.'

2. Narrative Minutes

This is a concise written record of events and debate leading up to the resolutions (decisions) and the resolutions themselves. Participants' speeches, comments, contradictions, agreements and suggestions are noted and participants are held accountable for words that they utter. The aim is to give a thorough insight into the feelings of participants without unnecessary irrelevant details. For example, 'The Chairwoman addressed the meeting and expressed her dissatisfaction that no compromise was reached regarding the formulation of a Company Mission Statement. She referred the meeting to Ms Moloney on this matter. Ms Moloney reported that since the last meeting in April, based on suggestions made to her, she had formulated two sample Mission Statements that she believed would be acceptable to staff. Mr Jones expressed dissatisfaction at not being consulted about the matter. The Chairwoman rejected Mr Jones's complaint out of hand and confirmed that every member of staff had been given detailed information on the requirements. The Chairwoman ordered that a vote be taken on the matter and then requested a show of hands to accept or reject the sample statements. *It was resolved* that sample Mission Statement 2 would serve as the Company Mission Statement for the foreseeable future and would appear in the next company prospectus and future brochures.'

3. Action Minutes

Following decisions (resolutions) taken, the chairperson has sometimes the authority to direct members' actions. This would be in the form of indicating what results are expected following the resolutions and who is responsible for each area. A separate column is often included on the right-hand side of the script to indicate the person who has been appointed to the specific area of authority or who volunteers to perform the duty.

MARYVILLE FOOTBALL CLUB

Minutes

These are the minutes of the Maryville Football Club Annual General Meeting held on 12 November xxxx in Glenstall Hotel, Maryville.

Present: All Members accounted for and present.

The meeting commenced at 8 p.m. The Chairperson Ms Marie O'Donnell opened the meeting and expressed her satisfaction at the attendance at the meeting. She also spoke of the future envisaged success of the club and future involvements.

1. Apologies for absence.
2. Minutes of the last Annual General Meeting:
    The Secretary Mr Frank James read out the Minutes of the last AGM held on 11 November 1996. The Minutes were then approved and signed by the Chairperson, Ms Marie O'Donnell.
3. Matters arising from the Minutes of last year's AGM:
    The Chairperson referred to the updated report on estimated expected rise in subscriptions and consequent revision needed in facilities on the premises. With reference to the agreed proposal at last year's meetings she referred to the fact that work had already begun on extending the clubhouse and improving the pitch. A new bar and changing area for women would be incorporated in the plans. The cost of the work was detailed and distributed to members and the source of the funding was also detailed in this report.
4. Chairperson's Report:
    A copy of the report was circulated to members and the chairperson referred to the need to review security in the club due to theft of equipment and belongings in the recent past. The Chairperson proposed that 'a special meeting should be held in the club to discuss the matter on 30 November xxxx'. This proposal was seconded by Mr Frank James, Secretary.
5. Treasurer's Report:
    The Treasurer, Ms Regina White, distributed copies of last year's Treasurer's Report and she explained details of outgoing money and incoming money for the last year as well as new subscriptions.
6. Elections of Officers:
    The election of a new Secretary was held as follows:

    Kathleen Johnson was proposed by John Franklin.
    Seconded by Mary Smith.

The election of a new Treasurer was held as follows:

Seamus O'Connor was proposed by Darren Walters.
Seconded by Donnacha O'Neill.

Ms Marie O'Donnell agreed to remain in the position as Chairperson. This was proposed by Frank James and seconded by Seamus O'Connor.

Voting for the elections was by 'a show of hands' and in each case the motions were accepted unanimously.

7. Any Other Business:
The Chairperson Ms O'Donnell announced the recent resignation of Mr John McCarthy, the senior grounds supervisor. She thanked him for his years of service and she welcomed Mr Frank Fahy to the position. The Chairperson also thanked Ms Mary Fox for agreeing to organise the club's Annual Presentation Night and Dance which is to be held on 7 December xxxx starting at 8 p.m.

8. Date of Next Meeting
The Chairperson announced that the next regular club meeting would be held on 2 February xxxx at 8 p.m. at the Clubhouse.

Signed: _____   Seconded by _____
                Marie O'Donnell
                Chairperson
Date: 12 November xxxx

Signed: _____
                Kathleen Johnson
                Secretary

There was no other business to be discussed and the meeting was brought to a close.

Note: Minutes are sometimes numbered in ascending order (going up) and continue from meeting to meeting. In this example, the last minute is numbered 8, therefore the first minute of the next meeting should be numbered 9.

Purpose of Writing a Report of a Meeting

The report of a meeting is a summary of the minutes and must be either sent to members of the club or organisation or posted on a prominent notice board that deals with official business.

1. It serves as a means of communicating information to members. Good communication is the key to good organisation.
2. It can be referred to when convening the next meeting and is a record of what took place at the meeting – a more formalised structure to back up the minutes of the meeting.
3. Only actual decisions and resolutions that were agreed upon at the meeting, as well as other facts, are noted in the report without any narratives. This provides clarity to members.

MARYVILLE FOOTBALL CLUB
Report

Report of the Annual General meeting of Maryville Football Club.

The above meeting was held in Glenstall Hotel, Maryville, on 12 November xxxx at 8 p.m. All Members were accounted for and present at the meeting.

The following officers were elected by a show of hands:

Secretary – Kathleen Johnson

Treasurer – Seamus O'Connor.

The Chairperson Ms Marie O'Donnell is remaining as Chairperson of the Club.

A Special Meeting will be held in the Club on 30 November xxxx to discuss security problems.

Mr Frank Fahy has been appointed Senior Grounds Supervisor in the place of Mr John McCarthy who has resigned.

Ms Mary Fox is to organise the club's Annual Dance and Presentation Night to be held on 7 December xxxx starting at 8 p.m.

The next meeting is to be held on 2 February xxxx at the Clubhouse.

Report compiled by Kathleen Johnson (Secretary).

A Sample Student Summary of Meetings

Compiled by Jean Ryan
Computer Applications and Business student in Crumlin College 20XX–20XX

Meetings as a Form of Communication

Communication involves the exchange of information between people, and it successfully occurs when the receiver understands what the sender means to convey. In other words, communication is a two-way process which not only requires the message being received, but also understood. Communication is an essential activity for any organisation. The communication process must be both effective and efficient. An effective method, used by organisations to communicate with their employees, is by the means of meetings.

A **meeting** may be defined as the grouping of two or more people to discuss business of common interest. Meetings are a form of oral communication and may be formal or informal. An effective meeting is a highly efficient tool of communication for organisations. It enables organisations to discuss and co-ordinate various activities, give briefs on particular issues, consult with each other, make decisions, solve problems and set future goals and objectives. Formal meetings are conducted under strict guidelines, whereas informal ones are less organised. There are different types of meetings which may be classified as follows:

1. AGM – Annual General Meeting
2. EGM – Extraordinary General Meeting
3. Board meetings
4. Statutory meetings
5. Executive meetings
6. Consultative meetings
7. (a) Committee meetings
   (b) Sub-committee meetings
8. Review meetings
9. Ad-hoc meetings
10. Inaugural meetings
11. Ordinary meetings
12. Video Conferences

Functions of the Chairperson

- to plan in consultation with the Secretary, the dates and times of the meeting.
- to draw up the Agenda, again in consultation with the Secretary.
- to keep order and prevent disruption.

- to maintain the policies of the organisation.
- when a vote is tied, he/she must use a casting vote.

The Role of the Secretary

- to draw up the Agenda in consultation with the Chairperson.
- to set out the Notice of the Meeting.
- to circulate the Minutes from the previous Meeting (draft minutes).
- to write up the Minutes of a Meeting.
- to plan the next Meeting with the Chairperson.

The Duties of the Treasurer

- to receive yearly subscriptions from members.
- to issue receipts to members.
- to pay the bills on behalf of the organisation.
- to lodge all the organisation's money into bank accounts.
- to keep account books of all transactions made by the organisation.
- to prepare the Financial Report for the AGM.

Notices

NOTICE OF A MEETING

For meetings such as Committee Meetings, General Meetings, or Extraordinary General Meetings, written Notices must be prepared and sent to those entitled to attend. A Notice should contain details of the subject matter, the place, time and date of the meeting.

An Agenda

AN AGENDA OF A MEETING

The secretary, in consultation with the chairperson, is responsible for drawing up the Agenda of a meeting. An agenda is a list of subjects to be covered within the duration of the meeting. A meeting will be far more effective if those attending know in advance what is to be discussed. They will then be able to sort out their ideas, gather data, find out views of colleagues, and come well informed and ready to contribute. It also ensures that every item of importance will be reviewed, and no topic will be overlooked. This is known as meeting preparation, and is of vital importance in order for a meeting to be successful.

The list or programme of items to be discussed at a meeting is generally listed in order of priority, and is usually numbered for easy reference. On the right-hand side of an Agenda a space may be included for the recording of decisions taken on each item of business.

How to Plan for a Meeting

(A simple student account – in the capacity of secretary to the meeting)

1. Before the meeting, I consulted the Chairperson about the number of participants expected to attend the proposed meeting in order to choose a suitable room/venue.
2. I decided on the seating arrangement to suit the numbers attending and the general mood of the chairperson (negotiating style) – as this was a type of brainstorming session, where new ideas would be embraced!
   Note: Room layout styles are illustrated in the next section.
3. I made sure that OHP equipment (machine and pens) and Internet/computer facilities would be available to the group as one participant wished to use visual aids (Microsoft Powerpoint).
4. I placed a clip notepad, pen and mineral water at each participant's space.
5. I then checked with the chairperson about the date, time and agenda of the meeting before I posted the notice and agenda in a prominent place, well in advance of the meeting.
6. When everyone was seated and the meeting was about to commence, I put up a poster on the outside of the meeting room door 'Meeting in Progress, Please Do Not Disturb'.

Layout Plan of a Meeting

Room Layout

The Secretary should always ensure that the meeting room is laid out properly. The chosen meeting room should be laid out in whatever style is appropriate for the size, degree of participation and formality of the meeting.

The way in which the furniture is arranged for meetings can have a big effect on the atmosphere and efficiency. For example, a meeting held round a boardroom table has a completely different atmosphere from one in which participants are free to place their chairs where they wish. The following are eight common arrangements and layouts of the meeting room:

1. Boardroom
2. Round table
3. Negotiating
4. Freestyle
5. Theatre style
6. Schoolroom
7. Horseshoe
8. Herring-bone

The following are eight arrangements of a meeting (note X will indicate where the Chairperson is seated).

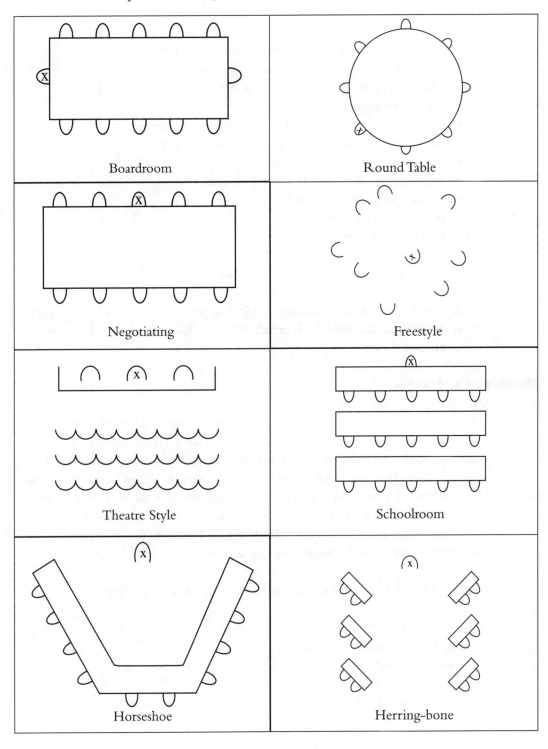

Boardroom

Round Table

Negotiating

Freestyle

Theatre Style

Schoolroom

Horseshoe

Herring-bone

When laying out the plan of the meeting, the following are some of the considerations required to be taken into account beforehand.

(a) The time and place of the meeting should be known well in advance.
(b) Agendas must be circulated well before the date of the meeting.
(c) Minutes must be written up as soon as possible after the meeting.
(d) The meeting room shall possess the following:
- inform reception
- notice on the door notifying that a meeting is in progress
- refreshments available if a long meeting is expected
- files, reports and attendance sheets
- spare agendas, paper and shorthand notebook
- graphs and charts (if needed)
- direct incoming calls
- tape recorder (if required)
- cloakroom facilities
- adequate heating, lighting and ventilation.

In all formal meetings the following seating arrangement is a must. The Chairperson must sit in the middle with the Secretary sitting on his/her right-hand side, and the Treasurer seated on the left.

Minutes of a Meeting

THE MINUTES

After the closure of a meeting, the secretary has the responsibility of writing up the minutes of the meeting. The minutes of a meeting are a written account of what was discussed and what decisions were taken at a meeting. At a subsequent meeting the minutes should be read, proposed and seconded and then signed by the chairperson when adopted, thus ensuring accuracy. The minutes of a meeting are of extreme importance. If a dispute arises, the court can ask to see the minutes of a meeting. Therefore they must be accurate. With regard to the Companies Act 1963, all companies must keep the minutes of meetings held by directors and shareholders.

Information which should be included in the minutes of a meeting are:

- the type of meeting
- the date, time and place of meeting
- names in attendance
- names of absentees
- the approval of previous meeting Minutes, containing signature of chairperson showing/indicating approval

ELEMENTS OF A REPORT

TITLE

CIRCULATION

. . . .
. . . .
. . . .
. . . .
. . . .

PREPARED FOR

BY

DATE . . . .

MAIN PART

- *Work description*
  - *scope*
  - *methods in detail*
  - *facts*
  - *calculations*
  - *analysis*

- *Discussion of above*
  - *pros and cons*
  - *arguments*

CONTENTS	PAGE
SUMMARY	. . . .
INTRODUCTION	. . . .
MAIN PART	. . . .
CONCLUSIONS	. . . .
RECOMMENDATIONS	. . . .
APPENDICES	. . . .

- *In large Reports list subheadings*

CONCLUSIONS

- *List conclusions in order of importance.*

- *These should not come as a shock to your reader.*

- *Should be obvious from the data in the main part.*

SUMMARY

- *Of complete Report*

- *Max. two pages typed*

- *Assembled from topic sentences*

RECOMMENDATIONS

- *List action to be taken as a result of conclusions.*

- *It is useful to evaluate different courses of action.*

INTRODUCTION

- *Why writing*

- *Terms of reference*

- *History and background*

- *Work methods*

- *Explain technical terms or jargon*

APPENDICES

- *Contain any information which is not needed by the general reader, but for the specialist reader.*

- summary on matters arising from Minutes
- the resolutions passed or motions rejected
- the adjournment, postponement until a later date, or conclusion of the meeting
- the date of the next meeting (if decided).

Reports

A Report of a meeting is a small summary, or an account, of what happened and of what decisions were reached. A Report should be laid out and presented clearly to its readers. Reports are needed for many reasons such as:

- giving information about work done
- assessment of a situation
- recommending a course of action
- circulating new information or ideas
- keeping others informed of progress on particular projects.

The following are the rules which apply when writing up a Report.

Accuracy – the Report should be correct and exact.
Brevity – the Report should be of a reasonable length.
Clarity – the Report should be clear and understandable
Simplicity – the Report should be simple, not complicated.

Conclusion

When studying this topic **'Planning Meetings'**, it became obvious that an effective meeting is an extremely efficient tool in the communication of an organisation. Communication is of vital importance for an organisation in order for it to be successful and gain profits. Meetings inform those within a company of important issues, decisions, problems, goals, objectives and potential new developments. Meetings help to keep those within an organisation up to date with company activities, its financial position and how it compares with competitors.

Meetings – the Top 20

The following are guidelines which directors, chairpersons, managers and supervisors should follow in order to maintain an effective meeting at any hierarchical level.

TOP 10 DOS

Set clear objectives for every meeting
Circulate agenda and papers in advance
Complete thorough personal preparation
Choose a suitable room and lay it out carefully

Stick firmly to the agenda

Use visual aids as a help to control discussion

Time your contributions carefully

Use the skills and knowledge of all participants

Use time sensibly throughout.

TOP 10 DON'TS

Don't hold a meeting unless it is really necessary

Don't invite people who need not attend

Don't wait for latecomers unless there is a special reason to do so

Don't let personal feelings affect meeting behaviour

Don't mix creativity with criticism

Don't take part in more than one discussion at one time

Don't force a decision before adequate debate

Don't argue directly with other participants; debate through the Chair

Don't, when in the Chair, express your own views unless it is essential to do so.

A page from an Appointments Diary

Monday	Thursday . . . .
Tuesday	Friday . . . .
Wednesday	Special Notes . . . .

PRACTICE QUESTIONS

1. Who are the main Officers at a meeting?
2. What are the functions of the Chairperson of a meeting?
3. What is a Chairperson's Agenda? Draft your own example.
4. What are the functions of the Secretary of a meeting?
5. What are the functions of the Treasurer of a meeting?
6. Explain the following terms:
   (a) Motion
   (b) Quorum

(c) Point of Order

(d) Through the Chair

(e) Casting Vote

(f) Unanimously Carried.

7. What *three* main unwritten rules govern most formal meetings?

8. In what different ways can a vote be taken?

9. What do the following terms mean with regard to meetings?

(a) Notice

(b) Agenda

(c) Minutes.

10. Explain the *three* categories of Minutes of a meeting?

11. What are the reasons for compiling the Report of a meeting?

Sample Assignment Brief – Meetings

1. You are the secretary to a meeting. Explain the plans that you put in place in advance of the meeting. Support your plans with illustrations as appropriate.

2. Having attended the meeting, please submit the following business documents:

(a) Notice of the meeting.

(b) Agenda of the meeting.

(c) Minutes of the meeting (please attach written notes).

Please note – all formal documents should be formally presented, with particular attention paid to layout, spelling and punctuation.

Sample Student Assignment

1. Plans I put in place in advance of the meeting:

- I chose a suitable room that would suit about 15 people.
- I decided on a horse-shoe room layout style having consulted with the chairperson.
- I made sure all participants had pen, pencil and paper at their station as well as mineral water.
- I checked with the chairperson regarding equipment that might be needed if any of the participants were giving a presentation (e.g. overhead projector, OHP pens, flipcharts and pens, computer for Powerpoint presentation, TV Video, DVD, CD players). However, none was needed.

- I checked with the chairperson regarding the agenda and the time and length of the proposed meeting and then posted the Notice and Agenda on the main notice board.
- On the day of the meeting, just before it started, I posted a notice on the outside of the meeting room door 'Meeting in Progress, Please Do Not Enter'.

Layout and Seating Plan

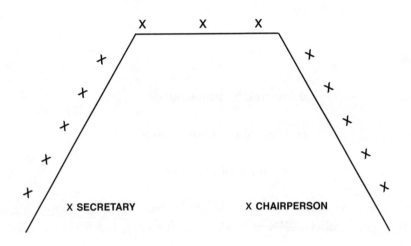

2. a. Notice

NOTICE

A Meeting of the Limerick Senior College
Fashion Show Committee will take place

on

Thursday 18 October 20XX

at

9.30a.m.

in

Room 1, Top Floor
Limerick Senior College

2. b. Agenda

AGENDA

1. Apologies
2. Date, Time, Venue and Refreshments
3. Sponsors, Advertising and Tickets
4. Models and Clothes
5. A.O.B.
6. Date of next meeting

Sign

```
┌─────────────────────────────────────────────┐
│                                               │
│           MEETING IN PROGRESS                 │
│                                               │
│                                               │
│           PLEASE DO NOT ENTER                 │
│                                               │
└─────────────────────────────────────────────┘
```

2. c. Minutes

Limerick Senior College

Fashion Show Committee

Minutes of Meeting

These are the minutes of the meeting of the LSC fashion show Committee that was held on Thursday 18 October 20XX at 9.30a.m. in Room 1, top floor, Limerick Senior College:

PRESENT

Ms Jane Fitzpatrick (Chairperson)
Ms Miriam Ryan (Secretary)
Ms Susan Browne
Ms Fiona White
Mr Joseph Black
Mr Frank Walshe
Ms Joan McCarthy
Ms Vera Lynn
Ms Jacinta Henderson
Ms Gemma McDonnell
Ms Roisin Wren
Mr David George

APOLOGIES

Ms Mary Ryan was unable to attend due to work-related matters.

DATE, TIME, VENUE AND REFRESHMENTS

It was agreed that the show should be staged on 5 December 20XX and that it will commence at 8p.m. with a 7.30p.m. wine and cheese reception. It was also agreed that the interval should happen at 9p.m. for a duration of 15 minutes.

Fiona suggested that the venue should be Jurys Hotel, based on a proposed discount offered by them. She also informed the meeting that she had checked the costs of ramp, host and lighting/music and all amounted to €500.

SPONSORS, ADVERTISING AND TICKETS

It was agreed that the chosen charity would be ISPCC Children's Charity.

Frank agreed to research sponsors by getting a list of existing suppliers to the college.

Susan proposed that an 'event publication' with different sized advertisements might be offered in return for contributions of money, services or goods on the night. Joan said that she would encourage Graphics students to help with the publication. Vera also said she had some desktop publishing skills that might be of use.

Joseph agreed to get the tickets printed for free by a printer that he knows.

MODELS AND CLOTHES

It was agreed that there would be six male models and twelve female models, all of whom will be students of the college. Miriam and George agreed jointly to look after the clothes, where some previous student designs could be showcased as well as a good selection of shops. A selection of evening casual, sports and bridal wear could be organised.

Gemma agreed to train the students on Wednesday of each week commencing next week with auditions in the afternoon.

ANY OTHER BUSINESS

Susan agreed to deal with the raffle and to source prizes from different businesses in the city and from staff in the college.

NEXT MEETING

It was agreed that the next meeting will take place on Thursday 25 October at 9.30a.m.

_____

Secretary

_____

Chairperson

_____

Date

6. Processing of Business Documents

Definitions and Explanations of Documents and Business Terms including Discounts and VAT

The different types of business organisations discussed in Chapter 1 must all involve themselves in paperwork in order to track transactions. The Documents that are part of everyday business are:

1. LETTERS OF ENQUIRY

The formal procedure to enquire about a prospective supplier's prices and terms of trade is for the business that is enquiring to write a 'letter of enquiry' stating 'Please send me information on the following good etc.' This form of enquiry has in recent times been replaced by just telephoning and the subsequent receipt of a fax including the information asked for.

The Internet mode of communication has also replaced 'the letter of enquiry'. It is, however, important to be able to structure any enquiry using the appropriate letter presentation (sample given later).

2. PRICE LISTS AND QUOTATIONS

Customers that do not trade with the business on a regular basis usually ask for a Price List. Regular traders that aim to have future accounts with the business usually request a Quotation.

The Quotation is an important document as it is proof of the prices offered and any trade agreements made between traders that operate on a credit basis (do not pay immediately – buyers that have an account with different suppliers). Accounts are usually set up if the buyer is a regular customer and discounts are built into the transaction.

TERMS OF TRADE These are the trade agreements made between the supplier and the purchaser (seller and buyer) regarding Trade Discounts and Cash/Settlement Discounts, and these are indicated on the Quotation. Sixty days' Credit means that the Supplier allows the buyer approximately two months to pay the Invoice (Bill). Most Suppliers offer 30 days' (or net one month) credit to buyers.

Usually if a bill or invoice is dated 2 June and 60 days' credit is allowed, this means that the buyer does not *strictly* have to pay within 60 days. It does mean, however, that this invoice must be paid by 31 August. The same would apply if the invoice were dated 30 June. A longer payment period is gained if the invoice is dated at the beginning of the month.

The three types of discount that exist are:

(a) Trade Discount: given by suppliers to regular buyers on a long-term basis. This discount is a form of recognition for staying with the same supplier and ensuring them of your continued business. The percentage allowed is often 10%.
(b) Settlement Discount: given only if amounts due are paid within a specific time period (often 14 days); can be between two and five per cent.
(c) Cash Discount (COD): given if the buyer pays cash immediately over the counter (varies depending on the bill).

Most traders 'shop around' and try to get the best quotation possible, keeping an eye of course on quality.

3. PURCHASE ORDERS

This is a letter sent from the buyer to the supplier to order a certain amount of goods. The buyer usually keeps one copy to check it against the delivery docket and the invoice. Goods are more often ordered directly over the phone and the order is entered into an order book on both the buyer end and the supplier end. This is an important exercise because the volume of transactions in one day makes it impossible to keep a mental track of every order made. This order will subsequently be checked against the delivery docket when the goods arrive. Often Purchase Orders are faxed to the supplier and confirmation of receipt of the fax might be in the form of a return phone call.

4. DELIVERY DOCKETS

These are Dockets that arrive with the goods supplied. When the goods are dispatched (sent out), the warehouse supervisor who releases the goods checks them against the purchase order and retains the top copy of the Delivery Docket. The goods are usually dispatched by road, rail or air transport, and the person delivering the goods asks the person receiving the goods to sign the second copy which duplicates on to a third copy underneath it. The delivery person takes the second copy back to the suppliers' headquarters and this is verification that the goods were delivered. The third copy remains with the goods and the buyer.

5. INVOICES

An Invoice is a bill sent by the supplier to the buyer, charging him/her for the goods that were delivered. A reference Delivery Docket Number and Purchase Order Number (where required) appears on the invoice in order to make it easy to match the documents mentioned.

Pro-Forma Invoice (PFI): This document looks like an invoice but is only a sample. It gives details of what would appear on a valid invoice to inform the customer in advance of deciding to purchase, about cost, carriage (transport costs) and VAT charges.

Cash Invoice – is an invoice given to a buyer if they pay over the counter immediately whether by cash, cheque or credit card.

Credit Invoice – is an invoice that the supplier sends to the buyer. The buyer is given either one, two or three months to pay the bill.

VAT

VAT means value added tax. It appears on invoices. It is an indirect tax levied on goods and services by government. This means it is collected by different parties and paid to the government. The VAT rates that apply are 0, 12.5 and 21 per cent.

VAT is a regressive tax (it does not take account of the ability to pay). For example, a pensioner and a millionaire might want to buy furniture at a selling price that includes 21% VAT. This 21% will not be reduced for the pensioner.

DIFFERENCES BETWEEN ZERO-RATED *VAT* AND EXEMPT FROM *VAT*

Some sellers like those who sell goods for charity are exempt from VAT. They are regarded as non-profit making organisations and cannot claim VAT back on purchases made. Other sellers, like those selling bread, do not charge VAT because it is regarded as a necessity. However, because these sellers are officially trading, they are allowed to claim VAT back on their purchases. They are therefore zero-rated suppliers/sellers. Other zero-rated traders might be funeral undertakers and sellers of books and periodicals.

Most goods have VAT levied on them at the point of sale. Goods are usually subject to 21% VAT, and services are usually subject to 12.5% VAT.

WHY BOTHER CROSS-CHECKING PURCHASE ORDERS, DELIVERY DOCKETS AND INVOICES?

Possible mistakes can be made, such as

- the wrong order being delivered (due to a mix-up/mistakes made by the clerk or dispatcher), or
- too few goods sent or too many goods sent.

If discrepancies are undetected, a business can lose a lot of money and cost effectiveness is one of the main objectives of successful firms.

Purchase invoices received are entered into the Purchases Book to keep an account of the volume and type of goods received.

Sales invoices that are compiled by businesses and sent to their customers are entered into the Sales Book to keep an account of the volume of sales, how many debtors there are, and how much each debtor owes.

WHAT TO DO WHEN DISCREPANCIES ARE DISCOVERED.
Credit Notes

A Credit Note is sent by the supplier giving the buyer recognition of credit given for the return of goods due to:

1. The goods being damaged in transit (while being transported), flawed or faulty.
2. An overcharge, where too many goods were delivered and charged for on the invoice. (The delivery does not match the original Purchase Order.)
3. Wrong goods were delivered. (Possibly a mix-up with another customer's order.)

Debit Notes

If a buyer realises that he/she has been undercharged, human nature tells us that the likelihood that the buyer will run to the phone and inform the supplier is fairly slim!

If, however, the supplier detects the mistake, it will be brought to the attention of the buyer and a Debit Note will be sent to the customer to make up the difference, i.e. the undercharge.

A Debit Note is like another invoice that was forgotten about, except for the important difference that it is directly connected with a particular invoice that was sent previously. The reference invoice number will appear on the Debit Note. When the buyer receives the Debit Note, a copy of it can be clipped directly to the corresponding invoice.

Statements

This is a document that is sent to the buyer to inform him/her about how much is owed to the supplier. It is usually sent out by the supplier every month, listing all the invoices that have been sent out, any Credit Notes and Debit Notes sent out, and any payments made by the buyer.

PRACTICE QUESTIONS

1. What *nine* business documents do businesses send out and receive on a regular basis? Define *each* briefly.
2. Distinguish between a Price List and a Quotation.
3. What are Credit Terms?
4. Name *three* discounts that business people avail of and distinguish clearly between them.
5. What is the difference between a Credit Invoice and a Cash Invoice?
6. Explain in detail what VAT is.
7. What are the differences between 'Zero Rated VAT' and 'Exempt from VAT'?
8. Why is it necessary to match up documents?
9. In each of the following cases, what document is compiled to indicate
   (a) an undercharge
   (b) a return of goods
   (c) an overcharge
   (d) an omission from an invoice?

SAMPLE QUOTATION

No. 12212

NEERY FIREPLACES LTD
21 REDROSE INDUSTRIAL PARK
KELLS
CO. MEATH

Customer Name: Mr Michael Walsh

Customer Address: Edenfoley Builders Ltd,
Athboy,
Co. Meath.

Telephone: (042) 431212

Date: 2/5/XX

The following are the terms of agreement that we wish to offer you with the view to doing business with you in the near future.

Terms:
60 Days' Credit
Trade Discount 12.5% on all orders
Cash/Settlement Discount 5% extra if paid Net one month
Carriage paid

- **Prices and the terms of agreement will be reviewed every six months and are subject to change. We ensure that we will give you due notice of any such planned changes.**

We hope that the terms that we are offering you are to your satisfaction and we anticipate trading with you soon.

We will be glad at any time to clarify any queries that you might have regarding our product range.

Yours faithfully

Mary Malone
Mary Malone
Sales Manager

Choosing Suppliers, Pricing and Assessing Quotations

When a person starts in business, he/she may decide to purchase raw materials from suppliers in the local area to minimise transport costs (Carriage).

Carriage Inwards: is a *trading cost* of transportation that suppliers put on bills when they invoice a buyer. The supplier has at this stage already paid the cost.

Carriage Outwards: is an *expense* to a supplier when he/she delivers goods to a buyer and bears the transportation cost.

Quality and Cost Minimisation (keeping costs at a minimum) are both difficult to weigh against each other. It is often said that you pay for what you get. However, it is worthwhile remembering that:

1. If you wish to follow the Economic Route the larger stores are able to sell at cheaper prices (because they buy in bulk and are able to avail of large trade discounts) and a lot of their products are of good quality. This is called an 'Economy of Scale' – one of the benefits of larger-scale operations
2. If you wish to specialise, specialist shops and outlets are relatively more expensive but their turnover is good in their own 'Niche Product Areas'.

It is only with some experience that businesses find suitable suppliers who charge prices that make it cost effective for the business that is buying to trade.

It must be remembered that a Mark-up on cost prices must be estimated and be worthwhile for the business. The cost price must be low enough for the business to sell their products or service successfully at a profit. Breakeven Analysis, discussed in Chapter 2, outlines how a breakeven price can be arrived at.

PRACTICE QUESTIONS
1. What is the difference between Carriage Inwards and Carriage Outwards?
2. Why is it difficult to reach a happy medium between maintaining Quality and keeping Costs down?
3. What is the meaning of the term 'Niche Product Area'?

Example 1: Purchase Order Cash Invoice Exercise and Suggested Solution

Ms Fitzpatrick was redecorating her house and she had previously visited and spoken with a sales consultant in All Weather Paints. She sent a Purchase Order by fax to Jim Smith of All Weather Paints, having written a Letter of Enquiry addressed to him also. Jim faxed the Price List to her and, having delivered the goods, he subsequently sent her the Invoice. Note how the Invoice figures are calculated by reference to the Price List and the Purchase Order.

- When compiling the Invoice it is important to remember that Discount is always subtracted before VAT is added.

LETTER OF ENQUIRY

12 The Lawns
Clonmel
Co. Tipperary
Tel: (0504) 22422
Fax: (0504) 22423

10/7/XX

Mr Jim Smith
All Weather Paints
Weatherfield
Thurles
Co. Tipperary

Dear Jim,

Following our phone conversation, kindly forward to me a current Price List of your products. I hope to purchase some of them in the near future.

Yours truly,

Jane Fitzpatrick

Jane Fitzpatrick

PRICE LIST OF PAINTING AND DECORATING PRODUCTS

ALL WEATHER PAINTS

PRODUCT CODES	DESCRIPTION OF PRODUCTS	VAT	PRICE (in euros)
P(IN) 75	Interior Matt 1 lt	B	7.50
P(IN) 50	Interior Gloss 1 lt	B	9.00
P(IN) 80	Interior Vinyl Silk 1 lt	B	7.50
P(IN) 100	Interior Eggshell (Alkyd) 1 lt	B	11.00
P(IN) 110	Interior Eggshell (Acrylic) 1 lt	B	8.50
P(Ex) 150	Exterior Matt 2.5 lt	B	12.00
P(Ex) 90	Exterior Matt 10 lt	B	37.00
P(Misc) 120	Scrumble Trans Oil Glaze 2.5 lt	B	45.00
Br200	Badger Softener	B	41.00
Br195	Stencil Brush	B	1.50
Br90	Sable Writer	B	7.00
Br12	Paint Brush 1.5 inch pure Bristle	B	6.00
Br14	Paint Brush 2 inch pure Bristle	B	10.00
Br16	Paint Brush 2.5 inch pure Bristle	B	12.00
Br18	Paint Brush 3 inch pure Bristle	B	15.00
Br20	Paint Brush 4 inch pure Bristle	B	25.00
Br22	Paint Brush 6 inch pure Bristle	B	30.00
Sp110	Sea Sponge (Synthetic)	B	7.50
Sp120	Marine Natural Sea Sponge (Lge)	B	40.00
Sp80	Marine Natural Sea Sponge (Sm)	B	30.00
Pap100	Wall Stripper	B	250.00
Pap120	Wallpaper Table	B	15.00
Pap130	Wallpaper Hanging Brush	B	20.00
Pap133	Seam Roller	B	4.50
Sc170	Scaffolding 4ft h x 3.5 ft w	B	72.50
WSp 12	White Spirit (Sm)	B	2.00
WSp 14	White Spirit (Lge)	B	4.75
Ro186	Roller (9 inch)	B	12.50
Ro120	Roller (6 inch)	B	6.50
Ro124	Roller Extension Poll	B	15.00
SERVICE	INTERIOR DESIGNER	A	QUOTE

Large Range of Paints and Wallpaper available

Wallpapers Prices from €10 to €150 per roll

Wallpaper Borders from €10 to €20 per roll

VAT CODES	A = 12.5%	B = 21%

WRITTEN PURCHASE ORDER

12 The Lawns
Clonmel
Co. Tipperary
Tel: (0503) 22422
Fax: (0503) 22423

Date: 15/7/XX

Mr Jim Smith
All Weather Paints
Weatherfield
Thurles
Co. Tipperary

Dear Jim,

Please supply me with the following goods as soon as is convenient.

CODE NUMBER	QUANTITY
P(IN) 80 (Rose Colour)	5 Lt
P(IN) 110 (Rose Colour)	1 Lt
Br195	2
Sp110	1
WSp12	1

Please include on the bill that you are sending to me, an amount of €30 plus VAT that I owe your Interior Design Consultant.

When you deliver the goods I will pay cash on delivery. Please phone me in advance to arrange a time of delivery.

Yours truly,

Jane Fitzpatrick

Jane Fitzpatrick

Having received this written purchase order from the cash customer, All Weather Paints allocates an Order Number to it for reference purposes. The Order Number is 4567.

DELIVERY DOCKET

From: All Weather Paints   No: 230
        Weatherfield   Date: 20/7/XX
        Thurles   Order No: 4567
        Co. Tipperary

GOODS:

5 lt Interior Vinyl Silk – Rose Colour	Ref: P(IN) 80
1 lt Interior Eggshell (Acrylic)	Ref: P(IN) 110
2 Stencil Brushes	Ref: Br 195
1 Sea Sponge (Synthetic)	Ref: Sp 110
1 Small Bottle White Spirit	Ref: WSp 12

Received the above goods:

Signed:

Jane Fitzpatrick

CASH SALES INVOICE
ALL WEATHER PAINTS

Weatherfield
Thurles
Co. Tipperary
Telephone: (0504) 21331
Fax: (0504) 21332
VAT No. IE 1234567 D
Purchase Order Number: 4567
Invoice Number: 1101

Ms Jane Fitzpatrick
12 The Lawns
Clonmel
Co. Tipperary

Date: 20/7/XX

Product Code	Q	Description of product	Price p. unit	Vat 12.5%	VAT 21%	Total
P(IN) 80	5 lt	Interior Vinyl Silk-Rose Colour	€7.50 p Lt			€37.50
P(IN) 110	1 lt	Interior Eggshell (Acrylic)	€8.50 p Lt			€8.50
Br 195	2 no.	Stencil Brushes	€1.50 ea.			€3.00
Sp 110	1 no.	Sea Sponge (Synthetic)	€7.50 ea.			€7.50
WSp 12	1 no.	White Spirit (Sm)	€2 ea.			€2.00
SERVICE		Interior Design Service	€30	€30.00		
Totals				€30.00	€58.50	
		Less Cash Discount 5%		€1.50	€2.93	
				€28.50	€55.57	
		Add VAT		€3.56	€11.67	
				€32.06	€67.24	
Total						€99.30
Plus Carriage						€10.00
Total Invoice Price						€109.30

Since Ms Fitzpatrick has agreed to pay cash on receipt of the goods, the Cash Invoice serves as the Delivery Docket and she has been given a 5% Cash Discount because she is paying COD. This type of gesture by a business helps to give the business a competitive edge and entices the customer to return again to purchase goods – maintains consumer loyalty.

Example 2: Credit Invoice Exercise and Suggested Solution

QUESTION

Kelly and Sons Painting and Decorating Subcontractors have been trading regularly with All Weather Paints and can avail of an ongoing 10% Trade Discount which is deducted from every bill irrespective of when it is paid. This agreement was reached when the two parties began trading a long time ago. On 7/8/XX Kelly and Sons placed the following order for goods.

You are required to compile

1. The Purchase Order dated 7/8/XX
2. The Delivery Docket dated 8/8/XX
3. The Credit Invoice dated 10/8/XX

Code No.	Quantity
Br20	5
Sc170	1
P(EX) 150 Magnolia	2 tins
P(IN) 75 White	10 lt
P(IN) 50 White	10 lt
P(IN) 80 White	10 lt

SOLUTION

PURCHASE ORDER

No: 4898

Customer Name: Kelly and Sons Painters & Decorators
Customer Address: Randles Park
Clonmel
Co. Tipperary
Telephone: (0506) 31212

Date: 7/8/XX

TO:　　Mr Jim Smith
All Weather Paints
Weatherfield
Thurles
Co. Tipperary

Code Ref.	Quantity	Description	VAT Rate (%)	Unit Price
Br 20	5 no.	Paint Brush 4"	B	€25.00 ea.
Sc 170	1 no.	Scaffolding 4'h x 3.5'w	B	€72.50 ea.
P(Ex) 150 Magn	2 tins	Exterior Matt 2.5 lt	B	€12.00 p. lt
P(IN) 75 White	10 lt	Interior Matt 1 lt	B	€7.50 p. lt
P(IN) 50 White	10 lt	Interior Gloss 1 lt	B	€9.00 p. lt
P(IN) 80 White	10 lt	Interior Vinyl Silk 1 lt	B	€7.50 p. lt

Delivery Instructions: Delivery by transit van on 8/8/XX

Signed　*Mick Kelly*

Purchasing Officer

DELIVERY DOCKET

From: All Weather Paints   No. 234
       Weatherfield   Date: 8/8/XX
       Thurles   Order No: 4898
       Co. Tipperary

GOODS:

5 no.	Paint Brush 4"	Ref: Br 20
1 no.	Scaffolding 4'h x 3.5'w	Ref: Sc 170
2 lt	Exterior Matt 2.5 lt	Ref: P(Ex) 150 Magn
10 lt	Interior Matt 1 lt	Ref: P(IN) 75 White
10 lt	Interior Gloss 1 lt	Ref: P(IN) 50 White
10 lt	Interior Vinyl Silk 1 lt	Ref: P(IN) 80 White

Received the above goods:

Signed: *Mick Kelly*

CREDIT INVOICE
ALL WEATHER PAINTS

Weatherfield
Thurles
Co. Tipperary

Telephone: (0504) 21331
Fax: (0504) 21332
VAT No. IE 1234567 D
Purchase Order Number: 4898
Invoice Number: 1102

Date 10/8/XX

Kelly and Sons
Painters & Decorators
Randles Park
Clonmel
Co. Tipperary

Product Code	Quantity	Description of Product	Price p. unit	VAT 12.5%	VAT 21%
Br20	5 no.	Paint Brush 4"	€25.00 ea.		€125.00
SC170	1 no.	Scaffolding 4'h x 3.5'w	€72.50 ea.		€72.50
P(Ex) 150 Magnol	2 lt	Exterior Matt 2.5 lt	€12.00 p. lt		€24.00
P(IN) 75 White	10 lt	Interior Matt 1 lt	€7.50 p. lt		€75.00
P(IN) 50 White	10 lt	Interior Gloss 1 lt	€9.00 p. lt		€90.00
P(IN) 80 White	10 lt	Interior Vinyl Silk 1 lt	€7.50 p. lt		€75.00
Total					**€461.50**
		Less Trade Discount 10%			€46.15
					€415.35
		Add VAT			€87.22
Total Invoice Price					**€502.57**

Terms of Trade: Net One Month; Trade Discount 10%, Cash Discount 5%, 14 days 2.5%

Example 3: Routing an Invoice – Student Exercise

This means sourcing an invoice or tracing its origin. It involves compiling the corresponding
1. Delivery Docket.
2. Purchase Order.
3. Quotation.
4. Letter of Enquiry.

Refer to the appropriate Practice Question at the end of the chapter.

Example 4: Identifying Discrepancies on Orders and Invoices

(includes a Credit Note and Debit Note):

Refer to the All Weather Paints Price List at the beginning of the section:
On 12/8/XX Mary Jones, Limerick Builders Ltd, Main Street, Limerick, telephoned the following order to All Weather Paints:

Quantity	Product Code
10	P(IN) 75 Burnt Sienna
3	Br 195
4	WSp 14

She received the correct goods and checked the Delivery Docket that arrived with the goods to verify this. On 14/8/XX Mary received the Invoice for the goods. However, when she checked the Purchase Order Form she realised that the Invoice stated P(IN) 50 in error. She immediately phoned All Weather Paints and they confirmed the mistake and forwarded the Credit Note to Mary a day later thereby acknowledging the overcharge.

Refer to the All Weather Paints Price List at the beginning of the section:

CREDIT NOTE

ALL WEATHER PAINTS

No: C/N676

Weatherfield
Thurles
Co. Tipperary
Telephone: (0504) 21331
Fax: (0504) 21332
VAT No. IE 1234567 D
Reference Purchase Order Number 2323
Reference Invoice Number 3424

Ms Mary Jones
Limerick Builders Ltd
Main Street
Limerick

Date: 15/8/XX

Date	Details	Price	Total
	Incorrect Product Code P(IN) 50 Burnt Sienna Should be P(IN) 75 Burnt Sienna Subsequent Overcharge	10 x €2.50	€25.00
	Add VAT @ 21%		5.25
	TOTAL CREDIT GIVEN		€30.25

Important Note:
As already mentioned, Credit Notes are also sent by suppliers when a buyer returns damaged goods or goods which were not ordered.

Example 5: Debit Note – Question and Solution

Refer to the All Weather Paints Price List at the beginning of the section:

On 20/8/XX Mary Jones, Limerick Builders Ltd, Main Street, Limerick, telephoned the following order to All Weather Paints:

Quantity	Product Code
14	P(EX) 90 Magnolia
1	P(EX) 150 Magnolia

She received the goods the day after she phoned and she checked the Delivery Docket to verify that she had received all the goods she had ordered. She received the Invoice for the goods the next day and realised that Product Code P(EX) 150 had not been charged for. She received a phone call from Jim Smith, All Weather Paints, that day to inform her of the error. He said that he would send on a Debit Note to rectify the undercharge, and this arrived two days later.

DEBIT NOTE

No: D/N389

ALL WEATHER PAINTS
Weatherfield
Thurles
Co. Tipperary

Telephone:(0504) 21331
Fax: (0504) 21332
VAT No. IE 1234567 D
Reference Purchase Order Number 2848
Reference Invoice Number 3797

Date: 24/8/XX

Ms Mary Jones
Limerick Builders Ltd
Main Street
Limerick

Date	Details	Price	Total
	Item omitted from Invoice No. 3797		
	P(EX) 150 – undercharge	1 x €12.00	€12.00
	Add VAT @ 21%		€2.52
	TOTAL		€14.52

Important Notes:

Once an Invoice is sent out it cannot be changed. This is why Credit Notes and Debit Notes play such an important part in the correction of errors when traders are engaged in transactions.

• In the last two examples, Trade Discount was not allowed to Limerick Builders.

Payment Methods

Money is Legal Tender, that is, a means of payment that must be accepted by law in return for payment of a debt. The most common payment methods to date are payments by:

1. Cheque (Cheque Card Validation)

A Cheque Card is given to all creditworthy current account holders. It is nearly always requested by the shop or outlet to verify the authenticity of the cheque – to ensure that the cheque will not 'bounce' (not enough money in the account to meet it). If there is a shortfall in the account the bank will allow the account to go into debt (the red) because they trust the customer to restore the balance in the account to a credit balance (money in the account) as soon as possible. So if you have a cheque card to accompany cheques, any embarrassment will be avoided.

2. Credit Card

Payment using a credit card is immediately validated by computer (e.g. in super-markets) or payment via phone or Internet with card number.

Credit cards are generally given to creditworthy customers. The bank or financial institution sets a Credit-Limit and it allows the customer to use the money reserve whenever he or she needs to do so. However, a set minimum amount of the debt must be cleared when the Statement of Account arrives at the end of the month. Otherwise large amounts of interest will accrue on the debt.

3. Charge Cards

Charge cards are issued by businesses to their regular customers, allowing them a money reserve that is based on the same principle as credit cards. The difference is that the customer is confined to shopping in that store or business when availing of the money reserve. The shop issues the customer with a bill and a minimum amount of the debt must be paid off at the end of the month to avoid large interest charges.

Credit and Charge Cards are very useful if the bills received are managed tightly. They give the customer a sense of security always knowing that money is available if needed (positive cash flow). On the other hand, they can work out to be a debt-generating habit, that is, prone to getting out of control.

4. Cash Availability from Banks or Financial Institutions (Plastic Cards/ATM)

The Irish refer to the ATMs (Automatic Teller Machines) jokingly as 'The Hole in the Wall' or 'The Drink Link'. Most are open twenty-four hours a day. This method of using the Plastic Card, keying in a PIN Number (Personal Identification Number) and withdrawing money is, nowadays, the most convenient and common method of withdrawing cash. Cash can also be lodged in this way by using a 'Lodgment Envelope'. During office hours, cash can also be withdrawn using a Withdrawal Docket in the bank or financial institution.

5. Bank Giro / Credit Transfer

The method used to pay a person to whom you owe money (creditor) by bank transaction (filling in a bank giro form) allowing for the transfer of money directly into the creditor's account. It avoids having to wait for a cheque and the inconvenience of having to get to a bank to lodge it.

6. Bank Draft / Money Order

If you have not got a cheque book, then buying a bank draft in the bank will allow you to send money safely by post. The person or firm that is named on the draft will be paid by lodging it to their own bank account.

7. Postal Order

Postal Orders can be purchased from Post Offices if you do not have a cheque book and you need to pay a smaller sum of money to a creditor. They are a similar type of payment method to bank drafts. The banks, however, handle small as well as larger sums of money.

8. Direct Debit Mandate

The Direct Debit Mandate is under the control of the financial institution that sets it up for the customer. It cannot be cancelled without the agreement of the financial institution. Most mortgages (house loans – long-term loans) are paid off by direct debit. The money is taken out of the bank account that the customer nominates. If the customer defaults on payment, there is a risk that, for example, a house might be repossessed by the bank or financial institution the mortgage is taken out with.

9. Standing Order

A Standing Order is under the control of the customer. The customer can cancel the Standing Order at any time. Short-term and medium-term loans are usually paid off by the customer setting up a Standing Order allowing the institution (for example, the credit union) to take the money that is owed to it out of the customer's bank account.

10. Traveller's Cheques

When people travel abroad they usually bring enough money with them but do not carry it in cash. Instead, they change it into Traveller's Cheques and keep receipts of them in a different location in case they are lost or stolen. They are only accepted by banks for cash. In the foreign country the bank will convert the cheques at the current exchange rate into the foreign country's currency. The adoption of the Euro currency in many countries has lessened the need to carry Travellers' Cheques because cash can be withdrawn using Bank Cards at ATM machines in these countries. Bank charges for these services can, however, be expensive and there is also a risk of travellers losing Bank Cards.

11. *Eurocheques* (Eurocheque Card Validation)

The difference between Traveller's Cheques and Eurocheques is that Eurocheques are like regular cheques where the Eurocheque Book holder can write cheques in foreign currency and the amount when reconverted into Irish will be taken out of the Eurocheque holder's bank account.

It means that the person writing these cheques has to be absolutely sure of the exchange rate and sure that there are enough funds in his/her account to meet the amounts written on the cheques. The accompanying validation card is always requested by those accepting the cheques as a guarantee that the bank regards the customer as credit worthy and reliable in this regard.

Example 6: Statements of Account and Cheques – Questions and Solutions

A Statement of Account is a document that is sent out by the supplier to inform the debtor (person that owes money) how much money he/she owes or if anything is owed at all. If too much is paid, it will indicate this too. Most businesses send out monthly statements to their debtors.

In the case of Bank Statements, the customer can request weekly Statements of Account and in this case the balance on the account will be shown as well as other bank charges, withdrawals and lodgments.

Statement of Account Example – Question and Solution

PRACTICE QUESTION

Kelly and Sons traded with All Weather Paints in the month of July and received the following documents and made the following payments during the month:

Documents Received:

4/7/XX Invoice Number 1181	€250.20
18/7/XX Invoice Number 1311	€100.80
6/7/XX Credit Note Number 1767	€28
20/7/XX Credit Note Number 1858	€18.50
29/7 XX Invoice Number 1102	€476.68
31/7/XX Debit Note D/N 865	€26.14

Payments made:

2/7 XX Kelly wrote a cheque for €100

• Kelly and Sons had a carry forward balance of €200 from June.

You are required to:

(a) Show the Cheque that was sent by Kelly and Sons on 2/7/XX

(b) Compile the Statement of Account for the month of July

SOLUTION:

(a) Cheque

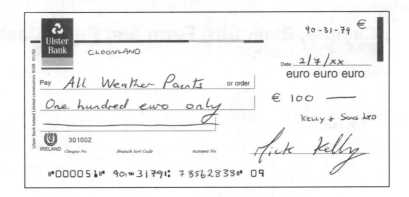

- Cheque Guarantee Card will usually be requested to back up the cheque and to verify the signature.

(b) Statement of Account

All Weather Paints
Weatherfield
Thurles
Co. Tipperary

Statement

To: Kelly and Sons
    Painter and Decorator
    Randles Park
    Clonmel
    Co. Tipperary

Date: 2 August XXXX
No. 89

Date	Ref No	Details	Debit €	Credit €	Balance €
1/7/XX	–	C/f	–	–	200.00
2/7/XX	121214356	Cheque	–	100.00	100.00
4/7/XX	1181	Invoice	250.20	–	350.20
6/7/XX	1767	Credit Note	–	28.00	322.20
18/7/XX	1311	Invoice	100.80	–	423.00
20/7/XX	1858	Credit Note	–	18.50	404.50
29/7/XX	1102	Invoice	476.68	–	881.18
31/7/XX	865	Debit Note	26.14	–	907.32

Cheque, Bank Giro Form and Petty Cash Voucher

Cheque

Bank Giro Form

Petty Cash Voucher

PETTY CASH VOUCHER

Date:———————————— No:———————

Purchase(s) :

	AMOUNT	
	£	p
TOTAL OF PURCHASES :		

Signed:————————————————

Authorised by: ————————————————

PRACTICE QUESTION 1

Yvonne's Boutique, Harold's Cross Road, Dublin 6 (VAT Number 943126) purchased the following items from Fashion House, Dame Street, Dublin 2 (VAT Number 23165).

10 Handbags @ €25 each
30 Leather Belts @ €15 each (Ref: 62)
28 Hair Clips @ €5 each (Packet number: 101)

Draw up the following documents based on this information:

(a) Purchase Order, no. 231, date 26/4/XX
(b) Delivery Docket, no. 561, date 28/4/XX
(c) Invoice, no. 326, date 28/4/XX

   VAT = 21%

(d) Yvonne found that 15 leather belts were scratched and so she returned all 15 of them. You are required to make the appropriate adjustment by compiling the Credit Note no. 846, date 4/5/XX that was sent out.

(e) Draft the Statement Number 922, dated 7/5/XX that Fashion House sent to Yvonne's Boutique.

(f) Draft the Bank of Ireland Cheque dated 10/5/XX that Yvonne's Boutique sends to Fashion House to clear the balance on the account.

PRACTICE QUESTION 2

(a) Route the following Invoice:

INVOICE

ALL WEATHER PAINTS
Weatherfield
Thurles
Co. Tipperary

Telephone: (0504) 21331
Fax: (0504) 21332
VAT No. IE 1234567 D
Purchase Order Number: 4568
Invoice Number: 1102

Date 10/8/XX

Kelly and Sons
Painters & Decorators
Randles Park
Clonmel
Co. Tipperary

Product Code	Quantity	Description of Product	Price p. unit	VAT 12.5%	VAT 21%
P(IN) 80	5 lt	Interior Vinyl Silk – Rose Colour	€7.50 p. lt		€37.50
P(IN) 110	1 lt	Interior Eggshell (Acrylic)	€8.50 p. lt		€8.50
WSp 12	1 no.	White Spirit (Sm)	€2.00 ea.		€2.00
Br22	5 no.	Paint Brush 6"	€30.00 ea.		€150.00
P(IN) 75 White	10 lt	Interior Matt 1 lt	€7.50 p. lt		€75.00
P(IN) 50 White	10 lt	Interior Gloss 1 lt	€9.00 p. lt		€90.00
P(IN) 80 White	10 lt	Interior Vinyl Silk 1 lt	€7.50 p. lt		€75.00

Total				€438.00
	Less Trade Discount 10%			€43.80
				€394.20
	Add VAT			€82.78
Total Invoice Price				€476.98

Note: In the office the exercise would be to locate and match up the documents.

(b) Write your own account of what you think the Supplier's Office Procedures would have entailed from the moment the Letter of Enquiry was sent. Explore and expand on the ways the Order could have first been received, the Delivery Instructions up to and including when the Invoice was sent out and received by the buyer.

PRACTICE QUESTION 3

Jim's Drapery, Mary Street, Cork (VAT Number 43434342 K) purchased the following from Fashion House, Dame Street, Dublin 2 (VAT Number 23165).

35 Handbags @ €25 each
45 Leather belts @ €15 each (ref: 62)
10 Hand and face towel sets @ €25 each set
20 Children's sun caps at €5.50 each
- Trade discount allowed is 15%
- VAT is charged at 21%

You are required to:

(a) Draft the Invoice that Fashion House sent out to Jim's Drapery – Invoice No. 2343, date 23/7/XX.

(b) Fashion House realised on the day after they sent the Invoice, that the Purchasing Manager in Jim's Drapery had phoned Fashion House after the above order was taken, to order an extra 10 children's sun caps. This extra order had not been included in the Invoice.

Based on this information you are required to complete the Debit Note No. 2425 and date it appropriately to rectify the omission.

(c) Given that the following additional documents were sent by Fashion House to Jim's Drapery and the following payments were made by Jim's Drapery in July, compile the July Statement of Account and show the correct balance that is owing.

Documents Received

1/7/XX	Invoice No. 2020	€300.00
2/7/XX	Invoice No. 2031	€400.50
18/7/XX	Invoice No. 2158	€80.50
20/7/XX	Credit Note C/N1255	€30.50

Payments made

3/7/XX	Cheque No. 10005	€400.00
20/7/XX	Cheque No. 10010	€100.00

The Carry Forward Balance from the previous month was €233.55.

Purchases Book, Sales Book and VAT Returns

Purchase Invoices, Sales Invoices, Credit Notes and Debit Notes are the documents used to compile VAT (Value Added Tax) Returns every two months.

Purchases are divided into

1. Non-resale items – items that are purchased but not sold back to the public, like office furniture or mobile phones, used as part of the daily business routine. Goods that are hired, insurance bills and accountants' invoices are also non-resale items.

2. Resale items – items that are purchased and resold back to the public like a builder's blocks, because they are going to be used to build a house that will be sold to the public later.

• Make sure to categorise Purchases correctly in this way.

Sometimes small businesses enter their Purchases Returns (Credit Notes) into their Purchases Book together with Purchases, but *write them in red* to denote that they must be subtracted from Purchases. The same applies to VAT on Purchases and Purchases Returns (Credit Notes).

A Self-employed Sales Distributor had the following purchases in March and April XXXX. His VAT Registration Number is IE 5678785 T.

10/3/XX	Purchased €40 worth of diesel from Grange Service Station (VAT included @ 21%).
15/3/XX	Purchased a mobile phone from NCA Mobile Phone Shop which cost €39.00 inclusive of VAT @ 21%.
24/4/XX	Purchased a computer from Filine Technology costing €899.00 inclusive of VAT @ 21%.
25/4/XX	Truck cleaned – a full valet provided by Valetet cost €55.00 inclusive of VAT @ 12.5%. 12.5% VAT is charged because it is a purchase of a service as opposed to a purchase of goods.
20/3/XX	Returned the mobile phone because it was faulty and received a full refund and a Credit Note.
15/4/XX	Purchased bread and confectionery wholesale from Betterbuy Bake to resell to his own customers. The bill was €2,277 inclusive of VAT. There is no VAT on bread. However, there is 21% VAT on confectionery. €130 of the €2,277 was confectionery.

Sometimes only the Selling Price is quoted on the Invoice so it is important to be able to convert back to the figure before VAT and to find the VAT itself. The *quick* way to do this is:

Take €40 divided by 121% = €33.06

(the figure before VAT) also known as the Net Figure.

Take €33.06 multiplied by 21% = €6.94

(the VAT itself).

Take the entry required for 15/4/XX – the following is the breakdown.

€2,277 *minus* €130 = €2,147.

• So €2,147 is the cost of the bread (no VAT)
• €130 divided by 121% = €107.44 (the figure before VAT) and €107.44 multiplied by 21% = €22.56 (the VAT itself)

- Check:

	Bread	Confectionery
	€2,147	€107.44
VAT	0	€ 22.56
Total		€2,277

Note that this entry is recorded under 'Resale' in the next section.

- *Note:* You enter the Invoices into your own books by allocating your own Invoice Reference Number to them in the order that you locate them. Only Invoices, Credit Notes and Debit Notes that are dated in March or April can be included in the March/April VAT Returns.
- (Purchase Invoices received as well as Returns, i.e. Credit Notes received, are entered here in this case. This is not always feasible because the larger the business, the greater the need to have individual Purchases Returns and Sales Returns Books.)

Sample extract from a Sales Distributor's Book (Jim Jones) :

Jim Jones
PURCHASES BOOK

March/April XXXX

Date	Details	Inv/Cn No.	0%	Non-Resale 21%	12.5%	0%	Resale 21%	12.5%	VAT
10/3/XX	Purch Grange Service St	201		33.06					6.94
15/3/XX	Purch NCA Mobile Ph Shop	202		32.23					6.77
24/4/XX	Purch Filine Tech & Computers	203		742.98					156.03
25/4/XX	Purch Valetet	204			48.88				6.11
20/3/XX	*Return NCA Mobile Ph Shop*	*205*		*32.23*					6.77
15/4/XX	Purch Betterbuy Bake	206					2147.00	107.44	22.56
Mar/Apr Totals				**776.04**	**48.88**		**2147.00**	**107.44**	**191.64**

Purchases VAT = €191.65

- Check:

	(Selling Prices)		
	Net	VAT	Gross
Non Resale (21%)	776.04	162.97	939.01
Non Resale (12.5%)	48.88	6.11	54.99
Resale (21%)	107.44	22.56	130.00
Resale (12.5%)	0	0	
Total VAT on purchases		191.64	

- The self-employed sales distributor made sales in March and April XXXX and the transactions are shown in the Sales Book as follows:

Sample extract from a Self-employed Sales Distributor's Sales Book:

Sales Book: Jim Jones
March/April XXXX

Date	Details Inv/Dn No.		0%	Net 21%	12.5%	VAT	€ (Gross) Selling Prices
2/3/XX	Franco's	121	32.00	12.00		2.52	46.52
14/3/XX	Betterbuy A/c	122	1172.00		40.42	5.05	1217.47
14/3/XX	Commission	122		182.43		38.31	220.74
20/4/XX	Patricia's Deli	123	30.00	15.00		3.15	48.15
15/3/XX	Betterby A/c Debit Note	124	15.00			0.00	15.00
	Mar/Apr Totals		**1249.00**	**249.85**		**49.03**	

Summary of March/April VAT Return XXXX – Purchases and Sales

Purchases VAT Figure	€191.64	(Rounded to €192)
Sales VAT Figure	€49.03	(Rounded to €49)
VAT Reclaimable (Repayable)	€142.61	(Rounded to €143)

- Since the VAT on Purchases is higher than the VAT on Sales, the sales distributor can claim back the difference – €142.61. (Rounded to €143)
- If the VAT on Purchases had been lower than the VAT on Sales, the sales distributor would have had to pay the difference to the Revenue section of government.

A Sample Euro VAT Form:

In all correspondence please quote:

Registration No: IE

Notice No: 02782366-16579P

Period:

Office of the Revenue Commissioners
Collector-Generals Division
Sarsfield House
Francis Street
Limerick

17608 181010 17520 160678 030902VAT3EE

Enquiries: 1890 203070

Payment due by:

VAT 3 RETURN

Please print one figure only in each space using a black or blue ball-point pen.

1. VAT

€ : ENTER WHOLE EUROS ONLY

VAT on sales*   T1   4 9   •00

VAT on purchases*   T2   1 9 2 •00
*See notes part 1 overleaf

OFFICE USE ONLY
AMD A1 ☐ GCD: 014
O/S A2 ☐ UNIT: 101
DRS CSZ: I

Net Repayable   OR   Net Payable

T4   1 4 3 •00   T3   •00
(Excess of T2 over T1)   (Excess of T1 over T2)

2. TRADING WITH OTHER EU COUNTRIES

Total goods to other EU countries   Total goods from other EU countries

E1   •00   E2   •00

3. BANK DETAILS FOR REPAYMENTS/REFUNDS

SORT CODE B1 ☐ ☐ ☐   ACCOUNT NUMBER B2 ☐

Only complete if you have not previously advised us of account details or you wish to amend previously submitted details.
Any repayment of VAT will be repaid to the bank or building society account as notified.

I declare that this is a correct return of Value Added Tax for the period specified:-

Signed:- *Jim Jones*   Status:- *Director*   Date:- *19th May xxxx*

PRACTICE QUESTIONS

1. What books are required to be written up in order to do a VAT return?
2. A self-employed bread sales agent, John Ryan, has the following Purchases and Sales for May–June XXXX, VAT Number 48567591K

Purchases (Purchases Invoices and Credit notes)	**Sales** (Sales Invoices)
5/5/XX €40 Trailer Service Station (VAT 21%)	2/5/XX Mary's Deli €500 (VAT 21%)
6/5/XX €980 Computer Literate (VAT 21%)	8/6/XX Superbuy €1,000
	(VAT €800 @ 12.5% €200 @ 0%)
15/6/XX €20 Trailer Service Station (VAT 21%)	10/6/XX Monalisa €550 (VAT 21%)
16/6/XX €1,000 Betterbuys – Bread for resale (VAT 0%)	20/6/XX Monalisa €550 (VAT 21%)
17/6/XX €29 Return of Bread to Betterbuy (Credit Note) (VAT 0%)	26/6/XX Superbuy €950 (VAT 0%)

All figures above are *inclusive* of the VAT stated

You are required to:

(a) Enter each transaction into the appropriate books and make appropriate pre-calculations.

(b) Complete the VAT Return for John Ryan for the period May–June XXXX.

Note: Be careful to categorise Purchases in Resale/Non-Resale form and do a summary of the return before you enter anything in the VAT return form itself.

Sample Assignment
PART 1 (Kelly & Sons Ltd Question): .

	PRICE LIST OF PAINTING AND DECORATING PRODUCTS		
	ALL WEATHER PAINTS		
PRODUCT CODES	DESCRIPTION OF PRODUCTS	VAT	UNIT PRICE *per tin, per bottle, each etc.*
P(IN) 75	Interior Matt 1 lt tin	B	€7.50
P(IN) 50	Interior Gloss 1 lt tin	B	€9.00
P(IN) 80	Interior Vinyl Silk 1 lt tin	B	€7.50
P(IN) 100	Interior Eggshell (Alkyd) 1 lt tin	B	€11.00
P(IN) 110	Interior Eggshell (Acrylic) 1 lt tin	B	€8.50
P(Ex) 150	Exterior Matt 2.5 lt tin	B	€12.00
P(Ex) 90	Exterior Matt 10 lt tin	B	€37.00
P(Misc) 120	Scrumble Trans Oil Glaze 2.5 lt tin	B	€45.00
Br200	Badger Softener	B	€41.00
Br195	Stencil Brush	B	€1.50
Br90	Sable Writer	B	€7.00
Br12	Paint Brush 1.5" pure bristle	B	€6.00
Br14	Paint brush 2" pure bristle	B	€10.00
Br16	Paint brush 2.5" pure bristle	B	€12.00
Br18	Paint brush 3" pure bristle	B	€15.00
Br20	Paint brush 4" pure bristle	B	€25.00
Br22	Paint brush 6" pure bristle	B	€30.00
Sp110	Sea Sponge (Synthetic)	B	€7.50
Sp120	Marine Natural Sea Sponge (Lge)	B	€40.00
Sp80	Marine Natural Sea Sponge (Sm)	B	€30.00
Pap100	Wall Stripper	B	€250.00
Pap120	Wallpaper Table	B	€15.00
Pap130	Wallpaper Hanging Brush	B	€20.00
Pap133	Seam Roller	B	€4.50
Sc170	Scaffolding 4' h x 3.5' w	B	€70.00
WSp12	White Spirit (Sm)	B	€2.00
WSp14	White Spirit (Lge)	B	€4.75
Ro186	Roller (9")	B	€12.50
Ro120	Roller (6")	B	€6.50
Ro124	Roller Extension Pole	B	€15.00
SERVICE	INTERIOR DESIGNER	A	QUOTE

Large range of paints and wallpaper available

VAT   A = 12.5%
CODES B = 21%

Wallpaper prices from €10 to €150 per roll
Wallpaper borders from €10 to €20 per roll

You are employed as a sales clerk in the offices of All Weather Paints, Weatherfield, Thurles, Co. Tipperary.

On 29 July XXXX you receive an order from Kelly and Sons, Painters & Decorators, Randles Park, Clonmel, Co. Tipperary, for the following:

Code No.	Quantity
P(Ex) 150 Magnolia	12 tins
P(IN) 75 White	10 tins
Br12	8
Br14	8
Br20	4
P(Misc) 120	2

QUESTIONS

1. Enter this information on a Purchase Order Form and for use in your firm.
2. Prepare an Invoice to send to Kelly and Sons, dated 30 July XXXX, Invoice Number 1343 and assume it is posted that day. Apply a 10% Trade Discount and VAT at 21%.
3. On 2 August XXXX Kelly and Sons receive the goods. Draft the Delivery Docket.
4. They discovered that 2 of the items, Code Number Br20, are damaged, as well as finding that 2 tins of the items Code Number P(Ex) 150 Magnolia are Gloss Code P(IN) 50. The damaged items were returned and the other items were simply exchanged. Kelly himself is unhappy with the service on this occasion.
   (i) Draft the Letter of Complaint that he sends to you in All Weather Paints
   (ii) Prepare the document you would send him to rectify the mistake dated 5 August XXXX, Document Number 2454.
5. Prepare the Statement of Account at the end of the month.
6. Prepare the cheque which Kelly and Sons send to pay for the goods on 10 September XXXX.

PART 2 (Frank's Newsagent's Question):

Read the following Purchase Order and also study the corresponding Invoice that follows it.

ORDER FORM

FRANK'S NEWSAGENT'S
Main Street, Monaghan.

Order no: 3335/20

BOOKSTORE SUPPLIES
Main Street, Ennis.

Date: 10 July XXXX

QUANTITY	DESCRIPTION	PRICE €
20	Financial Extracts, Pelican, Byrne and Smyth ISBN 2322	15.50
10	DIY Domestic, Pelican, Lee and Lee ISBN 1451	9.50
5	Painting and Decorating, Folens, Rodgers and O'Rourke ISBN 2828	12.20
12	Feathered Friends, O'Brien Publishers, O'Neill and O'Neill ISBN 2222	6.50

INVOICE

BOOKSTORE SUPPLIES
Main Street, Ennis.
Tel: (0503) 23244
Fax: (0503) 23245
VAT No: 1212435F

Invoice No: 1010
Order No: 3335/20

FRANK'S NEWSAGENT'S
Main Street, Monaghan.

Date: 15 July XXXX

QUANTITY	DESCRIPTION	UNIT COST €	TOTAL €
19	Financial Extracts, Pelican, Byrne and Smyth ISBN 2322	15.00	285.00
10	DIY Domestic, Pelican, Lee and Lee ISBN 1451	9.50	95.00
5	Painting and Decorating, Folens, Rodgers and O'Rourke ISBN 2828	12.20	70.00
12	Feathered Friends, O'Brien Publishers, O'Neill and O'Neill ISBN 2222	6.50	78.00

With reference to Order Number 3335/20 and Invoice Number 1010:

(a) Assume that the prices on the Order form are correct. Note the discrepancies and work out the correct total. Exclude VAT and Discount.

(b) State whether an overcharge or undercharge occurred and name the appropriate document to correct the mistake.

(c) Finish off the incorrect Invoice Number 1010, above, and leave it in its uncorrected form by sub-totalling it, deducting 12% Trade Discount and adding VAT at 21%.

(d) Compile the document that will rectify the mistakes occurring in part (b), above, and deduct 12% Trade Discount and add 21% VAT. (Document Number 1586 dated 17 July XXXX.)

(e) If on 1/7/XX a balance of €212.40 exists on Frank's Newsagent's account and if a further two Invoices and one Credit Note were sent to Frank's newsagent's as follows:

> 22 July XXXX Invoice Number 1888   €345.50
>
> 23 July XXXX Invoice Number 2898   €100.20
>
> 25 July XXXX Credit Note Number 1090   €20.20

and if €400 was paid by cheque on 30 July XXXX (cheque number 10058) by Frank's Newsagent's to Blank Documents that can be Duplicated

Blank Documents that can be Duplicated

SAMPLE QUOTATION

                                                        No:

                                              Supplier Name:

Customer Name:

Customer Address:

Telephone:

                                                        Date:

The following are the items of agreement that we wish to offer you with the view to doing business with you in the near future.

Terms:

- **Prices and the terms of agreement will be reviewed every 6 months and are subject to change. We ensure that we will give you due notice of any such planned changes.**

We hope that the terms that we are offering you are to your satisfaction and we anticipate trading with you soon.

We will be glad at any time to clarify any queries that you might have regarding our product range.

                                              Yours faithfully

                                        _____

                                        Sales Manager

LETTER OF ENQUIRY

Customer Address:

Date:

Supplier Name and Address:

Dear

Following our phone conversation, kindly forward to me a current Price List of your products. I hope to purchase some of them in the near future.

Yours truly

_____

PURCHASE ORDER

No:

Customer Name:
Customer Address:

Telephone: **Date:**
To:

Code Ref	Quantity	Description	Vat Rate (%)	Unit Price

Delivery Instructions: Delivery by   on

Signed: _____
        Purchasing Officer

DELIVERY DOCKET

From:

No:
Date:
Order No:

Goods: **Quantity** **Description** **Code No.**

Received the above goods:

Signed:

INVOICE

Supplier name and address:

Telephone:
Fax:
VAT No:
Purchase Order No:
Invoice No:
Date:

Customer Name and Address:

Product Code	Q	Description of product	Price p. unit	VAT 12.5%	VAT 21%	Total

Total

    Less Trade Discount
    Add VAT

Total Invoice Price

Terms of Trade:

CREDIT NOTE   Credit Note No:

Supplier Name and Address:

Telephone:
Fax:
VAT No:
Reference Purchase Order Number:
Reference Invoice Number:

Date:

Customer Name and Address:

DATE	Q	DETAILS	PRICE	TOTAL

Add VAT @ 21%
Total Credit given

DEBIT NOTE   Debit Note No:

Supplier Name and Address

Telephone:
Fax:
VAT No:
Reference Purchase Order Number
Reference Invoice Number

Date:

Customer Name and Address:

DATE	Q	DETAILS	PRICE	TOTAL

Add VAT @ 21%
TOTAL

STATEMENT OF ACCOUNT

Supplier Name and Address

Statement

To: Date:

No:

Date	Ref No.	Details	Debit €	Credit €	Balance €

7. Retail Administration

'The retail sector is becoming an increasingly professional one with skills in IT, HR and marketing being in constant demand.' *Sunday Tribune* – June 2002

Many multi–national giants have set up shop in Ireland in recent times due to our positive economic performance – stores like Tesco, BHS, Marks & Spencer and Boots to name just a few.

Rising tide of retailing

The retail sector is becoming
an increasingly professional one,
with skills in IT, HR and marketing
being in constant demand. By **Leslie Faughnan**

Modern retailing is fast-moving, exciting and constantly evolving with FMCG (fast moving consumer goods) at the top of the marketing status tree. Food retailing has become a highly specialised industry while the sheer range of other types of goods is so vast that it can only be defined as 'non-food' retailing.

Perhaps the biggest changes in Ireland over the last decade have been stirred by the rising economy, the effect of which has attracted many UK multinational giants to set up shop on our shores. From pioneer BHS to Marks & Spencer and Boots – not to mention Currys and Dixons and the rest of the brown goods brigade – the evidence is there that this island is a natural market unit for UK retailers. It's English speaking, has very similar tastes and habits to the UK and it's served by the same television channels and other media.

The traditional Irish retailing names were – and many still are – multi-generation family concerns, from Arnotts, Clerys and Dunnes stores to Heatons. One of the traditions fostered by this family structure was that there was comparatively little career mobility in retailing and although promotion could certainly be gained, usually on the basis of seniority, in many cases the very top was reserved for the proprietorial extended family. It must sound like ancient history today to the thousands of young people working in vibrant shopping centres and city streets, yet in most provincial towns it still has a high degree of validity with family businesses dominating. But the main picture is of vitality, with attractive career paths for those who like retail management itself as well as for the many specialist roles that have come into the business. IT people, for example, are in demand as smarter systems permeate the shop floor and back office operations. In fact retailing is generally regarded as one of the leading sectors in the application of IT, from point of sale all the way back along the increasingly integrated supply chain through logistics and physical distribution to the manufacturers. Marketing skills are also sought after and rewarded while the breadth of skills and experience required means the HR and training departments are always busy.

Ireland today has close to a quarter of a million people working in retail, a sharp increase on the last census figure of 203,000. At that time there were 33,000 different enterprises in the retail sector of which just 325 companies, about 10%, accounted for over 40% of total national sales. This is becoming an increasingly professionalised sector, with the traditional on-the-job training supplemented by third level qualifications at certificate, diploma and degree level. The School of Business at DIT incorporates the old College of Retail Distribution in Mountjoy Square in Dublin and this year produces its first 32-strong crop of graduates who have specialised in services and retailing.

'By and large retailing still recruits people in the traditional way, often as school leavers,' says Edmund O'Callaghan, lecturer in retail and services management at DIT. 'So our courses in general are part-time. But they offer complete flexibility for people to progress up the levels from certificate to degree. The structure reflects the huge changes that have occurred in the sector in recent times with multinational companies entering the Irish scene and broadening the opportunities — and indeed some Irish companies like Dunnes Stores spreading abroad.' The DIT full-time degree students undergo a six-month work placement. According to O'Callaghan, a few years ago the placement officer might have had a little difficulty finding placements whereas today the larger organisations are actively seeking talent with third level qualifications for their management teams.

One of the UK giants with a 1,500-employee presence in Ireland is Marks & Spencer. It exemplifies in some ways the mix of sophistication and tradition in the sector today. As well as marketing and technological expertise that keeps it near the top of European retail groups, M&S has a long reputation as a good employer. 'We have no vacancies to speak of at the moment,' says recruitment and development manager Linda lynch, 'because we really have minimal staff turnover. That is in large measure because we allow and encourage people to change jobs and career direction within the firm. We always look to our own people when a vacancy or a need comes up – say for people on a project team introducing new systems or planning a new branch. Our philosophy is that everyone should be learning and developing all the time.'

Different Types of Retail Outlets in Ireland

1. Irish multi-generation family concerns – Arnotts, Clearys, Dunnes Stores, Heatons.
2. Multi-national Giants (European retail groups) – BHS, Marks & Spencers, Boots, Dixons, Currys.
3. Multiples – The Musgrave Group (started life 126 years ago as a family owned shop in Cork run by two Co. Leitrim brothers – it is still a family run concern). Musgraves' rapidly expanded its Centra and Supervalu operations in the 1990s thereby quadrupling its business. Other symbol groups include Londis and Spar. These shops are franchised out by Musgraves' and owned by independent operators. 90% of the stock however is sourced from Musgraves'.
4. Other Multiples are Tesco and Dunnes Stores.
5. Other Food Retailers/grocery sector – SuperQuinn.

Features of Different Types of Outlets

MULTIPLES

These are large business operations. Some oversee the operations of multiple shops that are franchised out by it, e.g. The Musgrave Group. Multiple shops are shops that have branches throughout a region or a country e.g. Supervalu, Londis, Centra.

The characteristics of multiples are:

1. Similar range of products and prices available in each branch.
2. Similar branch layout and appearance.
3. Central control of purchasing in Head Office.
4. Independent manager and sometimes owner (in the case of franchises) per branch hired by head office.
5. No credit offered to the public.

Advantages of Multiples

1. No bad debts due to no credit purchases by public.
2. Bulk buying means trade discounts can be gained and competitive selling prices offered to public.
3. Slow selling products can be transferred to other policy branches where demand is greater.

Disadvantages of Multiples

1. No credit given to customers.
2. Less personal consumer attention.
3. Local managers have less input into decision-making at head office.

Acquisition shopping as it should be

Paul O'Kane

The Background

Brothers Thomas and Stuart Musgrave opened their first shop in Cork in 1876. They set up their business as a partnership in 1887, trading as Musgrave Brothers. Seven years later it became a limited company.

The Church of Ireland brothers has an abhorrence of alcohol. Articles of association prevented the company from buying, selling or manufacturing alcoholic liquor. This was why the Musgrave-owned Metropole Hotel in Cork didn't obtain a bar licence until 1956.

By 1899 the company had a turnover of over £67,000 – almost 8.5m in today's terms. By the mid-1920s Musgrave was almost exclusively a wholesale business and by the 1930s it was selling to retailers all over Munster.

In the early 1950s Jack Musgrave took over the reins. Musgrave obtained the VG franchise for Ireland from the Netherlands in 1958 for a nominal £1. By the 1970s Musgrave narrowed its focus, eliminating sweet manufacturing in 1977 and its tea business in 1972. It began opening massive cash and carries in the 1970s and by 1977 turnover was almost £30m.

In 1979 Musgrave began to change its VG stores into the new 'voluntary multiples' it had developed, SuperValu and Centra. By 1990 Musgrave had turnover of £380 m and pre-tax profit of £9.9m. The group grew rapidly in the '90s, moving into Northern Ireland and into Spain in 1994. In 2000 it paid almost stg£90m to German food distributor REWE for an effective 43% holding in Budgens.

Despite being a 3.5bn operation Musgrave remains a family company: Thomas and Stuart's descendants still own 76% of the firm.

It's a long way from tea blending, boiled sweets and small shopkeepers.

The acquisition of the British retailer Budgens will transform the Musgrave group. Adding Budgens to Musgrave will grow the company's annual sales from 2.3bn to 3.5bn at a stroke and the move also sets the pattern for future growth at the company, according to Musgrave group managing director Seamus Scally. Although Musgrave also has a business in Spain, Britain will now be the focus for expansion.

Musgrave has owned a stake in Budgens since August 2000 when it acquired a 28% shareholding in the business and convertible loan stock which gave a total effective holding of 43% for 138m. Ten days ago it agreed to buy the remainder of the business for 275m in a deal that values Budgens at 492m. During Musgrave's two years as a minority shareholder with board representation, Scally

said the Irish company 'saw nothing that discouraged us from taking the remaining stock'.

Musgrave which started life 126 years ago as a family-owned shop in Cork run by two Co. Leitrim brothers, has finally arrived in the British market. In a way the company's huge success in Ireland in recent years has forced it to look east. During the 1990s Musgrave quadrupled its business by rapidly expanding both its Centra and SuperValu operations. These fascias replaced the VG stores that had been operated by Musgrave and its partners.

'We have 22–23% of the retail market in the Republic so the opportunity for significant growth here is fairly limited,' according to Scally. 'We're building a successful business in the North and felt that the British market most suited us.' Last year the company made pre-tax profits of 47m on sales of 2.27bn.

SuperValu and Centra have made Musgrave a 'virtual multiple', as although the group doesn't physically own any shops in Ireland it has a presence throughout the country. The company has used this system to its advantage when dealing with media, government and regulators. Its executives will argue that small shopkeepers who are part of Centra or SuperValu struggle daily against big bad multiples such as Tesco and Dunnes. But in fact Musgrave is a large multiple, albeit one that uses a franchise-like model. The shops are owned by independent operators but typically more than 90% of stock is sourced from Musgrave. It also advises on site selection, store layout, staffing and training.

The so-called independent grocery sector, which includes symbol groups such as Centra, SuperValu, Londis and Spar, now has 45–50% of the Irish market, according to Scally. While the sector has been aided by the expansion of almost all symbol operators, Musgrave has been responsible for most of the growth. During the 1990s, at a time when Musgrave and its 'small grocers' were threatened by a powerful new arrival in the shape of Tesco, the Cork-based group quadrupled its turnover.

Despite talk of the threat from the multiples, SuperValu and Centra have blossomed, due in part to the public's willingness to pay over the odds for convenience. The group hopes to continue its success by building a new type of convenience operation in Britain. 'The convenience sector was not particularly well done in the UK. It's a stg£100bn market but the independent sector has less than 20%.'

Scally said shortly after Musgrave began to research the British market they came across Budgens and were impressed by the quality of its stores and its track record. 'They [Budgens]

are very close to the business and they see opportunities and gaps created by the multiples when they move to large centres.'

Budgens has 245 outlets in the south of England, mostly convenience stores. It has been adding 15 to 20 shops a year and Musgrave hopes to continue the expansion. Unlike its Irish parent, Budgens actually owns most of its stores, although it also has a small franchise operation. Scally said Musgrave had no plans to sell any Budgens stores to franchisees as 'the [Budgens] model was working very well' but added that buliding the franchise operation would be 'speeded up'.

The acquisition will leave Musgrave with debts of 450m– 500m. Scally said the acquisition would result in a debt to EBITDA ratio of 3.5. 'That could be considered on the high side but in 2000 the ratio was 2.9 and by 2001 it had been reduced to 2.3. There's a very strong cash flow in this business.'

Scally admits that given the debt incurred as a result of the Budgens deal, Musgrave will probably not be in a position to make another large acquisition in the short term. 'All going well, after about five years we would take a big bite again.'

Budgens is a publicly quoted operation but Musgrave, which is committed to remaining private, intends to cancel the listing. There will be some savings from delisting but the deal offers few synergies as Musgrave has no existing British business and Budgens will be run as a separate entity. Scally said there may be benefits in terms of buying as the group would now have sales of 3.5bn in Britain and Ireland.

While the real expansion focus has shifted to Britain, Scally believes there is still room for organic growth in the Republic.

'We're adding Centra stores at the rate of 20 a year and we see that happening for the next five years at least, while SuperValu is growing by about five to six stores a year and that will also continue. That expansion should get us another 1–2% market share.'

But having invested so much in the deal, the real growth story over the next five years has to be Budgens. 'It's growing at 5% on a like for like basis, which is an attractive proposition. But Budgens has only stg£500m of sales in a £100bn market, that's only about half a percent of the market. It's much easier to grow that in percentage terms than it is when you have 15–20% of the market.'

If Musgrave's future is to stay bright, that future has to be British.

(Sunday Tribune, June 2002)

CHARACTERISTICS OF DEPARTMENT STORES, HYPERMARKETS AND SUPERSTORES

Department stores consist of a number of shops, each called a department, housed under the one roof. It is a spacious building with specialised shops/departments dealing in hardware, cosmetics, clothing, furniture, toys etc. The department store also offers other services to the consumer like restaurant facilities, coffee shops, post-office and banking services. Examples are Arnotts, Clearys, Roches Stores.

Hypermarkets are large stores with a large area of square footage, which usually have only one floor and deal in groceries, cosmetics and a large selection of household goods depending on the time of the year. Examples are Dunnes Stores, Cornelscourt, Dublin and LIDL (German).

Superstores are large stores that deal in a very large variety of housewares, clothes, food and in recent times different departments on different floor levels. Many Dunnes Stores outlets would fall into this category.

ADVANTAGES

1. Parking and improved infrastructure, giving the public ease of access and convenience.
2. Bulk buying means that companies get trade discounts. This results in lower and more competitive selling prices which are attractive to the public.
3. A wide range of goods and services are at hand under the one roof, making it easy for the customer.
4. Open display leads to impulse buying, and this is good for sales.

DISADVANTAGES

1. Lack of personal service to public.
2. Large population and catchment area needed for centre to be a success.
3. Goods may become damaged more quickly, due to open display.
4. Goods are generally mass produced and little attention is given to detail. Home produced goods are less common.

RETAIL CO-OPERATIVES

Some Co-operatives like Thurles Co-operative Creamery Limited have had a retail outlet attached to the Co-op. In this they sell fresh produce as well as a range of household items to the public. Retail Co-operatives like this are listed in the 'Registrar of Friendly Societies' under the section 'Industrial and Provident Societies – Dairy Section'. Other Co-operatives like Knitwear Co-ops can have shops attached to them also. They are listed under the Other Productive Societies section of the same publication.

The Impact of the Size and Type of a Retail Organisation

1. OWNERSHIP

The larger retail organisation usually has an ownership structure consisting of shareholders, private or public limited companies or, in recent times, they are multi-national companies. e.g. Tesco, Boots, Currys, Dixons. Multiples, department stores, hypermarkets and superstores also generally consist of this type of ownership structure.

The smaller shop/newsagent can be a sole trader or a partnership. Specialised shops are smaller and are usually units in shopping centres, with independent ownership per unit.

The larger retail organisations are highly competitive, and have been mostly responsible for putting the smaller corner store, drapery etc. out of business. However, they have provided a larger variety of choice for the consumer, employment for people and modern facilities for greater convenience.

2. PROFIT SHARING

The small retail outlet, shop, newsagent, either claims all profit for himself/herself, if they are a sole trader, or if it is a partnership, profits will be divided in agreed ratios, according to the Deed of Partnership. (Refer to the section on partnerships in Chapter 1). There is a greater possibility of owners/shareholders making greater profits in larger retail outlets, because investment capabilities are much greater with more investors as well as bulk buying abilities and the ability to avail of large trade discounts. This means that costs per unit sold are minimised and sales are maximised. They also have the added advantages of reputation. Moreover, advertising in the large outlet is cheaper per unit sold. These benefits due to larger size are called Economies of Scale and are the reasons why larger retail outlets can generate greater profits, despite these profits having to be divided out between the shareholders usually in line with their profit-sharing ratios.

The large retail outlets that are owned by multi-nationals repatriate profits (bring back profits to their own countries) and this is not good for the economy of the country in which the stores are located. There is also the danger that businesses like the British multi-nationals will in time move back to their home country causing a large loss of jobs in the country in which they have temporarily located. This is why establishing home-based Irish retail businesses, that start off small and have the possibility of becoming larger with time and track-record, is very much encouraged. This will lead to home-based profits and Irish jobs will then be guaranteed.

3. MANAGEMENT

In general, the larger retail outlet has a head-office with Chief Executives and Assistant Executives who monitor the activities of the different branches. Area managers are usually allocated certain branches in a part of the country and each branch has a Manager, Assistant Manager and Supervisors in different departmental areas.

The bigger the retail organisation, the more complex the management structure will be. The smaller retail outlet will probably have one manager who is the owner and possibility an Assistant Supervisor who will monitor activities in the shop/newsagent/corner shop when the owner is not present. (See tall and flat organisational charts in Chapter 1.)

4. ADMINISTRATION

The larger retail outlet will find it cost-effective to employ more modern technology to complete jobs more quickly and efficiently. Most administrative activities are likely to be computerised. There will generally be specialised areas that deal with administration, for example personnel department, sales and marketing department, buying and stores, financial and accounting etc. (Refer to the functions of management in Chapter 1.)

The smaller retail outlet will not be subdivided into departments and therefore the administration of the business will be probably confined to one office with one secretary or clerk in charge of all paperwork. There will be fewer employees and wages and bookkeeping might be done manually rather than by computer.

5. STAFFING

The staff structure of the larger retail outlet will be more complex than the small outlet. The larger outlet is likely to have a taller organisational structure, which means that a greater number of lines of authority exist and a greater variety of subordinates exist. Employees are usually directly answerable to one superior, who may be a supervisor or sub-manager. The large departmental structure leads to many heads of department. The smaller retail outlet has a smaller organisational staff structure, where staff are usually within close spatial proximity, and owner, supervisor, and usually a small number of other employees with one secretary/clerk make up the total staff. (Refer to Chapter 1.)

Factors that Affect the Location of a Retail Outlet

Retail outlets usually take the following factors into account when they decide to locate:

1. *POPULATION AND MARKET SIZE* – The larger the population in the catchment area, the greater the demand for goods.
2. *INFRASTRUCTURE* – The road network and accessibility to transport – rail, bus will make it convenient for shoppers and will stimulate demand.
3. *PROXIMITY TO BACK-UP SERVICES AND SUPPLIERS* – Reordering, repairs and maintenance services as well as suppliers should be located nearby, otherwise time and transport costs will pose a problem.
4. *PROXIMITY TO SKILLED LABOUR SUPPLY* – Local skilled labour is an advantage, as travelling expenses will not have to be paid to them and punctuality will be ensured in most cases.
5. *EXCESS LAND AREA/SPACE SURROUNDING OUTLET* – This applies more to the larger retail outlet, with the aim of providing car park space for customers, which is a major advantage with regard to convenience for the customer.
6. *PLANNING LAWS* – Planning permission and by-law considerations have to be taken into account when a retailer is considering setting up his/her business.
7. *CONSIDERING THE LOCATION OF THE NEAREST COMPETITOR* – The business should weigh up whether the competitor will have a significantly adverse effect on sales, or whether the business is diverse enough and popular enough to maintain consumer loyalty and not be affected by the competitor's location.
8. *GOVERNMENT LEGISLATION* – Tax incentives, if available, will encourage a business to locate in a particular area.

The Impact of Location on a Retail Outlet

When a retail outlet successfully locates, having taken into account the factors above, they set out with the aim of maximising sales and demand and minimising costs, thereby maximising profits. Successful location can lead to:

1. Higher profits, and plans to expand.
2. Higher demand for labour – employment.
3. Higher wages for employees and greater purchasing power as a result, as well as job satisfaction.
4. Greater usage of technology and computers – modern laser cash registers, credit card facilities.
5. Diversification of products – modification and improved products including branding goods, as well as new techniques to interest the customer and provide incentives to buy e.g. discount cards, stamps to avail of cheaper holidays or to purchase goods at a cheaper price.
6. Greater specialisation and management efficiencies.
7. More consumer friendly policy.

An Organisational Chart of a Large Retail Organisation

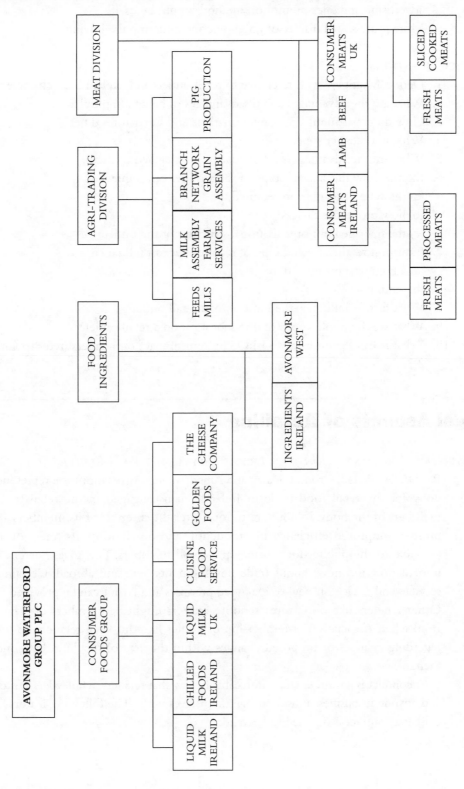

8. Advertising per unit output will be lower as the business grows so more advertising and sales promotion methods might be used.
9. More professional display of goods encouraging impulse buying.

PRACTICE QUESTIONS

1. Define 'Multiples' with reference to retail outlets and explain their characteristics.
2. What are the advantages and disadvantages of being a multiple?
3. How do department stores, hypermarkets and superstores differ?
4. What is a retail co-operative?
5. What are the advantages and disadvantages attached to them?
6. Explain how the size and type of retail outlet can influence:
   (a) the type of ownership required.
   (b) how profits are divided.
   (c) the management organisational structure of the outlet.
7. Explain how the size and type of retail outlet can influence:
   (a) administration procedures.
   (b) staffing levels.
8. What factors influence the location of a retail outlet?
9. What are the implications of good location on a retail outlet?
10. What is EPOS and how do EPOS Systems impact on retailers (refer to Chapter 2)?

Legal Aspects of Retailing

THE ESSENTIAL FEATURES OF CONTRACT LAW AS THEY AFFECT THE RETAILER

RGDATA (Retail, Grocery, Dairy and Allied Traders Association) is a representative body for the retail food trade in Ireland. Firms engaged in the retail trade are members of the body. Its aims are to look after the interests of its members and to promote improved efficiency in production and distribution. Its trade journal is available to the public (for a price) and to all members. This gives current trade information and news about trade developments here and abroad. Certain legal services and advice on new or extended premises and layout can be provided.

Other retailers like bookstores/school suppliers might be members of 'The Irish Booksellers Association'. Membership of bodies like this keep retailers up to date regarding changes or proposed changes within the area of retailing that concerns them.

A contract is an agreement enforceable by law that retailers, wholesalers, customers and anyone in business must concern themselves with. The following features must exist if a contract is deemed to be valid:

1. OFFER AND ACCEPTANCE

In order to ascertain whether an agreement exists, the offer must be clear, complete and unconditional. The agreement must match the offer exactly and must be communicated to the person who is offered it within a specific time limit in order for it to be legally effective. The offer and acceptance are valid if they are made by word, in writing or by conduct.

- *BY WORD*: In the retail trade, it is very rare that agreements are made orally. An example would be giving goods to a customer with a verbal promise that they would return in an hour's time to pay for them. A better example is the verbal agreement that a tenant makes agreeing to pay the required rent to a landlord or landlady.
- *BY CONDUCT*: In the retail trade, a customer in a supermarket or shop who fills their shopping basket with goods by his or her actions is offering to buy the goods. When the checkout assistant accepts the money for the goods, he or she is accepting the offer by actions or conduct.
- *IN WRITING*: When a retailer signs a 'terms of trade' agreement, agreeing to pay the sales agent at the end of every month or when they sign a lease agreement when leasing the business vehicle, the retailer has made payment agreements, the terms of which are outlined in writing.

2. CONSIDERATION

This is the **price** agreed by the parties to the contract. It is the medium of payment whether in the form of goods (barter) or money, a loss or responsibility that is given by one party and subsequently taken by the other party in return for goods or services rendered.

For example Mary offers to purchase Jim's house for €100,000. The €100,000 is the consideration. Even if the house is worth more it is the agreed price that is the consideration. In the retail sector, when the customer indicated his or her intention and offer to purchase by actions and by handing the checkout assistant €100, this is the consideration for the contract. When the checkout assistant takes the money this is the acceptance involved in the contract.

3. CONTRACTUAL CAPACITY

The parties engaging in the agreement must have the capacity to make the contract. The age of majority is 21 years. Anyone entering into a contract with a party below this age is not legally bound to fulfil a contract when it concerns the repayment of money, unless special conditions are attached to it. The contract would be regarded as null and void.

For example in a supermarket, a checkout assistant accepting €5 from a two-year-old child for sweets would not render the transaction valid because of the child's age.

4. *INTENTION TO CREATE LEGAL RELATIONS*

The intention of the parties concerned that a legal contract exists must be clear. If you agree to visit a person's house at a particular time on a particular date, this is not a legal contract. 'Intention' alone does not constitute a contract however.

For example if I go into a supermarket or shop with the intention of buying items and I return home having bought nothing, I am not legally bound to fulfil any contract because the other features of Contract Law have not been adhered to in this case.

5. *LEGALITY OF OBJECT*

Some contracts must be in a specific form in writing before they are accepted as being valid. Direct debit mandates and standing orders (discussed in Chapter 2) must be signed before they are accepted. Hire purchase agreements and leases must also be structured in a particular form and signed by the customer of the person entering into the contract.

For example if a retailer wishes to insure his premises against fire and theft he/she must sign a specifically worded insurance form that is issued to him/her by the insurance company with details of what the insurance does and does not cover.

The Implied Conditions That Underlie a Contract For a Sale of Goods Under The 'Sale of Goods and Supply of Services Act' 1980

The following conditions are implied in all sale agreements, unless specifically stated:

1. *MERCHANTABLE QUALITY*

It is presumed that all goods for sale are of merchantable quality. This means that if any serious fault exists in the goods, the buyer can take action against the seller for a breach of the implied condition of sale. (Exceptions: a motor vehicle dealer where both parties agree that the vehicle requires repair before use.)

2. *SALE BY SAMPLE*

If, for example, a retailer gives a potential customer a sample of the goods on sale, it is reasonable to presume that the goods that will be received by the buyer will correspond (as far as is practicably possible) with the sample. This could be applied to the sale of paint – with colour cards being the sample, or curtains – where sample materials would be provided by the shop assistant.

3. *SALE BY DESCRIPTION*

For example, if a firm that fits windows and doors has a brochure with photos and descriptions of the different types of designs available. The buyer receives a door or window that does not fit the original description of the item that he/she agreed to buy. Then the buyer can take action against the seller for breach of the implied condition of sale.

4. Fit for a Purpose

Often when customers are buying, they are relying on the knowledge, expertise and advice of the seller. When a customer informs a seller of the reasons why the goods are required, the implication exists that the seller is verifying that the goods or services are fit for the purpose for which they are going to be used. The buyer can take action against the seller for breach of the implied condition of sale.

5. Implied Warranty

When an advertisement for goods or a service appears, and extra conditions are guaranteed with the purchase, such as after sales service, the buyer can take action if these conditions are not honoured.

Another example of a warranty is a guarantee that goods or services will be delivered or provided at the agreed date and time. When a situation occurs where goods are delivered late, the buyer cannot refuse to take them, but he can sue the seller for a decrease in sales and a loss of earnings as a result of the late delivery.

Other Consumer Considerations Relating to The Sale of Goods:

RECOGNITION OF CONSUMER RIGHTS AND REDRESS FOR THE CONSUMER: Statements like 'no liability accepted for faulty goods' CANNOT be publicly displayed and lead to prosecution. Recognition of consumer rights must take precedence.

If the consumer has a reason for complaint he/she must act promptly. Otherwise delays in examining the goods would weaken the case and imply that the fault was caused after the goods were purchased or the service was given.

The Consumer Association of Ireland and Consumer Choice

The Consumer Association of Ireland

The CAI was established in 1966. It investigates complaints regarding consumer goods and services and their conditions of sale. The Association is a non-profit company limited by guarantee.

It is the aim of the CAI to represent and educate Irish consumers within the EU. (It liases with the Director of Consumer Affairs and other Government bodies, as well as European consumer organisations.) Consumer rights that are represented by the Association include the right to be protected against and compensated for:

1. dishonest advertising or labelling
2. the marketing of unsafe goods and services
3. the marketing of goods and services where prices charged are clearly not in line with expected quality standards.

If the CAI's legal team feel that a particular complaint warrants representation, the consumer can apply for this representation for a set fee.

'CONSUMER CHOICE MAGAZINE' is produced by the Consumer Association and members of the public can subscribe to it to keep themselves aware of consumer issues and changes in legislation regarding consumer rights.

THE BANKS' CUSTOMER SERVICE CHARTER dictates that customers have the right to a prompt, fair and equitable investigation of banking problems and have also a right to redress if the bank is at fault.

Consumer Information Act 1978

Any breach of the conditions of the Act legally entitles the customer to a full refund or some amount of compensation.

The following is *a summary* of the situations in which such entitlements may arise:

1. *misleading information* on products or services and/or a false trade description of same – both producer and retailer would be liable (Act applies to supply, sale, possession and advertising of goods and services)
2. *false claims* about products or services made by, for example, a sales person – reckless claims makes this person liable
3. display products with accessories attached but the price of accessories not included in display price (implied warranty that goods are free from *hidden cost* to other parties)
4. a retailer is responsible under a manufacturer's *guarantee* and a consumer can claim off both
5. *unsolicited goods* – sending goods to people who did not order them and seeking payment. Any person that received such goods may keep them once they have given 30 days written notice that the goods were not required
6. motor vehicles – usual conditions of purchase apply, once the car is free from defect that might cause danger to the driver, public or passenger. The exceptions are:
   (a) where the buyer is in the motor trade (implied condition does not apply)
   (b) if both parties agree that the vehicle will not be used in the condition it is in.
7. The new NCT – National Car Test Certification guarantees that consumers now have peace of mind when purchasing a used car. The vehicle must meet the requirements laid down by the Department of Transport and is unlikely to be purchased without a recent NCT cert.

SMALL CLAIMS COURT

The Small Claims Court is a consumer service for complainants with claims for damages that amount to a relatively small sum of money. The Small Claims Registrar conducts the proceedings in the District Court. The good or service must have been bought for private use from a business. If the consumer purchases a faulty product and the retailer having been informed does nothing, the Small Claims Registrar will try to settle the dispute. If this fails, the parties will be referred to the District Court.

The Role of the Director of Consumer Affairs

The principal functions of the Director of Consumer Affairs are:

- To inform the public of their rights as consumers.
- To conduct investigations under a wide range of consumer protection legislation.
- To prosecute offences as provided for by statute e.g. breaches of the Consumer Credit Act 1995, false or misleading advertising under the provisions of the Consumer Information Act 1978, food-labelling regulations and general product safety legislation.
- To keep under review practices or proposed practices by business generally which could impact negatively on the rights provided by statute for the consumer.
- To license or authorise moneylenders, pawnbrokers, and mortgage and credit intermediaries as provided for in the Consumer Credit Act 1995.
- To seek High Court Orders in certain circumstances.
- To monitor customer charges by credit institutions and to issue directions in relation to increases in existing charges and charges for new services/products.
- To promote codes of practice.

The structure of the office is mainly divided into:
  (a) Consumer Credit Section.
  (b) Consumer Protection Section.

(Refer to **www.odca.ie** for more information.)
These functions may be changed or enhanced by the expansion of consumer protection at European Union level – as indicated in the Amsterdam treaty.

PRACTICE QUESTIONS
  1. What is RGDATA?
  2. List and explain the conditions that must exist for a contract to be valid.
  3. What is the Sale of Goods and Supply of Services Act 1980 and what conditions of sale are implied by this Act?
  4. What is consumer redress? List three organisations or institutions that consumers can turn to in order to gain redress.
  5. Write a note on the Consumer Association of Ireland (CAI).

6. What are the main conditions that underpin the Consumer Information Act 1978?
7. Write a note on the Small Claims Court.
8. What are the main functions of the Director of Consumer Affairs?

Retail Administration

Portfolio of Coursework – Sample Assignment

A CASE STUDY OF AN ORGANISATION

Note: Students should refer to Chapter 1 in particular – how students can research organisations, S.W.O.T. and P.E.S.T. analyses before attempting this assignment.

Choose an organisation with which you are familiar or one that will be easy to approach for information and examine a range of the following aspects of the organisation:

- location
- structure (organisational chart)
- ownership
- environmental factors (P.E.S.T. plus Competition – refer to Chapter 1)
- staffing
- administration
- stock control
- pricing strategy

Note: Any other details given are extra and will earn marks for initiative and originality.

- Work placements can be chosen for analysis.

A Retail Case Study – A School Bookshop

Introduction

This case study aims to explore how a retail outlet, in this case a bookshop/school book supplier, started business and progressed to its current state. Areas of analysis will include the history of the business, its start-up characteristics, advertising, pricing, costs, factors affecting location, safety, health and hygiene procedures and the life cycle of the business. An analysis of its strengths and weaknesses will be carried out. Future opportunities or plans will be enquired into and threats to the business will be pin-pointed. Finally, an analysis of political, economic, social and technological factors that affect the business, or have affected it in the past, will be carried out.

History of the Business

The business was originally established in June 1988. It was located in a first floor, rented unit over a bank in the main street of a small town in Ireland. The owners then decided to relocate at street level in another rented unit on the main street.

The son of the previous owners now owns the shop and has been trading as a sole trader since May 1995. The shop unit in which the business is now located, which was previously a drapery/wool shop, has a larger floor area – 490 square foot approximately.

Set-Up Procedure and Qualifications or Work Experience Necessary to be Successful

Before occupying the unit, it was necessary to invest €15,000 to refurbish it completely. Included in this cost figure was the cost of improvements like ceiling, carpets, walls, and lights. The layout of the unit had to be changed completely to make it suitable for a bookshop.

The owner concluded that previous experience of the school retail trade is not absolutely essential for success in retailing. However, some knowledge of the retail trade with regard to books together with appropriate work experience with either educational printers, publishers or suppliers like Folens would be an advantage. Experience in receiving orders (types of orders) and previous knowledge of teacher's margins (how many books they might order and under what criteria they order), and publisher's margins would give the entrepreneur wishing to specialise in school supplies (as opposed to more general books) the edge.

Market Research

The daughter of the former owners also takes an active part in the business and undertook the market research. She investigated other bookshops and realised while carrying out this fieldwork that this town was the only town in the region that didn't have a school supplier.

Insurance/Health and Safety Considerations

The business is covered by full Public Liability insurance.

Advertising Before and After Opening

It was estimated that €300 approximately was spent on printing flyers while renovations were being carried out on the unit. These were distributed around the locality. Shortly after opening, an intensive marketing strategy was undertaken by the owners in schools. They provided in-school demonstrations of products, backed up by a catalogue and back-to-school prices quoted for teachers. Most of the arrangements for meeting teachers were done through the principals in the schools and teachers were often invited back to the shop to view the products if time did not allow for it during the day. Long hours after normal trading hours were spent working in order to gain the existing market share.

Expert personal selling techniques and follow-up phone calls as well as call-in procedures used in order to secure sales, were regarded as key methods of gaining business.

Change in Work Philosophy, Advertising and Target Market

The owners decided to adopt a different work ethos that incorporated a change of emphasis on product range and mix. There was to be more direct selling to schools. The visiting of schools was a major generator of business. 20–25 schools are now ordering and buying from the shop whereas two years ago this was not the case.

In more recent times, as well as keeping up the momentum with regard to personal selling, the business has also purchased advertisements in local publications and sports clubs, and has sponsored jerseys for local soccer clubs. The shop holds a January and May Sale, the January Sale appears to be the most effective.

ORGANISATIONAL CHART

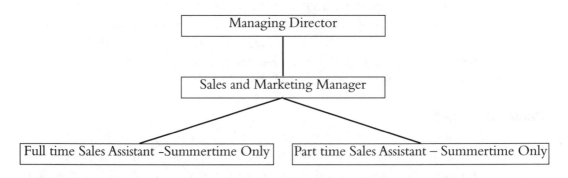

Functions of Staff

1. MANAGING DIRECTOR

The managing director controls the financial affairs of the business as he is a qualified accountant. He is responsible for the monthly management of accounts. Once a year he submits his tax and vat returns to be signed off by a firm of accountants. He also takes an active part in the running of the shop and the marketing of products.

2. SALES AND MARKETING MANAGER

The function of the Sales and Marketing Manager is to take charge of the overall marketing of products. She is directly involved in selling to schools, wholesale ordering, dealing with customers, agreeing the end-of-day till balance with opening cash and sales for the day and many other day-to-day routine business dealings.

Ordering is done during the day and in the evening. The efficient suppliers' fax lines are open in the evening and at night after business hours. This facilitates the ordering procedure particularly at peak trading times of the year.

3. FULL TIME AND PART TIME SALES ASSISTANTS

Both of those employees are employed in the peak summertime period only. They are responsible for looking after customer needs, handling cash and other means of payment as well as keeping an account of order requirements. They are also responsible for keeping the shop tidy and in good order.

Business Hours, Type of Stock for Sale, Suppliers and Trading Cycle

Regular business hours are from 9.30am to 6pm – Monday to Saturday.

The product and service range consists of:
1. School books (new and second-hand), school stationery and school supplies (arts and crafts).
2. Office and general stationery.
3. Novels and other books (adult, children's, – educational materials for younger age groups).
4. Services such as photocopying, faxing and laminating.

The stationery suppliers are Musgraves', Easons, Deales and Morton. The school book and other book suppliers and publishers are: Modern Languages (who have a shop and act as wholesalers), Fallons, Folens, Gill & Macmillan, Educational Company, Celtic Press, AIS, Veritas, Mentor Press, Exemplar Press and Topics Publications.

A large proportion of the annual turnover is generated in the period from 1 June to 30 September. This is mainly due to the demand for school supplies during this time. It is during this time that the demand for the two extra employees occurs every year.

With regard to the life cycle of the business, from 1995 to 1998 has been a 'Growth' stage and the business has not reached its peak as yet – that is, the 'Mature' stage of the life cycle.

October, November and December see a peak in demand for novels in the run-up to Christmas. The Christmas peak generally runs into January when a sale of goods is displayed in the shop front. January is also busy because of the Honours to

Pass or vice versa changes in schools and the demand for revision titles and exam papers.

February to May is the off-peak period and this time is used to plan for the forthcoming peak period. If any alterations need to be made to the way the business runs or to its premises, this is the time to make them.

Factors affecting Location

THE REASONS FOR THE CHOICE OF LOCATION

1. The town was the only town in the region that did not have a school supplier.
2. The young population meant that a sustained demand for schoolbooks existed in the region.
3. Previous experience in an upstairs location proved that street level was a priority for a retail outlet specialising in schoolbooks and supplies.

THE PROBLEMS WITH THE LOCATION

1. It is not close enough to suppliers. (Many suppliers won't deliver due to distance from Dublin.) Costs in terms of time and money are incurred because of delivery problems.
2. There is a shortage of adequate parking along the main street. This is one of the explanations for the stunted growth in retailing along the main street.
3. The lack of passing trade might also be caused by the commercial underdevelopment of the main street.
4. There are threats of future competition because of the relative closeness of the town to busy shopping areas.

Daily and End-of-Day Routine Regarding Cash and Stock Control, as well as General Yearly Stock Control

On a daily basis, the delivery dockets are checked against deliveries and then later checked against order forms and invoices received from the suppliers. When ordering is completed every evening, it is necessary to count the cash. The procedure referred to as 'Agreeing the Till' is undertaken. The control of cash is a priority in a retail outlet.

There are three stock-takes each year, one on 31 May, the second at the end of September/beginning of October, and the third in February/March. Everything in the shop is counted. Then the school order forms are counted and checked against stock.

A minimum stock holding is best in the area of school books because syllabi change yearly and surplus stock would be be impossible to sell into the school year and make a loss.

Pricing Policy

1. The retail outlet has no control over the prices of school books, other general books or novels. The publishers and suppliers have complete control over this. Retail shops, however, get 35% commission on novels and 20% commission on the sale of school books.

2. As regards stationery, the shop can price up from cost higher than the margin set by the suppliers. In this case a 40%–45% mark-up is worthwhile.

Quality and Quality Control

Customers demand that when buying a new book it must look untouched. As near to this as possible applies to second-hand books. School books have to be current and on the book list and in reasonably good condition.

Regarding 'returns' there is often the pretence that the book was bought in the retail outlet whereas in fact a price sticker indicates to the contrary. This is referred to as 'Swop Pretence'.

The customer will dictate the standards regarding quality, and will not buy the book or supply unless it conforms to a certain level of quality.

European Regulations

Novels published in the UK will be priced in both sterling and euro on the price form. Currently there is no VAT on books, however this could change depending on European regulations.

A S.W.O.T. Analysis of the Business

Strengths

- Location at street level on a main street.
- Family-run business, therefore security and customer loyalty through family links.
- Only school supplier in the town.
- School loyalty – unwritten guarantee of business.
- Good relationship with banks.

Weaknesses

- Shop layout and size.
- Parking problems.
- Passing trade problem due to underdevelopment of the main street.
- Schoolbook returns are approximately 5%.
- Delivery problems on supplier side, and time and cost of delivering to schools.
- Stock out too often – need to review stocking procedure.

Opportunities

- Expansion will depend on future competition in and near the area.
- Possible further diversification of product and service range.

Threats

- Other similar shops in nearby towns, as well as existing and planned shopping complexes where people can shop for everything including school books.
- The decision to make outlets on the main street residential rather than commercial premises. Passing trade would be virtually non-existent if this happened and would adversely affect the business.

A P.E.S.T. Analysis of the Business

Political Factors

Family links and good relationships with banks, Chamber of Commerce, clubs that the business sponsored, publishers and authors are factors that positively influence the business.

Economic Factors

- The 'boom' in the economy has meant more houses being built in the area and therefore a larger school-going population which translates into a higher demand for school books and supplies and other book store products and services.
- More finance is readily available from banks and financial institutions and interest rates are relatively low, so the cost of borrowing for renovations is low.
- More money has allowed the business to expand its range of products and services and to diversify.

Social Factors

- The change in the style of selling was part of a new work ethos fuelled by 'the competitive urge'. The success of the marketing strategy that has been employed since 1995 has brought in more customers. Personal selling has achieved the objective of gaining customer confidence as well as convincing them to sample the diverse product and service range that is readily available either in the shop, or which can be ordered in.

Technological Factors

- The business has made use of a new computerised ordering system called 'EROS' which is operated via Eason's Bookshop's modem. The procedure involves ordering through a bar code or by typing the title or author. The message is sent through via phone link, and provides an efficient and prompt service.

Conclusion

This sample retail case study of a bookshop has highlighted the importance of interpersonal skills and personality in the path to securing future business. Personal selling together with the knowledge that a sustainable market share exists and the youthful ambition to succeed describes adequately the work that was undertaken by the owners. The doubling of turnover since 1995 is evidence of the success of the venture. The diversification of products and services together with the structural improvements that were made to the unit equally contributed to the business' success to date. Finally despite the weaknesses that were listed, it is encouraging to see how a zestful, refreshing and ambitious marketing strategy can be successful.

8. Sample Exam Papers

Business Administration

Time Allowed: 2 hours

- Answer 10 out of 12 questions in Section A
- Answer two out of three questions in Section B

Section A

- Answer 10 out of 12 questions in this section.

1. List four environmental features that affect an organisation.

2. What are Quality Circles?

3. How does the Formal Organisation differ from the Informal Organisation?

4. List three functions of the Human Resources Department in an organisation?

5. With regard to meetings, what is a motion?

6. Explain the term EPOS.

7. Illustrate by sketching, the differences between a Component Bar Chart and a Multiple Bar Chart.

8. What is Factoring?

9. In each of the following cases, what document is compiled in order to indicate:
   (a) an undercharge
   (b) a return of goods
   (c) an overcharge
   (d) an omission from an invoice

10. With regard to Communication what is the difference between 'Effectiveness' and 'Efficiency'?

11. Who are the Social Partners and what is Collective Bargaining?

12. What is the purpose of a Cash Flow Chart?

Section B

- Answer two out of three questions from this section.

1. (a) Draw 'the Control Network Diagram' and the Gantt Chart.
   (b) Explain how quality control in business is maintained by linking the two illustrations mentioned in (a) to the four most widely used quality control measures.
   (c) Write a note on three quality marks that you are familiar with.

2. (a) Explain the procedures to convert from an Unlimited Partnership to a Private Limited Company.
   (b) What is the purpose of the Deed of Partnership and how is it connected with 'The Partnership Act 1890'?
   (c) What is the difference between the 'Certificate of Incorporation' and the 'Trading Certificate'?

3. (a) Explain the Principles of Insurance.
   (b) Write a note on each of the following:
      i. IBA.
      ii. Premium.
      iii. Comprehensive Insurance.
      iv. Fidelity Guarantee.
      v. Life Assurance.

Business Administration

Time Allowed: 2 Hours

- Answer 10 out of 12 questions in Section A.
- Answer two out of three questions in Section B.

Section A

- Answer 10 out of 12 questions in this section. (Two marks each)

1. List two purposes of the ICTU.

2. List two reasons for differences between a tall and a flat organisational pyramid. Illustrate.

3. List three benefits of a tight credit control policy.

4. With regard to insurance what is the meaning of Indemnity?

5. What is the 'Deed of Partnership?

6. List three Quality Awards.

7. What does a Gantt Chart measure?

8. What is a Certificate of Incorporation?

9. What is the meaning of 'Credit Terms'?

10. Name three common room layout arrangements made before a meeting.

11. What type of organisation is a Credit Union?

12. Give one Irish example each of the following:
   - A non-trading state body.
   - A trading semi-state body.

Section B

- Answer two questions from this section. (10 marks each)

1. (a) How do price lists differ from quotations?
   (b) Write a note on each of the following:
      i. Terms of trade.
      ii. Discounts given in business.
   (c) Examine the price list given (attached). The following was the order faxed to All Weather Paints from McCarthy & Sons Ltd., Cruises Street, Limerick on 21/1/XX.
   > 2 PIN 75 purple
   > 4 PIN 80 white
   > 6 PIN 110 yellow
   > 5 Sp 110
   > Interior Design Service (from a previous job, to be included in next invoice) €35 net figure. (VAT rates are indicated on the price list.)

Based on the information given:
   i. Compile the Invoice number 2200 sent to McCarthy & Sons Ltd., on 21/1/XX.

ii. Compile the business document sent to McCarthy & Sons Ltd., document number 511, on 22/1/XX when McCarthy returned five damaged tins of the six paint tins code PIN 110.

iii. Draft the January Statement of Account dated 31/1/XX, if McCarthy's balance owed to All Weather Paints for January XXXX was €200 and the following additional transactions had taken place in January:

- 4/1/XX Invoice number 2008 – €150 (Received by McCarthy).
- 14/1/XX Cheque Payment number 1000013 made to All Weather paints – €50.
- 18/1/XX Invoice number 2100 – €160.

2. (a) Give one example each of a short-term, medium term and long term manpower (workforce) gap.

(b) Distinguish between the terms 'Job Description' and 'Job Specification'.

(c) Explain and illustrate Maslow's Pyramid of Hierarchy of Needs.

3. (a) List and briefly explain the six main functions of management.

(b) Explain the differences between three different types of minutes that are taken at meetings.

(c) Write a note on the following terms used at meetings:

i. An Addendum

ii. A Resolution

iii. Standing Order

iv. A Quorum

PRICE LIST OF PAINT PRODUCTS

ALL WEATHER PAINTS

WEATHERFIELD, THURLES, CO. TIPPERARY
VAT NO. 2345678D   ALL PRICES QUOTED ARE IN EURO

PRODUCT CODES	DESCRIPTION OF PRODUCTS	VAT	PRICE
P(IN) 75	Interior Matt 1lt	B	7.50
P(IN) 50	Interior Gloss 1lt	B	9.00
P(IN) 80	Interior Vinyl Silk 1lt	B	7.50
P(IN) 100	Interior Eggshell (Alkyd) 1 lt	B	11.00
P(IN) 110	Interior Eggshell (Acrylic) 1 lt	B	8.50
P(Ex)150	Exterior Matt 2.5 lt	B	12.00
P(Ex)90	Exterior Matt 10lt	B	37.00
P(Misc)120	Scrumble Trans Oil Glaze 2.5 lt	B	45.00
Br200	Badger Softener	B	41.00
Br195	Stencil Brush	B	1.50
Br90	Sable Writer	B	7.00
Br12	Paint Brush 1.5 inch, pure bristle	B	6.00
Br14	Paint Brush 2 inch, pure bristle	B	10.00
Br16	Paint Brush 2.5 inch, pure bristle	B	12.00
Br18	Paint Brush 3 inch, pure bristle	B	15.00
Br20	Paint Brush 4 inch, pure bristle	B	25.00
Br22	Paint Brush 6 inch, pure bristle	B	30.00
Sp 110	Sea Sponge (Synthetic)	B	7.50
Sp 120	Marine Natural Sea Sponge (Lge)	B	40.00
Sp80	Marine Natural Sea Sponge (Sml)	B	30.00
Pap100	Wall Stripper	B	250.00
Pap120	Wallpaper Table	B	15.00
Pap130	Wallpaper Hanging Brush	B	20.00
Pap133	Seam Roller	B	4.50
Sc170	Scaffolding 4ft h x 3.5 ft w	B	70.00
WSp 12	White Spirit (Sm)	B	2.00
WSp 14	White Spirit (Lge)	B	4.75
Ro186	Roller (9 Inch)	B	12.50
Ro120	Roller (6 Inch)	B	6.50
Ro124	Roller Extention Poll	B	15.00
SERVICE	INTERIOR DESIGNER	A	QUOTE

Large Range of Paints and Wallpaper available

VAT CODES   A = 12.5%   B = 21%

Retail Administration

Time allowed: 2 hours.

Please answer four out of the following five questions.

1. Read the following extract and answer the questions that follow it.

Michael Jordan is Managing director of Leoware Ltd., a large multiple which incorporates multiple shops. A department store and hypermarket are located near one of the Limerick multiple Shops. This did not seem to affect business however. Michael believed that a mixture of consumer loyalty and a good marketing strategy were the reasons why the market share had not been affected. The future plan was to diversify and to do so Michael planned to look for either medium term or long term sources of finance. Michael planned to make other improvements in the business like tightening up the credit control policy in the business. This should help profitability and cash flow.

   (a) How do multiples, department stores and hypermarkets differ? Give a clear explanation.
   (b) In the context of retailing what is the meaning of 'to diversify'?
   (c) Distinguish between medium term and long term sources of finance? Give two examples each.
   (d) Outline the impact of a business' credit control policy on the profitability of a retail outlet.

2. (a) Define the meaning of 'Trade Union'.
   (b) Distinguish between the role of a Trade Union at:
      i. Workplace level.
      ii. Branch level.
      iii. National Level.

3. (a) With reference to stock control, what factors will affect a business that wishes to maintain an optimum level of stock? Explain these implications in your own words.
   (b) Differentiate between minimum stock and maximum stock and the problems with both.

4. Beauty Depot Supplies Ltd., delivered the following goods to Mary French & Company Ltd., Beauty Salon on 8/8/XX. (The following figures are selling prices inclusive of VAT.)

10 Boxes Maljay Moisturiser €500
15 Boxes Disposable Electrolysis Equipment €200
1 Box Sunbed Bulbs €120

(a) Work back to the figures before VAT was added, i.e. the net figures.
(b) Construct the invoice (number 18564) incorporating a 10% trade discount and then add the VAT at 21%.
(c) Distinguish between the use of a credit note and a debit note.
(d) Beauty Depot Supplies Ltd., undercharged Mary French & Co. by €20 (Figure inclusive of VAT at 21%). Draft the appropriate document that was sent to Mary French & Co. to correct the mistake – document number 35878, sent on 9/8/XX.
(e) On 10/8/XX Mary French & Co. paid €100 to Beauty Depot and paid off another €100 on 20/8/XX. Draft the Statement of Account dated 31/8/XX that Beauty Depot sent to Mary French & Co. taking into account that the opening balance of €50 existed on 1/8/XX.

5. Write notes on the following:

(a) Sale of Goods Act 1980.
(b) Roles of the Irish Ombudsman.
(c) Roles of the Director of Consumer Affairs.
(d) Indemnity (in the context of Insurance).
(e) Control – one of the functions of management.